A THEOLOGY
ON ITS WAY?

A THEOLOGY ON ITS WAY?

Essays on Karl Barth

by

Richard H. Roberts

T&T CLARK
EDINBURGH

T&T CLARK
59 GEORGE STREET
EDINBURGH EH2 2LQ
SCOTLAND

First Published 1991

ISBN 0 567 09585 1

British Library Cataloguing-in-Publication Data
A Catalogue record for this book is available
from the British Library

Typeset by Buccleuch Printers Ltd, Hawick
Printed and bound by Billing & Sons Ltd, Worcester

In memory of my friend
William George Wakefield (4.4.1942 – 16.7.1981)
Christian and theologian

Contents

Abbreviations   viii

Preface   ix

Acknowledgments   xi

Introduction   xiii

1. Karl Barth's Doctrine of Time: Its Nature
   and Implications   1

2. The Ideal and the Real in the Theology of Karl Barth   59

3. Karl Barth on the Trinity   81

4. The Reception of the Theology of Karl Barth in the
   Anglo-Saxon World: History, Typology and Prospect   95

5. Theological Rhetoric and Moral Passion in the Light
   of MacKinnon's 'Barth'   155

6. Barth and the Eschatology of Weimar: A Theology
   on its Way?   169

Name Index   201

Subject Index   205

Abbreviations

Karl Barth's *Church Dogmatics* are referred to throughout in the usual form of CD I/1, etc.

Indications are given where the early (Thomson) and the later (Bromiley) translations of *Church Dogmatics* I/1 are used.

The following abbreviations are also used:

Protestant Theology in the Nineteenth Century	–	PT
Fides Quaerens Intellectum	–	FQI
The Epistle to the Romans	–	ER
The Resurrection of the Dead	–	RD
Concluding Unscientific Postscript	–	CUP
God the Living and the True	–	GLT

Preface

I should like to recall the immense debt I owe to three great men, all Scots. The first, Donald MacKinnon, sometime Norris Hulse Professor in the University of Cambridge, was the Christian intellectual embodiment of Nietzsche's injunction: "Gefärlich leben!". The second, Thomas F. Torrance, sometime Professor of Christian Dogmatics in New College, Edinburgh, held without compromise to the pursuit of objective, self-authenticating theological truth in an era of relativity. To have heard, and later to have begun to understand, MacKinnon's lectures on theology and philosophical analysis, and then afterwards to have been able to proceed to doctoral studies under Professor Torrance's supervision was to experience something of an intellectual Golden Age. It is to them that I owe much of my persisting concern with the theology of Karl Barth and its ambiguous place in the socio-cultural history of the twentieth century.

These experiences were, however, to befall someone already marked by a third thinker, Ninian Smart, first and founding Professor of Religious Studies at the University of Lancaster. MacKinnon's agonistic struggle and Torrance's theological realism were encountered after initiation into the multi-disciplinary carving up of the cake of religion and its customs, characteristic of the pioneering Department in which, as M. B. Reckitt Research Fellow, I have recently had the privilege of temporary presence (1989–91). The successive impacts of Smart's aspectual (and sometimes reductive) analysis of religion as a human-all-too-human (albeit multi-dimensional) phenomenon, MacKinnon's search for clarity and the illumination of transcendence within the moral transcendental, and then an encounter with Torrance's assertion of the givenness of Christian x A Theology on its Way?

revelation were together more than sufficient to set the agenda for a lifetime.

I would, in addition, like to thank Professor (now Bishop) Stephen Sykes who invited me on two occasions to contribute to collections that sought critically to celebrate the genius of Karl Barth. It was a rare privilege to work with such a distinguished colleague for a decade in Durham. With all these writers I have on occasion disagreed, sometimes in the following pages: but in my view serious disagreement within the ambit of the Christian faith remains the inevitable burden of the theologian who seeks truth and resists its ideological manipulation.

I am as ever grateful for the patient and painstaking word-processing of Mrs Joan Trowbridge and for assistance with the index from Mr Henry Lupton. I should also like to thank Audrey Roberts for proof-reading and her unfailing support.

Lastly, I would like to recall the stimulus of my late friend, William George Wakefield (1942–1981), an Australian theologian and Christian minister whose love of Scotland and dedication to the theology of Karl Barth were intense and complete. To have walked together each week over the Pentland Hills and lived through the theological dialectic with him remains an unforgettable experience. To have known and loved him as a friend, is a life-long challenge and inspiration. His premature death remains our and Australia's loss. This book is dedicated to his memory in gratitude and respect.

Richard H. Roberts
Lancaster/St. Andrews
January 1991

Acknowledgments

The provenance of the chapters in this book is as follows:

"Karl Barth's Doctrine of Time: Its Nature and Implications". First published in S. W. Sykes (ed.) *Karl Barth Studies of his Theological Method* (Oxford: Clarendon Press, 1979), pp. 88–146.

"The Ideal and the Real in the Theology of Karl Barth". First published in J. D. Holmes, S. W. Sykes (eds.) *New Studies in Theology* I, (London: Duckworth, 1980), pp. 163–179.

"Karl Barth on the Trinity". First published in P. Toon, J. D. Spiceland (eds.) *One God in Trinity – An Analysis of the Primary Dogma of Christianity* (London: Marshall, Morgan and Scott, 1980), pp. 78–93.

"The Reception of the Theology of Karl Barth in the Anglo-Saxon World: History, Typology and Prospect". First published in S. W. Sykes (ed.) *Karl Barth: Centenary Essays* (Cambridge: Cambridge University Press, 1989), pp. 115–71.

"Theological Rhetoric and Moral Passion in the Light of MacKinnon's 'Barth'". First published in K. Surin (ed.) *Christ, Ethics and Tragedy: pursuing the thought of Donald MacKinnon* (Cambridge: Cambridge University Press, 1988), pp. 1–14.

"Barth and the Eschatology of Weimar: A Theology on its Way?". Originally delivered at the *Oxford Conference of Sociologists and Theologians*, January 1987.

Chapters 1–5 have undergone light revision and stylistic regularisation. Chapter 6 has been substantially revised and enlarged.

I am grateful to the University Presses of Oxford and Cambridge for permission to reprint Chapters 1, and Chapters 4 and 5, respectively.

Introduction

The theology of Karl Barth continues, despite all declarations of its obsolescence, to command interest and the partisan response. In this writer's judgment, as is argued below, Barth's work remains an achievement which exhibits both the grandeur and pathos of an oeuvre that recapitulates the fundamental loci of the Christian faith in interconnection, yet seems to do so at a distance from social reality in a quasi-autonomous, self-verifying sphere. This book contains six papers, the first three stem from my doctoral thesis[1] on eternity and time in the theology of Karl Barth. They were written with passion as I struggled to understand the reasons for the apparent self-enclosed nature of a great Christian theology. The last three papers were written after passing a year in Tübingen (1981–2) during which I became strongly impressed by German methods of total research, a methodology in which all sources, primary and secondary, are scrutinised and reviewed before a finger is laid upon pen or word processor key.

Whereas chapters 1 to 3 are expressions of aspects of the basic argument of my doctorate, chapters 4, 5 and 6 are reflections of different ways in which Barth's theology may be earthed in context. There is thus a counterpoise in the collection in which the first three papers probe the inner logic of Barth's thought and reach the broad conclusion that the investigation and analysis of the eternity/time axis reveals the precise pattern of proximity and distance of the ontology of Barth's theology from other realities. The remaining papers are reflections of the ways in which I have tried to investigate as it were the external relations of Barth's

[1] *Eternity and Time in the Theology of Karl Barth: An Essay in Dogmatic and Philosophical Theology* (PhD, Edinburgh, 1975).

work. Chapter 4 is a detailed exercise in "*Rezeptionsgeschichte*" in which the major (and some less important) responses to Barth's thought are assembled and classified. This investigation reveals considerable diversity and a major problem, a failure of interpretation on the level of totality. In Chapter 5 the early "Barthian" thought of Donald MacKinnon is examined in terms of its rhetorical characteristics, albeit in a preliminary way. Chapter 6 explores the cultural setting of Barth's early work and in it I try to formulate some of the theoretical insights that may be used in the interpretation of this episode. The growing international interest in and importance of rhetorical analysis has become increasingly apparent to me after contributing to the *Festschrift* in which this piece originally appeared.[2]

The theology of Karl Barth was at least in part forged in response to world events: it was not an aesthetic creation as such, compiled in privileged isolation. I intend at a future date to return to Barth's theology in something approaching the terms laid down at the end of Chapter 4. Meanwhile, I believe that the critique of Barth advanced in this book merits a response; in my view some of the global issues raised by a reading of Barth in these terms have yet to be addressed, never mind answered. In an era of resurgent fundamentalism it would be all too easy for conservatives to lay hold of Barth's theology and so to clothe themselves in it that they might appear to function with a robotic indifference to the actual conditions of the social and life-world we inhabit. If Christian theology is to survive in terms which transcend the ideological comfort provided by sub-cultural belief-systems then it will have to respond selectively and dialectically to its own historic resources. The lessons to be learned from serious appropriation of Barth's thought are based on the assumption that doing theology his way was *final* in the sense that he transmitted the tradition virtually entire at the cost of its alienation. Our present task is to expose and transcend that alienation.

If Christian theology is to proceed on its way in a distinctive yet benign form, then it must both take seriously the history of its

[2] See R. H. Roberts and J. M. M. Good (eds.). *The Recovery of Rhetoric: Persuasive Discourse and Disciplinarity in the Human Sciences* (Richmond, Va., University of Virginia Press, forthcoming). This work contains extensive bibliography and an introduction which affords basic guidance in this important field of study.

own religious alienation and be prepared to act and think proleptically within the life-worlds of the contemporary human condition. This will call for a daunting *kenosis* and a self-crucificatory journey of abnegation made in the hope of rediscovery. On many levels the new theological dialectic will require the holding together in a both/and of the either/ors that we inherit from twentieth century Christian theology and its *Sitz im Leben*. For a start, this way of rediscovery must be conducted in the context of the study of religion and religions, as such: contrary to the propagandists from both camps, the impulse of faith and the multi-disciplinary study of religion belong together, albeit in dialectical tension.

The theology of Karl Barth is, I believe, on its way; but it is not necessarily following those paths dictated either by its originator or its devotees or detractors. This theology is a great concatenation of texts, the intertextuality of which spans Western religious and intellectual history, and, properly understood, the fragmentation and pluralism of modernity and of post-modernity. A fuller reading of Barth's version of the metanarrative, the totality, requires creative misprision[3] on a grand scale. The greatest compliment we may pay the theology of Karl Barth is to resist the flattery of pointless imitation, to set aside the flawed author himself and to take up an engagement-in-context with the theological metatext of the twentieth century. Perhaps in this way we might emerge (albeit momentarily and through the pain of continuous effort) from the titanic clash of egos, the dialectic of self-aggrandisement that both Hegel and his inadvertent theological imitator, Barth, share. There can be no universality without power; yet there can be no *Christian* intellectual praxis without beneficent self-abnegation.

We cannot again risk Barth's dangerously close collusion between his voice and that of his God: the mediation of the tradition demands a hermeneutic that may one day evince a hearing and respect; in this humour and irony will have their

---

[3] I here borrow Harold Bloom's term from *The Anxiety of Influence A Theory of Poetry* (Oxford: Oxford University Press, 1973) and *Agon Towards a Theory of Revisionism* (Oxford: Oxford University Press, 1982). Theologians of the more traditional kind have much to learn from Bloom's literary theoretical analysis of the processes which take place when one text supersedes another.

place. Silent theological labour is required in the undergrowth of
the human and social world. The mechanisms of the kerygma
have been abused and are exhausted; in Western culture we live,
as George Steiner has argued, in the after-life of religion.[4]
Dissection of the decay of religious life-forms is but one aspect of
the task; but this should not divert us from that practical and
intellectual submersion in, and exploration of, the life-world that
may precede the discovery of new analogies within the reality with
which Christian theology must engage. Barth's theology provides
us with a resource, yet also with a warning: we must exploit the
former and comprehend the latter.

---

[4] The essays in this volume have a complementary relationship with my
collection, *From Hegel to Heidegger: Explorations in the After-Life of Religion*
(Bristol: The Bristol Press/Duckworth, forthcoming). The present collection and
From Hegel to Heidegger arise, as it were, from consideration of the "internal" and
"external" relations of a theological tradition, respectively.

I

Karl Barth's Doctrine of Time: Its Nature and Implications *(1979)*

Introduction

In this essay Karl Barth's conception of time (and its correlate eternity) is presented as follows. After some introductory remarks, Barth's theological method is set in the context of German idealism in the first section. In section two, Barth's own development is outlined from the 'theology of crisis' to the emergence of the first half-volume of the *Church Dogmatics*. Following this, in section three, the temporal vacuum of the eternal 'Now' moment inherited from the dialectic of idealism and *The Epistle to the Romans* is seen to become the vehicle of the time of revelation itself. In sections four, five, and six the fundamental concept of 'contingent contemporaneity' is then seen to undergird the doctrines of God, Christ, and creation, respectively. The so-called 'inner logic' of the *Church Dogmatics* is the axis of eternity and time unfolded through the motif of the 'analogy of faith'. Thus in the concluding section it becomes apparent that despite Barth's efforts to posit a resurrection of Jesus Christ in time in its 'simple meaning' he nevertheless provides a theology whose total structure remains enclosed within its own temporal envelope. The consequences of this are twofold: first, severe ambiguity of thought occurs whenever this structure encounters commonplace reality; second, the whole structure is a paradoxical combination of concrete assertion and unreality *in toto*.

Before proceeding in the directions outlined above, certain preliminary remarks must be made upon the general nature of Barth's theological endeavours in the *Church Dogmatics*. Barth makes a decisive and profound reassertion of the being of God in Jesus Christ. The act of God in Jesus Christ may be understood in a number of ways. Dr. Ford has addressed himself to what I regard as the exegetical norm of the 'story'. I direct my attentions to the ontological norm of God's being in act, understood in its significant persistence and continuity through the category of time. Indeed epigrammatically it might well be said that, for Barth, time is a surrogate for substance in general.[1] The relation of God's being in eternity to his being in time is understood in a mutual actualism in such a way that ontology and temporality are deeply enmeshed. It is my contention that having demonstrated and analysed the profound involution and convolution of these categories, it is then possible to map out the structure of being in the *Church Dogmatics* by tracing the application of temporal conceptions. In this way questions may be put to Barth's work that are normally pre-empted and repudiated by his method of deriving all theological explanation from the posited 'reality' of revelation, a reality that appears to demand conformity and submission rather than critical investigation.

In his posthumous Warfield Lectures, Ronald Gregor Smith made the following comment upon the *Church Dogmatics*, from which emerges an important question:

> In Barth we have the last, and possibly the greatest, certainly an awe-inspiring, effort on the part of traditional metaphysical theology to overcome the difficulty of relating 'God in his being for himself' with 'God for the world in Christ.' But if you begin with 'being', is there any way to the world of time and movement, the historical world where faith takes its rise?[2]

It is precisely this ontological 'way' from the being of God to the world of time and movement that is to lie at the centre of our attention in this essay. The very scale of Barth's achievement means that many issues can only be alluded to in an essay of these

---

[1] I have analysed this equation of time and substantial being and its consequences for the doctrine of analogy in 'The Ideal and the Real in the Theology of Karl Barth', originally in S. W. Sykes and J. D. Holmes (eds.), *New Studies in Theology* (London, 1980) and reprinted as chapter 2 below. I allude above to Dr. (now Professor) David Ford's paper 'Barth's Interpretation of the Bible' in S. W. Sykes (ed.) *Karl Barth: Studies of his Theological Method* pp. 55–87.

[2] R. Gregor Smith, *The Doctrine of God* (London, 1970), p. 91.

dimensions: they remain, as it were, unlit corridors leading away
from the primary passage being explored. It is my intention to
unravel something of what T. F. Torrance has called the 'inner
logic' of this theology in such a way as to show that the autonomy
of theology as conceived by Barth inevitably leads into a tortuous
ontological double-bind, an all-pervasive theological ambiguity
and unreality. In consequence it will become apparent that the
profound and legitimate mystery of Christ must not become
(albeit unwittingly) the cloak for mystification and the
infringement of the bounds of theological sense.

I   *Context and development*

The most relevant factor in the immediate historical context of
Barth's early development and his later, mature work concerns the
treatment of the axis of eternity and time, understood as
categories of infinite and finite existence, in both the evolution of
idealist thought in Germany and in its later dissolution in the face
of hostile philosophical criticism. Such a growth and subsequent
declension in European thought is, in the first instance,
'philosophical' by nature, but its ultimate origins, nature, and its
renewed criticism had undeniable and important theological
dimensions. Again such a context is relevant because Barth's
overall theological stance bears many signs of operating within
parameters laid down and dictated by the late German
Enlightenment as well as idealism. It is, however, necessary to
consider both these conditioning factors as well as general but
fundamental features of his theological method. Thus whilst
Kant, Hegel, and Kierkegaard have had their effect, their influence
must be understood in conjunction with the truly constitutive role of
analogia fidei, the 'analogy of faith' in the work itself. Whereas the
former thinkers (all intimately connected with the idealist tradition)
conditioned the theological possibilities open to him, it is Barth's
massive adherence to the principle of analogy of faith which comes to
motivate the interrelation of eternity and time and provides the
rationale for the dominance of the former over the latter.

   In the light of these remarks it may be seen that whilst Karl
Barth was not a philosopher, his comments upon the idealist
philosophers Kant and Hegel (made at some length in his
Protestant Theology in the Nineteenth Century) constantly reveal

his understanding of the theological significance of their work. Thus Barth sees an irony in the fact that Kant's segregation of philosophical and theological activity allowed for an emancipation of constructive theology outside the framework of the latter's own critical undertaking. This insight is that the 'biblical theologian proves that God exists by means of the fact that He has spoken in the Bible' (*PT*, 311–12). Indeed for Barth the problem to be solved was of how and where God had spoken once the Kantian emancipation of faith into its own discrete sphere had been accomplished.

According to Barth[3] there is thus a scientific living-space for theology in relation to its proper object and some indication as to the nature of this 'proper object' is apparent when an examination is made of the notable study of Anselm[4] originally published in 1931. In this he argued that theology should recognize the point of departure for its method in revelation and thus stand on its own feet in relation to philosophy. More specifically, Barth argued that Anselm provides 'a vital key, if not the key, to an understanding of that whole process of thought that has impressed me as the only one proper to theology' (*FQI*, 11). At the very core of this process of thought is Anselm's recognition of a '*ratio* peculiar to the object of faith' a '*ratio* of God', that is, a 'Word . . . not divine as word but because it is begotten of the Father – spoken by Him' (*FQI*, 45–6). Truth is thus the consequence of God's own action, not an attempt to produce or evince truth from autonomous human ratiocination. The 'analogy of faith' is, therefore, a grace-given correspondence between theological language and its object. Such a correspondence is not predictable or static in the manner characteristic of Roman Catholic analogy of being (against which Barth polemicizes) but given in the event of God's own self-revelation in his Word in Jesus Christ.[5] The very possibility of *theo*-logy is intrinsically conditioned by God's own

[3] We cannot concern ourselves with the adequacy of Barth's argument for the use of this presupposition but with its consequences.

[4] *Anselm: Fides Quarens Intellectum* (London, 1960). See the further discussion in Professor Sykes's paper, in S. W. Sykes (ed.) op.cit., pp. 36ff.

[5] Barth defines the analogy of faith as follows: 'The correspondence of the thing known with the knowing of the object with the thought, of the Word of God with the word of man in thought and speech even as it distinguishes true Christian prophecy taking place in faith from all that is untrue' (*CD* I/1, p. 279).

act and does not depend upon any persistent, given affinity between the being of God and the being of other entities.

The link between Barth's comments upon Kant and his analysis of Anselm's *Proslogion* is of major importance because it indicates in the barest outline the nature and the limitations of his understanding of the range of theology, and with it, the basis of his doctrine of time. The theological foundation of the first volume of the Church Dogmatics was laid therefore in Barth's study of Anselm in an identity of knowing and being, as 'It is in the Truth and by the Truth, in God and by God that the basis is a basis and that rationality possesses rationality' (*FQI*, 51).

In more specific terms it is necessary to see how the movement of idealist thought in respect of the antitheses of eternity and time, finite and infinite, brought about developments in Barth's own thought relevant to our argument. It must be remembered that Barth made no simple theological obeisance to Kant, but he quite clearly regarded the distinctions found most lucidly expressed in *Religion Within the Limits of Reason Alone*[6] between the rightful spheres of philosophy and theology, as in a certain relevant sense correct. Thus, far from *inhibiting* theological endeavour, Kant's work served to *free* it for its proper task, an unqualified adherence to the Word of God. This was but one aspect of Kant's influence upon Barth, for another crucial element concerned the basic assumptions concerning the relation of the categories of finite and infinite existence.

In the *Critique of Pure Reason* Kant argued that the antinomy of finite and infinite space and time, part of the traditional diet of metaphysical thought, was irresolvable and formed an aspect of those problems imposed upon the human mind by the nature of reason itself. The 'dialectical play of cosmological ideas' is something to which reason is subject whenever it attempts speculation in the 'endeavour to free from all conditions and apprehend in its unconditioned totality that which according to the rules of experience can never be determined save as conditioned'.[7] The attempt to think the 'unconditioned', that which lies beyond the 'universal laws of nature', is implicit in the

[6] Trans. T. M. Greene and H. H. Hudson, *Religion within the Limits of Reason Alone* (New York, 1960).
[7] Trans. N. Kemp Smith, *The Critique of Pure Reason* (London, 1968), p. 422.

illicit and futile strivings of metaphysical thought. The deep metaphysical agnosticism that resulted from Kant's limitation of reason found its corresponding expression in his conceptions of the religion of 'revelation' and 'biblical theology' in *Religion Within the Limits of Pure Reason Alone*. Any identity between speculative metaphysics and theology was abrogated and a 'religion of reason' replaced the pretensions of metaphysical theology.

The metaphysical agnosticism of Kant contrasts with Hegel's positing of absolute knowledge. Here the implications of the latter's thought for that of Barth can be initially traced in *Protestant Theology* where the wealth of references to Hegel's *Lectures on the Philosophy of Religion* is apparent. What is equally remarkable is the dearth of reference to Hegel in the *Church Dogmatics* itself, but this should not mislead the reader, for the implicit response of Barth is nevertheless pervasive. Indeed Hegel's virtual rediscovery of the doctrine of the Trinity subsisting in the divine act and of his concept of synthesis are clearly highly significant for Barth (*PT*, 413–17) and for his understanding of time.

The importance of Hegel's response to Kant as regards the problem of time is to be seen in the transformation of the antithesis of finite and infinite existence (conceived in theological terms as the contrast of time and eternity). In the dialectic Hegel subsumed all aspects of reality, including those in a state of apparent contradiction, such as time and eternity, into a single, overall process of noetic realization, that is in absolute thought. This ran counter to Kant's circumscription of possible human knowledge, for in the Hegelian dialectic thought and being enter into identity as the being of God and the being of man become one through the coming to self-consciousness of God through human self-consciousness. The very similarity between Barth's Christological synthesis and that of Hegel might raise certain difficulties, but at least Barth's intentions are clear when he contrasts the 'Hegelian concept of synthesis' and the 'incomprehensible synthesis of God' (*PT*, 417). The latter can only be understood upon its own terms, that is as related to its 'proper object' given in revelation.

It is precisely Barth's disagreement with Hegel over the nature of the 'proper object' of synthesis that indicates the nature and direction of his work and the context in which his emergent doctrine of time must be understood. Barth approved of Hegel's 'discovery' that 'Life itself is not a unity resting in itself, but a perpetual $a = non\text{-}a$, in despite of the whole of western logic' (*PT*, 413), but he indicates that 'in making the dialectical method of logic the essential nature of God' Hegel made impossible the 'knowledge of the actual dialectic of grace, which has its foundation in the freedom of God' (*PT*, 420; cf. *CD* II/1, 270). Barth's theological synthesis is of Hegelian proportions and involves the comprehensive embrace of diverse categories within a complex whole. Just as with Hegel the danger of reduction constantly threatened such a synthesis on the level of pure thought, so with Barth there is a threat of reduction of the diverse totality of being into the realm of the divine being in act.

As regards time itself, Hegel's conceptions bear a strong resemblance to those Barth adopts in his major work. In the *Philosophy of Nature* Hegel asserted that,

> In the positive sense of time one can therefore say that only the Present is, while what is before and after is not. The concrete Present is however, the result of the Past, and is pregnant with the Future. The true Present is therefore pregnant with eternity.[8]

The exploitation of eternity as the true indweller of the transient temporal present in the *Church Dogmatics* owes much to Hegel, but it is given its dynamic impulse by the principle of *analogia fidei* as Barth attempts to propound the nature of God's revelation in Jesus Christ. Barth's own response to the actual dialectic of the antitheses follows the breakdown of the idealist synthesis at the hands of Trendelenburg[9] and, following him, Kierkegaard. Out of this criticism arose essential elements in the so-called 'theology of crisis' or 'dialectical theology', in which Barth played a leading part in the years following the end of the First World War. It is most important to follow this development in some detail because its resolution raises questions which must be borne in mind in examining Barth's *magnum opus* and its doctrine of time.

[8] *The Philosophy of Nature* (Eng. trans. London, 1970), p. 86.
[9] Notably in *Logische Untersuchungen* (Leipzig, 1840). The only English translation of Trendelenburg's work appears to be 'The Logical Question in Hegel's System', trans. T. Davidson, *Journal of Speculative Philosophy*, V (1871), pp. 349–59; VI (1872), pp. 82–93, pp. 163–75, pp. 350–61.

Trendelenburg's critique of Hegel's use of Aristotelian categories was the product of the former's philological expertise and fidelity to the text of Aristotle. The synthesis of apparently incompatible categories was exposed as the radical confusion of such categories, real and logical. This exposure of the impossibility of a total identification of thought and that which existed was developed by Kierkegaard in a theological polemic. Using the logical tools forged by Trendelenburg, Kierkegaard forced apart the false and illusory categorical homogeneity of Hegelian idealism.[10] In specific terms this attack was concentrated upon Hegel's misuse of the Aristotelian concept of κίνησις in indicating the movement from possibility to actuality. This, according to Kierkegaard, cannot be expressed or understood in the language of abstraction, for, in the sphere of the abstract, movement cannot have assigned to it either time or space, its essential presuppositions.[11]

The noetic goal of identity in the Hegelian dialectic, achieved through the overcoming (*Aufhebung*) of contradiction, was supplanted in Kierkegaard's *Postscript* by an existential dialectic, in which the temporal is confronted by the eternal, in the 'either-or' experienced in the striving of the becoming subject (*CUP*, 270–1). The Hegelian stance, *sub specie aeterni*, is an illusion for it presupposes an abstraction from the inevitable and actual existential pathos of the individual. Whereas for Hegel 'The systematic Idea is the identity of thought and being', Kierkegaard argued that 'Existence, on the other hand is their separation' (*CUP*, 112). In consequence the most pressing problem is how it is possible for 'eternal truth ... to be understood in determinations of time by one who as existing is himself in time' (*CUP*, 172). Kierkegaard pointed to the theological implications of this reassertion of the *diastasis* (a radical disjunction) of the temporal and the eternal, in that 'the paradoxical nature of Christianity consists in its constant use of time and the historical in relation to the eternal' (*CUP*, 88). He

---

[10] Accounts of this critique may be found in H. Diem, *Kierkegaard's Dialectic of Existence*, trans. H. Knight (Edinburgh, 1959), and J. Collins, *The Mind of Kierkegaard* (Chicago, 1965).

[11] See *Concluding Unscientific Postscript*, trans. D. F. Swenson and W. Lowrie (Princeton, 1941), p. 306 and *The Concept of Dread*, trans. W. Lowrie (Princeton, 1957), p. 43, 'In logic no movement can come about for logic is and everything else logical simply is.'

asserted an existential paradox of encounter over against the Hegelian possibility of abstract synthesis:

> The eternal and essential truth, the truth which has an essential relationship to an existing individual because it pertains essentially to existence . . . is a paradox. But the eternal essential truth is by no means in itself a paradox; but it becomes paradoxical by virtue of its relationship to an existing individual. (*CUP*, 183)

Such an existential paradox shifts the focus of difference from an abstract contrast of being to an encounter of finite consciousness with an infinite Wholly Other God. The consequences of this new perspective for Christology and the doctrine of creation were completely realized by Barth in the theology of crisis, and in so doing he exploited anew with extreme destructive power the dialectic of eternity and time. This was quintessentially expressed in the epochal second edition of the *Commentary on the Epistle to the Romans.* The existential dialectic of the temporal and the eternal found in Kierkegaard, in which the existing individual '*in time* comes into relation with the eternal *in time*' (*CUP*, 506), becomes in Barth an eschatological crisis, a confrontation of the temporal by a consuming eternity. The underlying Christological equilibrium maintained by Kierkegaard was shattered in an eschatological annihilation of time by eternity.[12] Whereas we shall see that Barth perceived and rectified the Christological difficulties in his later work (and he must be given full credit for his remarkable capacity for self-correction), it is in his understanding of creation (and time as its basic form) that problems will emerge that are unresolved and even unacknowledged.

II *Römerbrief and the dialectics of idealism*

Having seen how certain important and influential factors condition the emergence of Barth's own theological theory of time we are now in a position to examine the actual development of his thought from the dialectical theology of the period immediately following the First World War up until the appearance of the Prolegomena to the *Church Dogmatics* proper.

---

[12] See J. Heywood Thomas, 'Kierkegaard's View of Time', *Journal of the British Society for Phenomenology*, 4, No. 1 (Jan. 1973), pp. 33–40 and 'The Christology of S. Kierkegaard and Karl Barth', *Hibbert Journal* (1954–5), pp. 281ff.

In the decisive edition of *The Epistle to the Romans* which appeared in 1922, Barth stated in well-known words that if he had a 'System' then it was 'limited to a recognition of what Kierkegaard called the "infinite qualitative distinction between time and eternity" – "God is in heaven and thou art on earth"' and that 'The relation between such a God and such a man, and the relation between such a man and such a God, is for me the theme of the Bible and the essence of philosophy' (*ER*, 10). Barth carried his theme further, for 'Philosophers name this KRISIS of human perception – The Prime Cause; the Bible beholds at the same crossroads – the figure of Jesus Christ' (loc. cit.). So Barth conceives of a theological triumph over what is regarded philosophically as *Krisis*. By a powerful conjunction of eschatology (inspired by its so-called 'rediscovery' by Schweitzer and Weiss) and the principle of justification on the basis of God's grace alone (a return to a radical Lutheran insight) Barth was able to pass beyond the dialectic of finite and infinite categories, that is, time and eternity. In the dialectical phase of Barth's development this overcoming of the antithesis was by the annihilation of time by eternity and in his later dogmatic work a renewed Christological synthesis was asserted. Demolition had to precede reconstruction and the development we are to examine has only the appearance of dramatic discontinuity. In reality there is a progression in which Barth brilliantly utilizes an extraordinary wealth and diversity of insights drawn from the Christian tradition. The *Church Dogmatics* embodies his own response to this dilemma: a massive effort of self-correction that has been aptly classified as a movement from dialectic to analogy, a transformation that has elements of both continuity and discontinuity. The temporal dialectic of *Romans* clears the ground for a theologically generated theory of time strictly analogous to the general structure of the *Church Dogmatics*. We must turn once more to *The Epistle to the Romans* in order to appreciate the sheer power and consistency of his theological transformation and positing of a new beginning.

The eschatological extinction of the fragile equilibrium of Kierkegaard's Christology of paradox in Barth's *Romans* is precipitated by an absolute and unmediated dichotomy between time and eternity, juxtaposed as a dialectical divine 'Yes' or 'No', for, in a mutual annihilation, 'time is nothing when measured by the standard of eternity' (*ER*, 43). In the *Krisis* of revelation a tangential intersection is posited in 'Moments' linked together in the 'crimson line' of points of intervention. Unlike Kierkegaard, for whom 'To believe is to believe the divine and human together in Jesus Christ',[13] Barth allows the consistent impulse of the dialectical tension of time and eternity to run freely against the merely asserted relation of the divinity and humanity of Christ, which is thereby overwhelmed. The ontological *diastasis*, the drawing-apart into antithesis of time and eternity (representing the categories of finite and infinite existence), becomes the real locus of theological power. The antithesis is empowered by realized eschatology understood as the judging and the justifying act of God. The eschatological crisis blasts away any reliance upon a liberal Christology focused upon the life of Jesus or an orthodox Christology of a risen, triumphant Christ.

The combination of this radical disjunction with the principle of divine justification means that eternity purges time and any 'magnificent temporality of this world that can justify man before God' (*ER*, 56). The Pauline extinction of human boasting apart from God's justifying act in Jesus Christ is interpreted in the temporal categories of the dialectic. The philosophical antithesis of the idealist tradition becomes the vehicle of radical theological insight. So Barth commenting on Romans asserts that, 'They knew the judgement of God to be *according to the standard of truth*; and if men are measured by the standard of the truth of God, who can withstand it? Can stability be attained anywhere or at any time?' (*ER*, 58). This demolition of human security includes Barth's own standpoint in time which has become highly problematic. His only recourse is to begin from outside of both speculative idealism and the passionate subjectivity characteristic of the existentialist alternative. In brief, Barth was to attempt to pass beyond the horns of a dilemma into what he came to understand and propound as the 'God-given'. In the years between the second edition of *The Epistle to the Romans* (1922) and the first volume (the Prolegomena) of the *Church Dogmatics*

---

[13] J. Heywood Thomas, 'Kierkegaard's View of Time', p. 36, referring to the *Papirer* IX, A101.

(1932) proper, he explored such ways of escape from the inevitable outcome of the theology of crisis.

According to Barth's interpretation of St. Paul in *Romans*, 'No road to the eternal meaning of the created world has ever existed, save the road of negation' (*ER*, 87) for the 'redemption that is in Christ Jesus' is 'the dissolution of history in history, the destruction of the structure of events within their own structure, the end of time in the order of time' (*ER*, 103). The disclosure of the 'timeless, necessary reality in the longitude of time' (*ER*, 116) is an exposure of the hidden victory of election over rejection, of life over death in a temporal dialectic. Barth's 'greedy dialectic of time and eternity' (*ER*, 530) is characterized as follows: 'Between the past and the future – between the times – there is a "Moment" that is no moment in time. This "Moment" is the eternal Moment – the *Now* – when the past and the future stand still, when the former ceases its going and the latter its coming' (*ER*, 497). Eternity is understood as the intrusion of a timeless 'Moment' that interposes 'between' the successive stages in the temporal order. As such it is the formal basis of the eschatological crisis, but offers little to a Christology that must not only mediate the encounter of judgement and justifying grace by divine *fiat*, but must also be related to creation and to the life and work of Christ and his salvation.

At this point a comparison may once more be drawn between the content of this essay and that of Dr. Ford. Given the empty 'Now' of the 'eternal Moment', Barth has provided a theological receptacle at the centre of his renewed dialectic. Dr. Ford's approach to Barth explores the method implied by the introduction of biblical narrative. R. W. Jenson's insight[14] that if the intersection of time and eternity were replaced with 'the story narrated by the second article of the Apostles' Creed, he would obtain the theology of the *Church Dogmatics*' is amply justified by Ford's analysis. It is my contention that such a substitution is fraught with difficulties which are exposed by analysis of the nature of time as it is exploited in Barth's new synthesis.

Barth's intermediate work between *Romans* and the first volume of the *Church Dogmatics* was extensive and much may be

[14] *God after God: The God of the Future and the God of the Past seen in the Theology of Karl Barth* (Indianapolis, 1969). Again I refer to Professor David Ford's contribution to S. W. Sykes (ed.) op. cit.

learnt, in particular, from his articles in *Zwischen den Zeiten* concerning his changing understanding of the nature of the theological task. In *The Resurrection of the Dead*[15] and the abandoned *Christliche Dogmatik* of 1927 Barth demonstrates a growing appreciation of the shortcomings of the post-*Romans* theological situation and of the difficulties of rebuilding theology. In the former, St. Paul is said to be speaking not only of the end of history and of time but also of a 'reality so radically superior to all happening and temporality, that in speaking of the finiteness of history and the finiteness of time, he is also speaking of that upon which all time and all happening is based' (*RD*, 110). Barth criticizes, moreover, the annihilation of time by eternity, for 'real eternity' is that which 'marks' time as infinite. Eternity as the timeless crisis of tangential intersection is ontologically inadequate, it provides no 'base', and is merely subversive of time, adding nothing to it at all. Above all, Barth argues, the insight that 'God's eternity sets a limit to the endlessness of the world, time, things and men must be made fruitful' (*RD*, 112). The change from a negative to a positive appreciation of the importance of the concept of eternity in relation to time is one gauge of the degree of transformation in Barth's theological thought. In the abortive *Christliche Dogmatik* Barth made his first statement of an allegedly emancipated theology, that is, one free from the extraneous philosophical and non-biblical allusion so characteristic of *Romans*. But the 'existentialism' of the *Christliche Dogmatik* was heavily criticized[16] and Barth recommenced in earnest in the Prolegomena of the *Church Dogmatics* proper, working within the limits and upon the theological foundations outlined in the opening paragraphs of this paper. It was, according to Professor T. F. Torrance, a way forward that

> must come from a concentration upon Christology, upon the Word made flesh, for therein there opened up the possibility of a dogmatics genuinely bound with a form taken from the Word rather than from contemporary and temporal philosophies . . . With the concentration upon the Incarnation of the Word, upon

[15] Trans. H. J. Stenny (London, 1933).
[16] See J. D. Smart, *The Divided Mind of Modern Theology* (Philadelphia, 1967), Ch. 10.

Jesus Christ, God and Man in one Person, dialectical thinking had to fall away and positive Christological thinking had to take its place.[17]

We may agree with Torrance that this change took place, but its consequences remain unclear and merit sustained analysis.

Thus it is the precise nature and implications of this 'positive thinking' as it bears upon the problem of time that lies at the centre of interest in this essay. The profoundly 'negative' understanding of eternity over against time is evident in the early thought of Barth. This is both as regards its theological impulse, which is governed by the eschatological motif, and its actual temporal content, a conception of apparently 'timeless' eternity inhabiting momentary interstices in the temporal order. The changing theological demands made by the progress of Barth's thought as outlined above, calls for a corresponding transformation not merely in the theological framework of the encounter of eternity and time but also in the actual content of his temporal conceptions. This latter transformation is of crucial importance and an assessment of it leads the reader into the labyrinthine depths of the *Church Dogmatics*. The universality of the category of time entails a corresponding breadth of theological response, and it is such a response that is to be found in Barth's *magnum opus*.

In the foregoing sections the context and the development of Barth's thought have been set out briefly so as to allow a systematic examination of the doctrine of time and eternity in the *Church Dogmatics* to take place. Here can be found an extended and complex doctrine of time, which, whilst uniting many features of Barth's theological thought, is nevertheless built upon deep problems inherited from the idealist tradition and, beyond that, from the recurrent Platonizing tendency of Christian theology. The range and profundity of Barth's work demand a comprehensive response; and the following sections attempt to achieve this comprehensive stance by means of a brief paraphrase of the *Church Dogmatics* from the standpoint of time, showing how certain fundamental conceptions form an indispensable aspect of the 'inner logic' of this theology.

[17] *Karl Barth, An Introduction to his Early Theology 1910–1931* (London, 1962), pp. 106–7.

III   *Time and God's act*

The theological integrity of Barth's thought allows of no simple distinction between conceptual bones and theological flesh. Thus it is only in the context of theological exposition that an analysis of the doctrine of time and of the conceptions employed can be made. Barth uses within a vast, variegated, but ultimately unified vision certain fundamental conceptions. If these are to be examined and criticized their function in this scheme must be understood. Indeed, the passage, 'Man in his Time' (*CD* III/2 para.37) (often regarded as most significant with regard to the problem of time) is but the culmination and anthropological application of a set of conceptions which operate throughout the whole structure of the *Church Dogmatics* as informed by the temporal and closely allied ontological ideas that form part of that basic structure. In this way the architectonic nature of the doctrine of time may be understood, as well as its consequences and particular applications.

The shift in Barth's method evident in the differences between the *Christliche Dogmatik* of 1927 and the first volume of the *Kirchliche Dogmatik* is expressed in their titles. The former retains the possibility of a subjective emphasis, the latter indicates *in nuce* the starting-point that Barth adopts, the given reality of the 'essence of the Church', Jesus Christ. In the *Church Dogmatics* the task of dogmatic theology 'presupposes the ascertainability by man of the proper content of Christian language about God' and, according to Barth, 'Language about God has the proper content, when it conforms to the essence of the Church, Jesus Christ'.[18] The Church has been and is constituted by the figure to which the New Testament narrative witnesses. The theological exposition whilst related to such narrative, relies upon and exploits a conceptual structure which allows the 'Now-moment' to undergo extension in time. It is this structure which must be perceived as it underlies and informs Barth's exposition.

It is on the basis of the 'free personal presence of Jesus Christ' that theology may take place, but dogmatics as such seeks an

---

[18] *Church Dogmatics* I/1, p. 11. In the following pages both translations of the first half-volume have been used. The version quoted is considered the most apposite translation and is indicated by the translators' names, G. T. Thomson and G. W. Bromiley, respectively.

explanation of this 'presence' which is indispensable and original, 'the uncontrollable presence of its ontic and noetic basis' (*CD* I/1, Bromiley). It is out of the 'reality' of this recurrent presence that the 'possibility' of theological explanation may be generated, resting upon what Barth terms 'the fundamental transcendence of all human possibilities' (*CD* I/1, 44, Thomson) which takes place not as some inherent essence in the Church, but as '*actus purus*', divine action beginning with itself ... free action, not a continuously present relation; grace is an event of personal approach' (*CD* I/1, 43, Thomson). The presence of God in proclamation, that is the realization of the Word of God, correspondingly occurs as 'man's language about God on the basis of an indication by God Himself fundamentally transcending all human causation, and so devoid of all human basis, merely occurring as a fact and requiring to be acknowledged' (*CD* I/1, 101, Thomson). The uniqueness of the divine presence in the self-objectification of God (*Selbstvergegenständlichung Gottes*) is secured by the unpredictable divine condescension, not by any immanent means of continuity. This emphasis upon the transcendent root of the occurrent divine presence gave rise to J. Hamer's mistaken charge of an 'occasionalism' directed at the early volumes of the *Church Dogmatics*.[19] It is towards the basis of the divine presence in Church proclamation that Barth turns, postulating no timeless foundation, 'temporarily hidden but peacefully abiding' (*CD* I/1, 112, Thomson). This is not open to a Neoplatonic recollection or *anamnesis*, but, on the contrary, asserts a dynamic duality of immanence and transcendence which is experienced as a *fulfilment*, not a *negation* of time.

In a passage of importance, Barth sums up the temporal dimensions of the 'fulfilled time' (*die erfüllte Zeit*) in terms not incompatible with the early conception of the 'eternal Moment – the Now', cited earlier from *The Epistle to the Romans*, in which 'the past and the future stand still, when the former ceases its going and the latter its coming' (*ER*, 497). Thus, the 'God with us' has happened 'in human history and as part of human history', yet, according to Barth, 'it has not happened as other parts of this

---

[19] J. Hamer, *Karl Barth* (London, 1962), pp. 33–5. It is precisely Barth's doctrine of God's temporal being that ostensibly overrides such a misconception as Hamer's.

history usually happen' for it is self-sufficient and 'self-moved being in the stream of becoming (*Strom des Werdens*)', a 'completed event, fulfilled time, in the sea of the incomplete and changeable and self-changing' (*CD* I/1, 116, Bromiley). Barth is to derive not only 'eternity' or 'fulfilled time' from the '*Deus dixit*, to which there are no analogies', but also time itself, through the so-called 'true time' given in the revelation of God in Jesus Christ. In what follows, the doctrine of time Barth provides has both to function theologically and also to provide a concrete account of time as it is experienced and understood outside the purlieu of theology. Without such an actual fulfilment the threat of unreality will loom over his efforts.

The actual explication of the temporal continuity of revelation, the so-called gracious divine presence, is made in terms of the doctrine of the Word of God as the direct sign and correlate of the doctrine of the Trinity, for the 'Word needs no supplementing by the act. The Word of God is itself the act of God.' (*CD* I/1, 163, Thomson) The 'natural and corporeal' realities of preaching, the man Jesus Christ, the Church, and the Word of God written are the vehicle of the 'fulfilled reality' which is underlaid and sustained by the 'contingent contemporaneousness' (*kontingente Gleichzeitigkeit*) of God's act. By this term Barth conveys to the reader (albeit inadvertently) the ambiguity of his conception of time in relation to revelation, for, as will become apparent, he is at pains to posit contingency on the basis of revelation, not upon the basis of what are normally considered historical acts. The derivation of the ultimate reality of all realities from revelation (given the validity of the eschatological purge entailed by Barth's conception of justification expounded in *Romans*) makes quite inevitable a persistent and often uncomfortable synthesis of conflicting attributes and categories, not least in the temporal dimension. This will become increasingly apparent as analysis of the theological basis of the early volumes of the *Church Dogmatics* proceeds below.

The initial presupposition in Barth's argument is that, 'God's word is God's act means first its contingent contemporaneousness' (*CD* I/1, 164, Thomson). Barth's meaning is adequately conveyed by the English etymology of the word 'contemporaneousness', that is a kind of 'temporal togetherness'. By means of this conception Barth argues that the 'times' of prophecy, apostolate, and Church, and so on, are at one with the 'direct, original utterance of God Himself in His revelation, the time of Jesus Christ' (*CD* I/1, 164, Thomson). Quite literally for Barth these times are 'together with Christ' by virtue of the fact that the 'Word of God is itself God's act' (*CD* I/1, 168). Such a temporal grasp by means of the actuality of the divine Word should not be taken as a sure and certain sign of a radical disregard for history on Barth's part. On the contrary it is his unending struggle to do justice to *both* temporal and historical diversity as well as to a final unity which informs his doctrine of time and eternity throughout the *Church Dogmatics*. If, however, Barth's understanding of history and time is not to fall back into a quasi-idealist de-temporalization of the biblical witness or Church history then he is bound to resist the tendency towards a negative atemporal conception of eternity that was characteristic of his thought in *The Epistle to the Romans* and is indeed still evident in the early parts of volume I/1 of the *Church Dogmatics*. It is by the positing of the 'act' of God as a dynamic, living basis of the unity of the Word of God that Barth strives to escape the constant threat of a Platonic dissolution of time into eternity.

The notion of the 'act of God' is therefore of decisive importance for it underlies the apparently distinct theological concepts of election, revelation, calling, new birth, and so on. This 'act' 'shatters the immanence of the historical connection from within', thus allowing, so Barth asserts, the time of Christ to be contemporary with the time of the prophets and the Church 'without removal of the difference' between them (*CD* I/1, 168, Thomson). The divine 'Now' to which the whole of biblical history and Church history relates is not a simple unity *per se*, but the ostensibly dynamic ground of the act of God. It is thus exclusively by reference to Jesus Christ (who is, as will be seen, the 'reality' of God's act) and to the Trinity, that the trans-temporal unity and thus the hermeneutical interconnection of the proclaimed, written, and revealed God is achieved.

What is the 'possibility' that can be deduced from the 'reality' that Barth posits? How is this 'act' to be understood? Answers to these questions will reveal a considerable amount about the nature and function of the concept of time in the *Church Dogmatics*. In congruity with Barth's epistemological principles[20] the 'reality' of revelation leads through analysis into an account of the Trinity as its 'possibility'. Correspondingly, the temporal structure of the inner possibility of the statement, 'God reveals Himself' is the Trinitarian foundation of the 'presence of the Word of God between the Times' (*CD* I/1, 334, Thomson). Barth adheres exclusively to the doctrine of the Trinity as the basis of the knowledge of God (*CD* I/1, 349–383, Thomson) and it is within these parameters that the doctrine of time must consequently be understood. The doctrine of the Trinity as an 'explanatory confirmation' of the revealed name Yahweh-Kyrios is the explication of 'a unique entity, of a single unique Willer and Doer, whom Scripture designates as God' (*CD* I/1, 400, Thomson). By such an identification Barth introduces the conceptions of being and act, entity and agent *in unity*, and thus he claims to build a bridge between the ontological thinking of the Greek Fathers and the revealing God of the Bible. The unhesitating equation that is made here between the biblical concept of revelation and the lordship of God, on the one hand, and on the other the language of essence and substance, characteristic of patristic theology, presages an integration of 'being' and 'act' of great significance and this has a consistently important influence upon the conception of time in the *Church Dogmatics*.[21]

The relative worth of Barth's doctrine of the Trinity developed in the latter parts of volume I/1 of the *Church Dogmatics* is not of prime importance here, save to note that it is above all the unity of the Godhead that he seeks to confirm. This is to be expected, as Barth must at all costs preserve the unity of the divine act, for 'all God's operation, as we are bound to conceive it on the basis of this revelation, is a single act, occurring simultaneously and unitedly in all His three modes of existence' and consequently it must be said 'Of creation, past revelation and reconciliation, to the redemption to come it holds good that He who acts here is the Father and the Son and the Spirit' (*CD* I/1, 430, Thomson). The unity of Barth's whole theological scheme can only be preserved if the unity of the divine act is sustained, because the doctrine of

---

[20] See *CD* I/1, (Thomson), p. 214, pp. 236–7 for an account of knowledge as 'acknowledgement'.
[21] Such an integration is not of course unique to Barth.

God's being-in-act is the ontological *fundamentum* of the *Church Dogmatics*, and the axis of eternity and time the medium through which this ontology is diffused throughout the theological structure of his work. So it is that the pattern of antecedence and consequence and the corresponding method of *analogia fidei* informing the *Church Dogmatics* take on an urgent importance in the context of the doctrine of time. Here the derivation of the fullest and truest reality from the divine arm of these dualities gives immense theological power to the doctrine of time, yet, simultaneously, this raises not inconsiderable problems.

Given the axis of antecedence and consequence, the Fatherhood of God is derived from his Fatherhood of Jesus Christ. As the functional reciprocity of Father, Son, and the Holy Spirit is realized in the life, death, and resurrection of Jesus Christ, so God the Father is revealed as Creator. It is from within the 'self-enclosed circle' of the doctrine of the Trinity that God the Creator is known (*CD* I/1, 436, Thomson). The status of this assertion is a factor of great importance because the whole *catena* of temporal conceptions must be understood in relation to the central revelatory events in which the Trinitarian life-in-act of God is realized. Indeed the ontology of human existence is likewise bound up with the 'Lordship' of God for 'our existence is held by him, and only by him, over the abyss of non-existence . . . It is real so far as He wills and posits it a real existence' (*CD* I/1, 446, Thomson). Human existence, and thus time which is 'real so far as He wills and posits it a real existence' raises a difficulty inherent in the *Church Dogmatics* as a whole: how does this 'real existence' relate to that existence experienced by the human subject as a mere percipient being? This problem is acute with regard to time, as will become apparent in the exposition of *Man in his Time* (*CD* III/2, para.37). Suffice it to note here that as Barth derives the Fatherhood of God from his antecedent, eternal Fatherhood of Jesus Christ, so, likewise, must time be derived from within the 'self-enclosed circle'. Furthermore, in the light of this antecedence and the centrality of the divine 'act' as the content of the 'presence' of Jesus Christ, the essence of the Church in revelation, so it is not time, *per se*, upon which attention must be concentrated, but eternity as the temporal *plenum* from which time takes its reality.

IV "*God's time is eternity*": *the central axis*

Having made an initial examination of the relation of time to the divine act in Jesus Christ and observed that this act is spelt out in Trinitarian terms it is now possible to proceed to a more detailed presentation of Barth's understanding of the nature and relation of eternity and time. This is most clearly expressed as regards eternity in the account of the divine perfections in volume II/1 of the *Church Dogmatics*. Here the 'act' of volume I/1 becomes the 'perfection' of God's eternity.

'Eternity' first emerges as an important theme in the exposition of the Niceano-Constantinopolitan Creed that concludes volume I/1 of the *Church Dogmatics*. Here it denotes the status 'before all time' of the Persons of the Trinity and it is at this point that the transformation of the temporal conceptions is once more apparent. The phrase 'before all time' indicates the mysterious inclusion of the time of revelation and that of the sinful creature (*CD* I/1, 425, Bromiley). The phrase (before all worlds) of the Creed does not grant a 'temporal definition' but, according to Barth, gives an indication of 'genuine and eternal transcendence' (*CD* I/1, 427, Bromiley). Despite this proviso, there is here the initial presentation of a conception that has ordinary temporal implications. The theological conditioning must now, however, shroud the logic of the concept of eternity and time being developed. In *Romans* there was the eternal '"Moment" that is no moment in time', a *Now* – when the past and the future stand still which becomes the 'unborn secret of revelation' qualifying the moments in common time (*ER*, 497). In the first volume of the *Church Dogmatics* the basis of such qualification is indicated, for once more the 'absolutely marked (i.e. distinguished) events in time' (*schlechterdings ausgezeichnete Ereignisse*) (*CD* I/1, 488, Thomson) are moments in which the eternal encounters time; but now, by contrast, the reader is initiated theologically into the 'unborn secret of revelation' (*ER*, 497).

What has happened is that the dialectic of antitheses in *The Epistle to the Romans* has given way to a dialectic informed by a new conjunction of transcendence and immanence, that is a creative 'inclusion' of time by eternity. The simple 'annihilation' of time has apparently been superseded. The distinction between the temporal concepts of *Romans* and those of the first half-volume of the *Church*

Dogmatics deserves qualified statement, for there remains both continuity and new development. The decisive temporal source (the 'Now' moment of *Romans*) is given temporal and historical extension as it becomes identified with God's act in Jesus Christ as propounded in volume I/1 of the *Church Dogmatics*.

Much now depends upon whether the actual content of the temporal conceptions can bear the positive (as opposed to the destructive) weight now laid upon them. The dialectic of *Romans* made highly effective use of the Platonizing dissolution of time into eternity through the eschatological annihilation of human (and therefore temporally bound) assertion in the *Krisis* of divine judgement. Whether the remnants of such temporal conceptions can function as adequately in the context of a positive theological exposition, such as Barth attempts in the *Church Dogmatics*, remains to be seen. In volume I/1 the beginnings of such a transmutation are evident, but the ambiguity of Barth's efforts are equally apparent given the incipient tension between theological intention, and the conceptual tools to be employed in the theology of eternity and time *per se*.

The ambiguity of affirming time and its reality through the 'analogical' use of eternity stems from the problematic 'temporal' nature of the latter. The weight placed upon the antecedent and essential concept of the divine act extended in 'contingent contemporaneity' is markedly increased by Barth's corresponding denial of natural theology. Once more we need not enter into the rationale of Barth's adoption of this stance, save to point out that it is entirely congruent with his uncompromising and consistent advocacy of the principle of justification by God's grace alone. It is the consequences of such a rejection that concern us, for, as we shall become aware, the denial of natural theology comes dangerously close to a repudiation of natural reality itself.

In the context of the uncompromising rejection of the pretensions of natural theology and of the analogy of being (which is to be understood in the light of the exclusive source of the knowledge of God, and God's identity with knowledge of himself *CD* II/1, 10–16), man is consequently denied 'independent existence' for the 'vitality of natural theology is the vitality of man as such' (*CD* II/1, 165). Once more the purge of human self-assertion is sustained with consistency, but a new element has appeared for 'Man exists in Jesus Christ and in Him alone.' Indeed, Barth asserts, 'The being and nature of men in and for themselves as independent bearers of an independent predicate, have, by the revelation of Jesus Christ, become an abstraction which can be destined only to disappear' (*CD* II/1, 149). This denial and Christologically-inspired affirmation must be stressed because it is in direct parallel with the assertion of humanity in Christ that temporality is likewise to be understood. These affirmations of man in Christ are the realization and correlates of the divine act in being, of the God 'who is in His act of revelation' (*CD* II/1, 262).

This 'act' is explicated in paragraph 28 of volume II/1, 'The Being of God in Act', where Barth asserts the divine being apart from, and over against, any doctrine of being *qua* being. The first declaration, 'that in God's revelation, which is the content of this Word we have to do with His act' is followed by an exposition which exploits and develops the temporal 'inclusiveness' advanced in the latter stages of volume I/1 and outlined in the preceding section of this essay. The being-in-act of God has immediate temporal implications, as might be expected if it is to contain within its 'simplicity' the total time-scale envisaged. The event is in the past yet it also happens now and will happen in the future, for the birth, death, and resurrection of Jesus are temporally unlimited. This because if the event is the act of God whose being as 'event' or 'act' is final, then there can be no further penetration, only the explanation (in effect the *exegesis*) of what is posited in his act. The theological spade turns upon the bedrock of the utterly surpassing actuality of the divine Word[22] – it is ultimate reality. God's act, his *actus purus et singularis*, exists in revelation in 'dialectical transcendence', that is, it is self-distinguished from 'general happening' within which the 'definite happening' (*bestimmtes Geschehen*) of revelation takes place (*CD* II/1, 264). The particularity and specific freedom of God's act, event, and life is by way of the concrete existence of Israel, the birth of Jesus Christ, his resurrection, and so on, which are the indispensable correlates of the divine act. In the briefest terms, 'the whole content of the happening consists in the fact that the Word of

---

[22] Close study of pp. 262–4 of *CD* I/1 is essential for a full understanding of Barth's argument at this point.

God became flesh and that His Holy Spirit is poured out on all flesh' (*CD* II/1, 267). Barth's integration of the *Deus in se* and the *Deus revelatus* in his active freedom is expressed in a doctrine of the divine perfections which extrapolates and integrates his emphasis upon the dynamic and the actual. The activity of God understood as the fulfilment of the statement that 'Jesus Christ is the same yesterday and today and for ever' (Heb. 13:8) is explicated in terms which stress the positive attributes expressing that activity, rather than as metaphysical statements and limitations. Against what he conceives of as a Hegelian depersonalized doctrine of Absolute Spirit, Barth stresses the 'particularity of the divine event in the particularity of the being of a person' (*CD* II/1, 267–71). This being does not subsist in holy isolation, but love and grace overflow, they take place in 'the whole intervention of the divine action and being' (*CD* II/1, 281). In the equation '"God is" means "God loves"', act, being, love, and person are unified in Jesus Christ. By locating his synthesis of categories in the divine act and by identifying this act with the person of Jesus Christ, Barth putatively escapes the reductive comprehensiveness of the Hegelian dialectic. The pattern of antecedence and consequence structuring in dynamic terms the divine act is realized in the concrete historical man Jesus Christ, in his time and in his person. In the account of the divine perfections the idea of eternity is developed, but it remains subordinate to Christology and the Father-Son axis which constantly informs Barth's exposition.

In the context of this framework there follows an account of the divine perfections in which the attributes of God are expounded as a positive doctrine of the 'Biblical idea of God' (*CD* II/1, 302). Included among these 'perfections', eternity is developed in the context of the discrete originality of the divine being, which is 'itself perfection and so the standard of all perfection' (*CD* II/1, 322). The perfections of God (as the Persons of the Trinity) are dynamically coexistent and consubstantial, as this doctrine is the 'development and confirmation of the doctrine of His being' (*CD* II/1, 327). The scholastic appearance of Barth's exposition is belied by his consistent attempts to avoid the pitfalls of the traditional arguments concerning attribution, which he sees as providing grounds for a rejection of metaphysical theology parallel to that of Kant. The being of God is not a speculative entity, but is one with his revelation, and thus the exegesis of the simplicity of God, as the foundation upon which constancy, eternity, omnipresence, omnipotence, and glory are built, is conducted in such a way as to avoid logical reduction. Again it is impossible to convey in outline the richness of Barth's exposition, as the essence of his argument consists not in an extended or connected logic in which each proposition follows from the former, but in a 'vertical' logic whereby the validity of the cohering assertions is given by the quality of purported witness each makes to the divine being. For Barth the very uniqueness of God would logically demand such an approach. Following the exposition of God's unity and simplicity, and his omnipresence and spatiality (all understood in the context of their utter prototypical superiority in God's active and dynamic being), comes the first extended consideration of eternity *per se*.

Having denied the participation of eternity in the finite-infinite dialectic (*CD* II/1, 188–9) and based his conception upon purely theological postulates, Barth contends that eternity,

> in itself and as such is to be understood as a determination of the divine freedom. Like the unity and constancy of God, it primarily denotes the absolute sovereignty and majesty of God in itself and as such, as demonstrated in the inward and outward activity of His divine being and operative in His love as the external love. God's love requires and possesses eternity both inwards and outwards for the sake of its divinity, its freedom. Correspondingly it requires, creates and therefore possesses in its outward relations what we call time. Time is the form of creation in virtue of which it is definitely fitted to be a theatre for the acts of divine freedom (*CD* II/1, 464–5).

Eternity and time are defined in terms of their functional roles in the doctrine of God as Revealer and thus any conceptions of omnipresence and eternity based upon an understanding of God as 'the supreme principle of existence and the universal' embracing space and time are ruled out. The latter stem from the 'problems of a created existence and a created world' and as such fail to relate to the God of Christian revelation. Infinity as such can form no adequate basis for a concept of eternity, for 'It speaks of the non-finiteness, the non-limitedness or non-limitableness, and therefore the timelessness and non-spatiality of God' (*CD* II/1, 465). The enduring criticism of a timeless eternity as an adjunct of the immanent antitheses of finite and infinite and 'the general concept of tradition' is made on the basis of its 'insufficiency' in describing what God is in relation to space and time. God's 'infinity' involves no contradiction with finitude, for his 'whole action posits beginning and end, measure and limit, space and time'.

It is now apparent that Barth's argument is double-edged at the very least. On the one hand he denies the involvement of true eternity with the dialectic of finite and infinite categories; on the other he affirms eternity as the total time-positing action of God. This position can only be consistently maintained if the temporal categories asserted by the latter at no point identify with the finite-infinite dialectic. This means that the vast and complete temporal system that emerges in the *Church Dogmatics* must never coincide with non-theological temporal categories in identity, only in the so-called dialectic of transcendence. Can, however, the 'time' that emerges be the time of the world of experience and the cosmos if it is systematically at one remove from it, as what Barth will term the 'true time' of revelation? If this 'time' is not so correlated then what consequences will there be? Can the most powerful theological assertions be made about the shared realities of human existence, if such theologically posited realities are absolutely undetectable outside the peculiar theological mode of their positing and perception? Indeed can such an entirely self-consistent system escape from a certain triviality or even logical circularity? More specifically, can the concept of time reside entirely within the 'theological circle' that Barth expands, without what may be called a logical implosion into timelessness, once the relationship and identity of this concept with the shared time of human and cosmic existence is systematically excluded? The doubts raised here must remain in mind as continuing examination is made of the concept of eternity and its temporal correlates.

On the basis of the foregoing exposition of the theological factors informing Barth's doctrine of eternity the passage 'The Eternity and Glory of God' (*CD* II/1, 608–77) can be seen to contain a new aspect of the synthesis between the systematic and the biblical in Christian theology. In this passage of Boethian conception, *Aeternitas est interminabilis vitae tota simul et perfecta possessio* (eternity is the complete and perfect possession of unending life) receives, according to Barth, its 'proper exploitation' as the legitimate fulfilment of both biblical and systematic insight. In a passage concrete yet rhapsodic in style, the ambiguity of Barth's thought is perceived in that it progresses towards the apparent, yet ostensibly resolvable contradiction of deriving time from eternity.

God's eternity, as an expression of the divine freedom, is 'pure duration' (*reine Dauer*). 'Pure duration' denotes the divine simultaneity (*Gleichzeitigkeit*) in which beginning, middle, and end are not three, but one, not separate as on three occasions, but one simultaneous occasion. Time, on the other hand, has beginning, middle and end which are distinct and even opposed as past, present, and future. In consequence, Barth argues, eternity is 'just that duration which is lacking to time'. In that eternity is simultaneity, so it is said to provide the duration lacking in time.

God, as the 'prototype and foreordination of all being, and therefore the prototype and foreordination of time' (*CD* II/1, 611), does not negate time because eternity as 'pure duration', the 'pure present', is only properly exploited when it 'includes' time. Time pre-exists in God's eternity, his endurance, 'duration itself', does not prevent him being 'origin, movement and goal' (*Ursprung, Bewegung und Ziel*). What distinguishes eternity from time is that 'origin, movement and goal', past, present, and future, 'not yet', 'now', and 'no more', rest and movement, potentiality and actuality, and so on, are all held in God's being, his eternity in a pure present. In eternity, therefore, these distinctions exist, but purportedly without the fleeting nature of the present, the separation between before and after.[23] Eternity is not the negation of time, an 'abstract non-temporality' in any simple sense, although it is 'certainly the negation of created time in so far as it has no part in the problematical and questionable nature of our

[23] There is an affinity here with the arguments advanced concerning the time orders of 'before' and 'after' and 'past, present and future' in J. M. E. McTaggart's *The Nature of Existence* (Cambridge, 1927), vol. II, Bk. V, Ch. 33.

possession of time', that is, 'to the extent that it is first and foremost God's time and therefore real time (*wirkliche Zeit*)' (*CD* II/1, 613).

With the introduction of the notion of 'God's time' and 'real time' on the basis of a positive 'proper exploitation' of the Boethian concept of eternity, Barth has carried his synthesis a stage further. The apparent contradiction of deriving the many from the one has now become explicit: 'God does not first create multiplicity and movement, but He is one and simple, He is constant, in such a way that all multiplicity and movement have their prototype and pre-existence in Himself' (*CD* II/1, 612). God, in his true being, in the begetting of the Son and the procession of the Spirit, exemplifies an order and succession in which 'unity is in movement' and in which there is a 'before and after' (*CD* II/1, 615). 'God's time' is 'the form of the divine being in its trinity' in which beginning and ending do not imply any limitation (*Begrenzung*) of God nor does this inner juxtaposition (*Nacheinander*) mean that there is any exclusion (*Auseinander*). So Barth develops his exposition of 'pure duration' upon an explicitly Trinitarian basis of prototypical interaction and reciprocity without division. The relationship between the Trinitarian and the temporal doctrines is enhanced by similar terminology used by Barth in both contexts, thereby implying a continuity of argument.

It would be possible at this stage in the exploration of the doctrine of time to turn to Barth's antecedents and compare his conception of eternity with those inherited from Parmenides, Plato, Plotinus, St. Augustine, and Boethius, and presented in systematic form in, for example, the *Summa Theologica* of St. Thomas Aquinas.[24] The importance of Barth's argument lies in its synthetic impulse and therefore in this essay attention must remain focused upon his goal of renewal and integration. The 'pure-duration' which stems from the informing of the Boethian *totum simul* by the Trinitarian impulse is then applied to the

[24] Consultation of F. H. Brabant's Bampton Lectures, *Time and Eternity in Christian Thought* (1936), and relevant chapters in E. Bevan's Gifford Lectures, *Symbolism and Belief* (1933–4), provide initial guidance. More recent discussion may be found in W. Kneale, 'Time and Eternity in Theology', *Proceedings of the Aristotelian Society*, vol. LXI, (1961), pp. 87–108.

biblical context. The 'from everlasting to everlasting' of Ps.90:2 which is 'so common in both Old and New Testaments . . . can be taken to mean from duration to duration, that is, in pure duration' (*CD* II/1, 609). The phrase, 'can be taken to mean' indicates in fact a substantial and methodological identity between the dogmatic conceptions that Barth has appropriated and developed and the biblical insights hinted at in Isa.43; Ps.90; 2 Pet.3:8; Ps.102, and so on. Barth's positive appropriation of the Boethian notion of a divine simultaneity, which is reasserted upon a Trinitarian basis developed in the first half-volume of the *Church Dogmatics* and now identified with biblical insight, is ready to be applied and exploited. Eternity, 'pure duration', is God's 'real time' and so now all God's revelatory activity in history, supremely (indeed in a sense, exclusively) in Jesus Christ can be conditioned by this positive theological conception of eternity.

In strictly temporal terms the *nunc stans*, 'the "now", the total and simultaneous present' which is the '*possessio vitae*, the total, simultaneous possession of unlimited life' is opposed to the merely negative 'now', the 'fluid fleeting present, which can be understood only as a mathematical point'. The theological elements underlying the former allow it to 'heal' the latter, as its 'duration' encounters the 'division' of mere (human) time. This juxtaposition is of course interpreted in positive theological terms and in correspondence with the initial exposition of the 'fulness of time which is identical with Jesus Christ' (*CD* I/1, 131, Thomson). As the Word became flesh, so eternity (without ceasing to be eternity) became time. In Jesus Christ it is not, Barth argues, merely that God has given us time, 'our created time, as the form of our own existence and world', but that 'God takes time to Himself, that He Himself, the eternal One, becomes temporal, and so, in consequence he not merely 'embraces' but 'submits' to it (*CD* II/1, 616). We have at this point accumulated the essential elements which allow us to proceed to review the systematic application of the basic equation of the divine being in act (with all its temporal implications) with the person of Jesus Christ. Eternity as the pure act of the divine being is the ground of the temporal unity and comprehensiveness of Jesus Christ, the 'essence of the Church'. Enormous weight is consequently laid upon Christology if the God-man is to be man in any acceptable sense and not merely the supra-philosophical expression of the divine being and the resolution of antitheses.

So it is that the very nerve-centre of Barth's theology is reached, that Christological concentration in which is located the realization of the divine being, expounded in the Trinitarian and ontological treatises of volumes I/1 and II/1 of the *Church Dogmatics* respectively. Christology, *per se*, has a temporal structure in which may be perceived three interconnected 'moments', predestination (or as Barth prefers, 'election'), incarnation, and resurrection. All three elements have a unified application in theological anthropology, that is 'Man in his Time' (*CD* III/2, para.37).

V   *The primacy of election*

'The election of grace is the sum of the Gospel' (*CD* II/2, 13). With these words Barth enters into his positive exposition of the doctrine of election and his dialogue with the Reformed tradition. The election of grace is 'the choice of God, which preceding all His other choices, is fulfilled in the eternal willing of the man Jesus and of the people represented in Him' (*CD* II/2, 25). Repudiating the classes of humanity, the elect and the reprobate, Barth places all men in a similar relationship to God in Christ, to the 'primal and basic act of God'. There can be no probing beyond the eternal choice of God already made in God's act, that is his own election of Jesus Christ. The eternal decision to elect Jesus Christ and to elect man in solidarity with him is realized in time. In becoming man, a particular man who represents the whole people, 'God Himself realized in time, and therefore as an object of human perception, the self-giving of Himself as the Covenant – partner of the people determined by Him from and to all eternity' (*CD* II/2, 53).

The eternal decision of God made in 'primal history' is realized in the concrete particularity and revelation of God in the history of Israel and in the Incarnation itself.[25] In Jesus Christ 'electing God' and 'elected man' are one, and it is upon him *alone*, Barth argues, that attention must be focused and not upon 'abstract

---

[25] H. Kung's excursus, 'The Redeemer in God's Eternity', pp. 272–88 of *Justification* (London, 1964), is relevant for the following exposition.

presuppositions concerning God or man, or of the abstract consequences of such abstract presuppositions' (*CD* II/2, 59). Progress in understanding should only be made in confirming and developing the presuppositions 'contained in the name of Jesus Christ'. It would seem possible at this point to draw out an invidious contrast between on the one hand the eternal basis of election in the 'perfect presence' of God in the pre-, supra-, and post-temporality of 'primal history' in which there is 'duration' (without, Barth argues, 'division') and on the other the realization of revelation from which all history ostensibly derives its contingency. In more general terms, however, it is possible to point to an incompatibility between election in the 'perfect presence' (a presence of 'duration' without the 'division' of before and after) and the contingent historical acts of salvation. If the latter are to be significant acts, then they certainly must have a distinct before and after. Without such 'division' nothing could have been achieved by the death of Christ, or indeed his resurrection, precisely because nothing could be said to have *happened* in a significant sense. The reality of what takes place is sapped by Barth's argument at this and other points.

The mutuality of electing God and elected man in the doctrine of predestination is the basis upon which a fully integrated Christology and soteriology is to be developed. The Johannine elements in Barth's thought now become apparent: the Word from the beginning is the Word which becomes flesh. This is to be expressed in a doctrine of the two natures from which all soteriological possibilities flow. In so far as God's works are done 'in time they rest upon the eternal decision of God by which time is founded and governed' (*CD* II/2, 99). Thus it is that grace precedes creation, for prior to the establishment of any reality distinct from God, 'God anticipated and determined within Himself . . . that the goal and meaning of all His dealings with the as yet non-existent universe should be the fact that in His Son He would be gracious towards man, uniting Himself with him' (*CD* II/2, 101). Creation and covenant as the consequence of the resolve of the triune God are derived from their central point in Jesus Christ. Without the unity of predestination and Christology eternal work and temporal event would fall apart. The very comprehensiveness and unity of Barth's vision, whilst entirely corresponding with the extensive dogmatic basis outlined here, is not without its dangers in that the distinction between the area of divine antecedence and that of temporal consequence, between the transcendent and the immanent, becomes blurred and ambiguous.

In the election and rejection of Jesus Christ sin is overcome and, therefore, 'In Jesus Christ we can see and know this sphere of evil as something which has already been overcome . . . which has been destroyed by the positive will of God's overflowing glory' (*CD* II/2, 172). 'Sin' must here be understood in the light of Barth's doctrine of 'nothingness' (*Nichtigkeit*) as the 'impossible possibility', that which exists in despite of the divine will. The overcoming of sin in Jesus Christ is the overcoming of 'nothingness' or non-being and its replacement or 'fulfilment' by the reality of revelation. The assertions also cohere with Barth's polemic against natural theology and compound the difficulty of his position. Inevitably 'sin' is in danger of being identified with the natural order as such which only becomes positively real as it is realized in the sphere of the analogy of faith. The relatively static and distinct categories of traditional theology (grace and nature, transcendent and immanent, and so on) are reinterpreted in the context of revelation and the analogy of faith in such a way that they appear as mere functions within a larger, dominant equation concerning the nature of the divine being.

The particular consequence of Barth's compression of election and rejection into the elected and rejected Jesus Christ is to shift the fulcrum of the divine action from Jesus Christ's act in history to God's act in him in eternity or the 'perfect presence'. A consequence of the surpassing completeness of the redemptive activity of God in his act in Christ is to make the path to salvation a merely noetic realization such that the 'godless man' comes to know that his choice is 'void' and that he is elected in Jesus Christ. The 'new creation' has taken place in Jesus Christ and the hearers and believers realize in their affirmation the completedness of the election of man made in Jesus Christ. Such a conception of election in its concentration upon the exclusive centrality in Jesus Christ is once more congruent with the utter self-sufficiency of the divine act as expounded temporally in the doctrine of eternity.

The problem is that given this exclusiveness, the temporal dimension of salvation becomes questionable, and what Barth calls the 'consummation' of the Reformation insight into the work of Christ and God's justifying act comes dangerously close to a *reductio ad absurdum*. The election of men in Christ 'transcending their own being, . . . also transcends the being of everything which God has created and which is distinct from Himself, with the exception of one man, Jesus of Nazareth'; as the 'eternal basis' of the existence of those who live as the elect this election is something which 'happened *to* and not *in* their human history and its development' (*CD* II/2, 321). Correspondingly men's 'special calling simply discloses and confirms the fact that they are already the elected' (*CD* II/2, 341) and that the 'rejected man' only exists as the 'object of the divine non-willing' (*CD* II/2, 450), that is, as sinners.

In overall outline Barth's doctrine of election is a reworking of the Protestant tradition in such a way as to integrate the Reformed emphasis upon the primacy of divine grace with the Lutheran concentration upon the utter exclusivity of the revelation of God in Christ alone. As noted above, the completeness of the election of man in Christ is congruent with the dogmatic ontology of the act of God, the *actus purus et singularis*, outlined in this essay. If, however, the act of God in Christ is not to remain unrelated to the human condition and to the sin-ridden complexity of individual human lives, then it must be expressed in adequate temporal terms, not only in relation to the shared human temporality of ordinary life, but also to the actual death and resurrection of the man Jesus Christ. Such an identity and involvement cannot remain frozen within eternal election, albeit an election in the eternal act of God (which contains within itself the pre-, supra-, and post-temporality of the divine being), but must truly enter time as it does in the 'story' of the Gospels.

Barth is aware in his own way of this danger of unrelatedness, which he sees as an adjunct of the traditional legalistic conception of election in an eternal decree dividing humanity into elect and reprobate. According to the traditional view, 'God was', for 'in time he predestinates no longer' (*CD* II/2, 182); the election exhibits a Deistic pattern, in which the divine decision is, once made, worked out without further reference to God. Such inadequacy may be countered, Barth argues, by exploitation of the full doctrine of eternity and its application to the doctrine of election. In his understanding of election, predestination ceases to be an *apologia* for God's absence, but becomes the means of his presence in time for the 'predestination of God is unchanged and unchangeably God's activity' (*CD* II/2, 183). So God's ontology of act conditions the doctrine of election, as it does all doctrines, for the pre-, supra-, and post-temporality of God in his eternity is the reality underlying election. The tension between eternal work and temporal realization is still problematic, however, so long as all the interpretative categories are grounded in and derived from the divine and eternal being of God. Thus a great deal depends upon the adequacy of Barth's conceptual distinction of, and relation between, eternity and time, as well as upon the purely theological exposition which is to reach its temporal consummation in the death and resurrection of Jesus Christ.

VI *Incarnation, Christology and the problems of the natural*
Karl Barth's doctrine of the Incarnation is determined by the pattern of thought expounded in his book on Anselm, according to which fact precedes interpretation, and so the 'simple reality of God' (*CD* I/2, 11) is revealed in 'God's time'. This simple reality is not a 'repeated or general event, like that of an event formulated in a law of causality', but a 'definite, temporally limited unrepeated and quite unrepeatable event' which has happened once for all, but which at the same time acts as the 'midpoint of time' (*die Mitte der Zeit*). The midpoint of time is the fulfilment of time with which are identical both the 'real temporal pre-existence of Jesus Christ in prophecy and his real temporal post-existence in witness' (*CD* I/2, 12). Cullmann's understanding of the 'midpoint of time' differs quite decisively from Barth's in that the latter is not contrasting eternity and time as mere finite (limited) and infinite (unlimited) duration but is once more asserting a temporal transcendence. The danger that we encounter in Barth's account is not merely that of an alien remnant of philosophy (Cullmann's charge)[26] but whether the

[26] See *Christ and Time* (rev. edn., London, 1962).

'mid-point' really is truly temporal, whether it does in fact determine human time or remains a purely theological construction, in danger of being what H. Bouillard terms a 'dream'.[27]

Barth proceeds to develop his doctrine of the Incarnation along classical Christological lines, 'the becoming flesh of the Word that remains the Word' (*CD* I/2, 38). In 'God's Time and our Time', the theme of the Incarnation is developed in specific and detailed temporal terms laying down the pattern of thought applied in the remaining two sections of paragraph 14, 'The Time of Revelation'. Barth's exposition is influenced by that of St. Augustine in the *De Trinitate*[28] but the former's work must remain at the forefront of attention. The statement 'God reveals Himself' is equivalent to the assertion that 'God has time for us'; this is 'the time that is real in this revelation' and this time-concept is determinative. No time-concept apart from that of revelation itself may be used, 'we must let ourselves be told what time is by revelation itself' (*CD* I/2, 45) and it is this principle that is applied with absolute consistency.

The completeness of Barth's account becomes even more obvious, but its problematic nature no less so. The difficulty concerns the relative spheres of natural and revealed knowledge in Barth's thought. According to T. F. Torrance, 'Barth's understanding of the Incarnation as the truth of God incarnate in space and time, encountering us in space and time, encountering us objectively in Jesus Christ, had the unavoidable effect of calling into question any idea that the truth about God arises within us.'[29] This is only half the truth for in his advocacy of 'the special concept of this special time' (*CD* I/2, 45) Barth is effectually calling into question not merely anthropocentric sources of revealed knowledge of God but natural knowledge of the natural world. The demand that the Incarnation be 'real', yet its reality lie in its own sphere and temporal reality, creates an unresolved tension and contradiction between it and the time experienced by extra-theological humanity. Such humanity cannot legitimately

[27] *The Knowledge of God* (London, 1969), p. 61.
[28] See Bk. IV, Ch. 19 and the *Confessions*, Bk. XI, esp. Chs. 16 and 39.
[29] 'The Problem of Natural Theology in the Thought of Karl Barth', *Religious Studies*, vol. 6 (1970), 24.

exist in terms of Barth's strict presuppositions: it exists only in so far as it affirms its reality in the elected and saving humanity of Jesus Christ.

The structure of human existence is temporality (for as Barth asserts: 'Humanity is temporality') and time thus has a corresponding position of 'unreality' outside the realm of revelation. In view of this juxtaposition does the knowledge and correlative reality experienced in God's grace actually effect a confirmation and fulfilment of nature, or its annihilation? The relation between the epistemological demands of faith and the ontological reality of the object of faith entails an inescapable contradiction, not merely between contrasting theological realities, but between reality as the purveyor of revelation and all reality apart from revelation. This contradiction necessitates a complete reconstruction of reality on theological foundations which strives towards completeness, but in so far as it remains dialectically transcendent, stays systematically at one remove from the texture of reality as normally experienced. An ontology and epistemology of the world are produced in direct correlation with those of faith and its object, Jesus Christ. Nature as such becomes wholly problematic in the face of this revelation.

Under the influence of St. Augustine, for whom in the Eternal, 'the whole is present' (*Confessions*, XI, 13), Barth rejects the former's 'subjectivism' and implicitly endorses his doctrine of eternity, giving it, as with Boethius' conception, a 'proper exploitation'. The positive elaboration of the temporal aspects of the Incarnation is matched by a correspondingly negative attitude towards extra-theological time. Barth begins to develop the logical content and fulfil the demands of a position which opposes theological and extra-theologically based time, for, as indicated above, there can be no peace between the two spheres of reality. There begins to emerge a positive theological development of the negative influence of eternity in the dialectic of *The Epistle to the Romans*. Eternity still annihilates time, but now instead of explosive demolition, a vast and 'unnatural' theological growth chokes and smothers the natural order and its reality, for grace consumes nature in putative, but merely apparent recreation. We are faced with a synthesis of reduction hidden in the folds of a theological cloak cast over the perennial dialectic of Western thought.

The power of Barth's doctrine of the Incarnation and his Christology is not an unambiguous triumph, but one underlaid by an epistemological and ontological repression, even, it becomes apparent, a repression of humanity precipitated by a profound confusion of theological and epistemological categories. Yet, here once more the reader is faced with the possibilities that Barth's thought may lead (as von Balthasar has said, doubtless without irony) to the true 'consummation of Protestantism', or, in reality, to the *reductio ad absurdum* of the principle of the Reformation, *sola fides, sola gratia*. Like some cancerous *Doppelgänger*, theological reality appears to inflate itself, drawing life from the reality it condemns, perfecting in exquisite form what could be seen as the most profound and systematically consistent theological alienation of the natural order ever achieved.[30] The theological evidence for this interpretation, that is the exclusive and irresistible progress of revealed reality enshrined in the dogmas of God, the Trinity, and God's act in eternity, is clear and indubitable. The impulse from eternity ostensibly encounters time in the Incarnation, but, as outlined above, this Incarnation 'is' in its own 'time'. A very careful analysis of the impinging of eternity upon time must now take place, in order, finally, to determine whether the ontological and epistemological alienation of the natural order is stemmed by the logic of Barth's temporal notions, or if at this fundamental conceptual level, an analogous logical parasitism does not confirm our analysis.

On the basis of the given time of God, 'the time we know and possess, is and remains lost time, even when we believe that God is the creator of time' (*CD* I/2, 47). Knowing neither time as 'fallen' nor time as 'created', the third 'time', that of revelation, eclipses both and must be 'a different time, . . . created alongside our time and the time originally created by God' (loc.cit.). Barth supports the denigration of the natural knowledge of time as

[30] A certain affinity exists here between the logic of Barth's position and that of Hegel as criticized by Karl Marx in the 'Critique of the Hegelian Dialectic and Philosophy as a Whole' in *The Economic and Philosophical Manuscripts of 1844*. Marx's comment upon Luther in 'Private Property and Labour', that he 'recognised *religion-faith* as the substance of the external *world*' indicates the direction of this criticism. That is in general terms the substitution of a spiritual, inner reality for the wider fabric of a reality of scientific, social, and economic relations, and the generation thereby of a 'false consciousness'.

either created (and subsequently 'lost') or experienced by an appeal to the 'three great difficulties in the common concept of time' (*CD* I/2, 47). These are the problem of the ungraspable present, the antinomy of the finitude or infinitude of time, and the relation of time and eternity. Revelation is able to 'assert the reality of time in the face of and in spite of these difficulties without the desire or ability to set them aside' (*CD* I/2, 49).

The contradictory nature of Barth's assertions is demonstrated in that using (as he will again later) the products of philosophical scepticism against the knowledge of time he paradoxically asserts the reality of revelation time, but denies the latter's ability to offer grounds of affirmation against sceptical negation. Man may know the 'lostness' of his time, but the response postulated with great concreteness and ontological zeal in revelation 'time' is 'known' by the noetic acknowledgment of faith alone.

An uncomfortable tension is apparent here which is indicative of the ambiguity of revealed and natural knowledge in Barth's theology. This ambiguity once more emerges in the relationship of the revelation's time to 'our' time. 'God's revelation', according to Barth, 'is the event of Jesus Christ' and 'We do not understand it as God's revelation, if we do not state unreservedly that it took place in "our" time.' This sanguine note is immediately confounded, for 'conversely, if we understand it as God's revelation, we have to say that this revelation had its own time' (*CD* I/2, 49). The time of revelation, 'God's time', 'time for us' has a present with past and future and is 'fulfilled time', with the expectation and recollection of its fulfilment and it is 'therefore real time'. This ambiguity between 'our time' and 'real time' stems, as seen above, from the fundamental assertion that 'we can only *believe* in the creation of time by God, as we believe in the creation itself, but we cannot *know* it.' It is only possible to believe in creation by virtue of belief in Christ and therefore all 'knowledge' (including explicitly that of the natural world and time) is consequent upon this prior 'belief'. The New Testament insight derived from Hebrews 11:3 has undergone an extraordinary universal interpretation, saved from absurdity by the mere assertion of the 'unreserved' happening of God's revelation in 'our' time. By faith, so argues the author of the Epistle to the Hebrews, we understand that the worlds have been framed by the Word of God. 'By faith' alone, Barth asserts, we may know the reality of creation itself. This is the consequence of his thoroughgoing subordination of cosmic and human reality to the epistemology (and the correlative ontology) of faith.

It is not possible to make a final judgement upon this crucial passage, for Barth makes extraordinary efforts to affirm the parallel between the Word's becoming flesh and its becoming time; but he remains ambiguous: 'It does not remain transcendent over time, it does not merely meet it at a point, but it *enters* time; nay, it *assumes* time; nay, it *creates* time for itself' (*CD* I/2, 50). Aware of the dangers of his position Barth immediately refers to *The Epistle to the Romans* knowing that the reader will not 'fail to appreciate that in it Jn.I,14 does not have justice done to it'. The positive theological conditioning of Barth's thought is obvious, but is there not the serious danger of a distinct Docetism exposed in his doctrine of time? 'Revelation has its time, and only in and along with its time is it revelation. How otherwise can it be revelation to and for us who are ourselves temporal to the core?' How indeed, for as the event of Jesus Christ is 'genuinely temporal', so it is 'not to be confused with any other time' (*CD* I/2, 51).

The temporal structure strictly analogous to that of the Incarnation, Christology, and the resurrection is couched in theological terms of an entry into, assumption of, and creation or healing of time. As 'man's existence became something new and different altogether, because God's Son assumed it and took it ever into unity with his God-existence, . . . so time, by becoming the time of Jesus Christ, although it belonged to our time, the lost time, became a different, a new time' (*CD* I/2, 51). The presence of Jesus Christ as the fulfilment of time does not allow any position from which 'to see through and regard any part of this old time as new, fulfilled time' (*CD* I/2, 58). The Word raises time into God's own time, which is 'alone real, self-moved, self-dependent, self-sufficient' (*CD* I/2, 52).

The incarnational initiative of volume I/2 of the *Church Dogmatics* underlies the Christological synthesis of volume IV in which Christology and soteriology interact in a full integration. Failure to observe the 'necessary connexion of all theological statements with that of Jn.I,14' is said to be prey to the 'devastating inrush of natural theology' (*CD* I/2, 123) – though one might add that the substitution of 'natural reality' for 'natural theology' would perhaps be more apt in indicating the truth of Barth's position. None the less it is of importance to note how Barth fully exploits the hypostatic union of patristic Christology and Protestant scholasticism and relates to it the categories of eternity and time. The 'assumption of grace' is central and thus the union of natures, (*unio naturarum*), is always regarded from the standpoint of the unity of person, (*unio personalis*). The supreme theological *locus* of the union of God and man in the Word become flesh subordinates all other categories. This union is propounded through the distinction of *an-* and *enhypostasis*, a Christological conception which presents its own difficulties, but which is, in this context, extremely important as an explanation of the basis upon which eternity and time are reconciled. Jesus Christ exists as man so far as he exists as God, and so in consequence his human nature does not exist apart from its divine mode of existence; it is ἀνυπόστατος. Positively the human nature acquires existence, that is subsistence, in the existence of God; it is ἐνυπόστατος. Christ's flesh has its existence 'through the Word and in the Word who is God Himself acting as Revealer and Reconciler' (*CD* I/2, 164). This unity of Godhood and manhood is no mere accidental co-location but is grounded upon the Ἐγένετο, 'the event of the incarnation of the Word'. God's being in the Incarnation is 'in becoming', thus 'being' (the 'person' of Christ) and 'act' (his 'works') are secured by reference once more to the ubiquitous divine act.

The corresponding and consequent relation of time and eternity is not simple but based upon the functional and unique co-location of God and man in the *unio hypostatica*. The temporal reality of the existence of Jesus Christ in which 'God is directly the Subject' is not only 'called forth, created, conditioned and supported by the eternal reality of God, but is identical with it' (*CD* I/2, 182). The problem of the identity of 'God's time', the time of revelation, with human time, is to be understood Christologically and its solution is directly analogous to that postulated in the doctrine of the hypostatic union. Such a development does, however, forge a further link in the theological chain of Barth's thought on time and renders the temporal sphere of revelation as problematic as the conception of the so-called 'impersonal humanity' of Christ. As the *vere Deus vere homo* of the Incarnation fulfils itself in the humanity of Christ (given its ontological ground in the Word of God's assumption of that flesh) so the 'temporal reality' of his humanity is likewise sustained. The 'self-enclosed circle' of the events of revelation bounded by the Virgin Birth and the empty tomb is constituted by the self-identification of God with man, and of eternity with time, in a unique collusion which provides the basis of the Christology-soteriology of volume IV of the *Church Dogmatics.*

The doctrine of reconciliation (*Versöhnung*) is a soteriological elaboration of the primary Christological postulates and in Barth's own estimation he has 'actualised' the doctrine of the Incarnation. All the main traditional concepts are understood as concentrically related terms describing one and the same ongoing process. Barth's statement of the doctrine of the Incarnation is in the form of a 'denotation and description of a single event' (*CD* IV/2, 105). On this basis he expounds the covenant of grace which is ontologically 'already included and grounded in Jesus Christ, in the human form and content, which God willed to give His Word from all eternity' (*CD* IV/1, 45). Jesus Christ is likewise the 'basis of the whole project and actualisation of creation and the whole process of divine providence from which all created being and becoming derives' (*CD* IV/1, 48). The eternal Word *is* Jesus Christ, very God and very man, preceding the creative will and accomplishing the Atonement. The foundation of such assertion is the self-interpretative Word of God whose being lies in the 'inner basis and essence of God' (*CD* IV/1, 52). Jesus Christ is consequently the 'decision of God in time' and the 'decision . . . made from all eternity'. In a renewed and integrated Chalcedonianism, Barth makes this the ground of the functional and systematic movement of soteriology in 'The Way of the Son of God' and 'The Homecoming of the Son of Man.'

The ensuing argument presupposes the mutual but distinct contributions of the 'omnipresent, almighty, eternal and glorious One' and the one 'limited in time and space' (*CD* IV/1, 184), as God 'acts as Lord over this contradiction even as He subjects Himself to it' (*CD* IV/1, 185). Correspondingly the *forma servi* and *forma Dei* of Jesus Christ are matched by his submission to time: 'The eternity in which He Himself is true time and the Creator of all time is revealed in the fact that, although our time is that of sin and death, He can enter it and Himself be temporal in it, yet without ceasing to be eternal, able to be the Eternal in time' (*CD* IV/1, 187–8).

Once again when confronted with Barth's assertion and defence of the Christological basis of this interaction the theological spade strikes bedrock and can penetrate no further. The 'greedy dialectic' has been resolved by a comprehensive Christological synthesis of great power, cohesion, and consistency. There remain, nevertheless, profound doubts about the tenability of this position, given Barth's explanation of the logic of the reality of the divine being. In other words the Christological resolution asserts an identity of the eternal and the temporal, but the doctrine of *anhypostasis* and *enhypostasis* also provides a rationale for the circularity in speaking of a divine act realized within its own time and of a time posited on the basis of divinity (that is, temporally speaking, upon a basis of God's being in eternal act). The significant time of revelation remains within the theological realm whose bounds have been traced from their ultimate ontological source.

In the foregoing section of this essay we have examined the interlocking circles that find their point of integration in the *locus* of the divine act. This eternal act, realized in the Incarnation and the hypostatic mutuality of divine and human being in the Incarnation, Christology, and the doctrine of reconciliation also underlies and realizes Barth's conception of creation itself. The resurrection and the temporally decisive 'forty days of resurrection time' is the consummation of the Incarnation and Christology but it takes place within the bounds of creation. Thus in pursuit of our investigation and in conformity with the logic of Barth's thought we may ask if the problems we have outlined are finally overcome. Does Barth succeed in sustaining the reality of the time of creation through the happening within it of the resurrection, the all-determinative temporal event, or are we merely left with the conceptual ambiguity of eternity and time writ large in the theological rhetoric of revealed 'reality'?

VII   *Creation and the dialectics of temporality*

The eternal act of God's being, realized in the Incarnation and the hypostatic mutuality of divine and human being in Christology and reconciliation, also sustains creation. Creation itself is the immediate context of theological anthropology and determines the application of the doctrine of time upon man. In the third volume of the *Church Dogmatics* the interaction of eternity and time is viewed in its closest relation to the existence and condition of common humanity and its shared and public world. It is in the spheres of creation and of 'Man in his Time' that the 'reality' and the logic of Barth's assertions may be tested, having explored the ontological substructure of his *magnum opus*. Whether the reader can emerge from this underworld into the light of experience and inter-subjective reality remains to be seen. The fabric of Barth's analogical recreation of temporal reality has been extended by Christology into the closest contiguity yet achieved with the 'fallen' and 'lost' world of man. The fabric of 'real' time has so far not been broken, however closely such a structure has moulded and conformed itself to the structure of what is commonly conceived as reality. In creation the temporal aspects of Barth's doctrine of man and the basic structure of his theological vision interact. Given such interaction it will prove possible to examine the conceptual interaction of eternity and time, the divine and extra-divine realms, and, in consequence to see how Barth's temporal 'negation of the negation', the supersession of time by 'God's time' (i.e., eternity) takes place in human existence itself, as manifested in the death and resurrection of Jesus Christ.

In this study, the pattern and impulse of Barth's thought has been followed. Now, in approaching the doctrine of creation additional complexity is encountered, but this dimension has yet once more to be approached in the light of the knowledge and the reality of faith. The priority of faith is both epistemological and ontological, for 'The insight that man owes his existence and form, together with all the reality distinct from God, to God's creation is achieved only in the reception and answer of the divine self-witness', and consequently this self-witness is 'in the knowledge of the unity of Creator and creature actualised in Him, and in the present mediated by Him, under the might and in the experience of the goodness of the Creator towards His creature' (*CD* III/1, 3).

Whether the distinction between Christ and creation is adequately sustained by Barth is a relevant question, especially in view of their close correlation, for creation is 'the external basis of the covenant', and the covenant 'the internal basis of creation'. This distinction is traditionally grounded upon a recognition of the eternal generation of the Logos and the temporal beginning of the creation. For Barth his all-pervasive actualism posits a single 'act' or 'event' of God that is unsurpassable (*CD* II/1, 263) and underlies both Christ and creation. Any distinction between God's 'essence' as it is in the Trinitarian relation of Father and Son and in the grounding of creation in the divine will ('externally' to the divine essence) is problematic in Barth's thought in the light of the exclusive power and function of God's benign act.

The God who self-posits himself 'in the Son by the Holy Spirit' determines that the eternal Father 'in the act of His free expression' and 'from within' is also the Creator. Only as 'Eternal Father' does God reveal himself as the Creator, that is for Barth, 'in Jesus Christ His Son by the Holy Ghost' (*CD* II/1, 11–12). In direct congruence with the consistent denial of natural theology there is an equally strict confinement of knowledge of the Creator to the Word and revelation. The local structure of Barth's argument is again such as to call in question the status not merely of the act of creation but of the created order, the world, and the cosmos themselves, which enjoy a merely derivative and secondary status over against the self-authenticating reality and objectivity of revelation. Barth's point is that creation, as divinely originated reality, is known only by the 'real analogy' evident in the logic of the revealed reality of the inner begetting of the Son by the Father, and, therefore, 'not at all in the life of the creature'. According to Barth's theological epistemology, the knowledge of creation itself is derived from revelation. Failing a theory of knowledge of creation as mundane, empirical reality (and such knowledge is systematically excluded by the logic of Barth's stance so far) an extremely insecure position results for natural knowledge of the natural world, and for individual man's place in it.

According to Barth, the 'fact that God has regard to His Son – the Son of Man, the Word made flesh – is the true and genuine basis of creation' (*CD* III/1, 51). Because of this dependence the doctrine of creation becomes deeply enmeshed in Christology and soteriology and the *circulus veritatis* is forged into ever more complete inner self-consistency. Not only creation itself, but

> The insight that man owes his existence and form, together with all reality distinct from God, to God's creation, is achieved only in the reception and answer of the divine self-witness, that is, only in faith in Jesus Christ, i.e. in the knowledge of the unity of Creator and creature actualised in Him. (*CD* III/1, 3).

Both creation and creature rest under the shadow of Christology and thus the temporal and dogmatic structures implicit in Barth's conception of Jesus Christ.

With regard to the specific problem of time Barth once more expounds the axis of eternal antecedence and temporal consequence in the light of the Christologically based creation. The covenant, the 'internal basis of creation', is the validation of the 'sphere of the creature' which God has determined from all eternity, and the history of this covenant is the sequence of events for which God 'gives time' (*CD* III/1, 59). Creation and history are thus made a function of the revealed purpose, and acquire their meaning and temporal 'fulfilment' from it. Indeed, here is found an echo of the statement of volume I/1, that history is the predicate of revelation, not revelation the predicate of history. It is in Christ that the 'fulfilment' takes place and once more in the context of creation Barth elaborates and 'properly exploits' the Boethian conception of eternity as the basis of this fulfilment in 'the organising centre of all God's acts', the reality of Jesus Christ. Predictably, eternity is 'supreme and absolute time, i.e. the immediate unity of present, past and future; of new, once and then; of the centre, beginning and end; of movement, origin and goal' which is the 'essence of God Himself' (*CD* III/1, 67). The supra-temporality of eternity is the active and creative being of God, expressing *ad extra* the inner covenantal decision and the reconciling purpose of God, thus constituting the possibility of creation. Only on the basis of the axis of eternity and time as unified in the Christological resolution of volumes I/2 and IV, can creation thus be the work of Christ, who, according to Barth, is the continuing reality of temporal fulfilment. So it is that the all-pervasiveness of the category of time becomes apparent again through its ontological and integrative role in the *Church Dogmatics.*

Only upon the foundation of the alleged 'temporality' and 'historicity' of God may Barth hold together and sustain his vision, for such derivation is absolutely essential, given the systematic exclusion, and therefore complete absence, of any immanent starting-point within his theological scheme. The involuted position to which this leads is demonstrated in such comments as 'Even the basis of creation in God's eternal decree is not a non-historical pre-truth, for this eternal pre-truth obviously has a historical character in the bosom of eternity.' Consequently, 'Not even the pure eternal being of God as such is non-historical pre-truth, for being triune it is not non-historical but historical even in its eternity.' (*CD* III/1, 66) In other words, a complex logical and conceptual reconstruction of creation statements in Trinitarian and Christological terms takes place. As regards the problem of time expressed in the contrasting thrusts of eternity and time, what distinction can there be if the 'history' and 'time' of eternity are translated into the history and time of God's will and purposes in the covenant?

It is at this juncture that Barth allows the formal contrast between eternity and time to emerge once again in explicit, logical terms. Eternity as the 'source of Time' is 'supreme and absolute time', that is, 'the immediate unity of present, past and future' and so on, which is the 'essence of God Himself'. God's eternity is the prototype of time and God is 'simultaneously before time, above time, and after time'. By contrast 'our time . . . is the form of existence of the creature' and, in contradistinction to eternity, it is 'the one-way sequence and therefore the succession and division of past, present and future; of once, now and then; of the beginning, middle and end; of origin, movement and goal' (*CD* III/1, 67–8). The contrast between the 'duration' of the simultaneity of past, present, and future and the 'succession and division of past, present and future' is the *only* logical or conceptual distinction between eternity and time. In 'healing' time, eternity implants its durational simultaneity into the succession and division of time. This is the distinction that arises in every context in which temporal categories are employed to sustain the structural unity of the doctrine of being in the *Church Dogmatics*. Correspondingly the same basic problems of the competing realities of the time of revelation and of the mundane temporal order recur and become extremely acute with regard to creation.

The complex nature of Barth's arguments concerning creation and Christ is matched by a corresponding analogical ambiguity in the explication of the creative interaction of eternity and time within the doctrine of creation. In a spate of double negations, Barth attempts to reconcile the positive creative aspect of 'God's time' with its not being 'fallen' time, that is the time of creation as it now is. God's eternal being as such, 'His pure, divine form of existence', is not in time, but even in this sense God is 'not non-historical and therefore non-temporal' because of the prototypical inner Trinitarian life. God is not 'non-temporal' because his eternity is 'not merely the negation of time, but an inner readiness to create time' (*CD* III/1, 68). God's supra-temporality, that is, his not being 'in time' but 'before, above and after all time' in such a way that 'time is really in Him', is the expression of his impulse towards the 'other', his creature. The theological impulse to create and sustain is explicated in terms of interacting conceptions of time, the nature of which are questionable at the very least. The distinctive feature of the time of the creature, its 'one way sequence, in that succession and separation, on the way from the once through the now to the then' (loc. cit.) is transformed by God's compassion and grace revealed in the act of his creation into 'His readiness for Time, as pre-temporal, supra-temporal (or co-temporal) and post-temporal and therefore as the source of time, of superior and absolute time' (*CD* III/1, 70).

Eternity and time are apparently distinct on the basis of the discrete theological entities to which they refer, but in strictly conceptual terms the ambiguity of Barth's argument stems from the illicit separation of the past, present, and future of time as 'simultaneous' and 'supra-temporal' from the succession of 'before and after'. The real contrast of eternity and time is temporally expressed solely in the contrast between 'contemporaneity' (in the full sense Barth intends) and 'division' and 'flux', respectively. Barth's equivocation regarding 'time' (that underlies the systematic and pervasive ambiguity of this concept in the *Church Dogmatics*) relies upon a conceptual distinction, the separation of a 'simultaneous' from a 'successive' time order in a contrast of 'duration' and 'division'. Is such a distinction not in fact a mere conceptual sleight of hand, in which two logically interdependent aspects of the idea of time, as used by Barth, are distinguished and subsequently hypostatized into deceptively distinct categories of reality? Whatever response may be made to this is it quite clear that the distinction is utterly pervasive and fundamental to the Church Dogmatics.

VIII   *Resurrection: time touched by Time?*

In the passage 'Man and his Time', Barth applies the doctrines that have been developed elsewhere, to the human condition as he understands it. Above all, the time of revelation as consummated in the resurrection becomes the actual prototypical basis of human time. In theological anthropology man is the central object of the doctrine of creation as 'the creature whose relation to God is revealed to us in the Word of God', but this means that 'the man Jesus is Himself the revealing Word of God, He is the source of our knowledge of the nature of man as created by God' (*CD* III/2, 3). This circumscription of the area of the knowledge of the creation and the consequent exclusion of knowledge of creation as cosmic totality is in entire congruity with the structure that has constantly emerged in Barth's thought.

As expected, the doctrine of time is governed by the insight that 'in practice the doctrine of creation means anthropology' (*CD* III/1, 3) and that the 'Word of God does not contain any ontology of heaven and earth themselves' (*CD* III/2, 6). Again using the principle of the analogy of faith, Barth asserts that in 'the disclosed relationship of God with man there is disclosed also His relationship with the Universe', and this is in congruity with Christological conditioning of the doctrine of creation. Human sin having made the understanding of human nature impossible, a new disclosure is necessary which is made in the one man Jesus, on the basis of which inquiry as to man in general may be made. The temporal structure of this 'disclosure' is what Barth explicates in 'Man in his Time'. It is inevitably preceded by a restatement of the eternity-time axis, that is, of simultaneity over against succession (*CD* III/2, 437–8), here designated by the terms of 'authentic' over against 'inauthentic' time.

According to Barth, man 'needs an inauthentic temporality distinct from eternity' in which past, present, and future are in succession forming a sequence 'corresponding to his life-act as a whole and in detail' (*CD* III/2, 438). Jesus, 'like all other men' is 'in His time', but in this time he lives hypostatically in virtue of his unity with God. He lives with God and for God, with men and for them as Representative and Judge in a twofold representation which 'makes the barrier of this time on every side a gateway'. Leading this life 'in His time' and in consequence 'His time becomes for God, and therefore for all men' (*CD* III/2, 439). The application of hypostatic unity to Christ's life in time is the basis of 'likeness' of his time with men's time, it being derived from the divine time. The *apparent* historical and temporal identity is always by virtue of the hypostatic unity, which works towards a 'fulfilment' of time ostensibly needed by the inauthentic time of men, a time that men in fact already have, and must have, if they are to live lives at all.

In the first section of 'Man in his Time', subtitled 'Jesus, Lord of Time', it is Barth's aim to establish by means of the integration of Christology and creation the absolute priority of the life of Jesus, as the life whose time will be 'at once the centre and beginning and the end of all the lifetimes of all men (*CD* III/2, 440). Thus it is that Jesus' time is all men's time in virtue of his supreme contemporaneity, his 'Lordship of time'. Jesus' time is the time of men in consequence of the hypostatic self-positing of God and not through any immanent, non-hypostatic identity. This hypostatic realization of time is consummated in the 'forty days of Easter-history and Easter-Time' subsequent to the resurrection. Barth asserts that in the resurrection an irreversible time-sequence is established (*CD* IV/1, 447) resulting in the 'forty days' of resurrection time, the end and goal of predestination. The culmination of Christology and creation in the resurrection is the fulfilment of time *par excellence*, and represents the application of the insight elaborated elsewhere, for example in volume IV/1, in the passage entitled 'The Verdict of the Father' (pp. 283 ff.). Here, 'the event of Easter Day and the resurrection appearances during the forty days were the mediation, the infallible mediation as unequivocally disclosed in a new act of God, of the perception that God was in Christ' (*CD* IV/1, 301). In the context of the doctrine of creation the resurrection-conditioned time of the 'forty days' becomes the foundation of the phenomenological and schematic account of time, 'Given Time', and 'Allotted Time' respectively.

In the 'forty days' of resurrection time the hidden mystery of the being of Jesus Christ was exposed, for 'during these forty days the presence of God in the presence of the man Jesus was no longer a paradox . . . He had been veiled, but He was now wholly and equivocally and irrecoverably manifest' (*CD* III/2, 449). With relentless consistency the theological and temporal dimensions correspond, for Jesus declared and known to be Lord is exalted from the dead and 'He was then the concrete demonstration of the God who not only has authority over man's life and death, but also wills to deliver him from death.' In addition, 'He was the concrete demonstration of the God who has not only a different time from that of men, but whose will and resolve it is to give men a share in this time of His, in His eternity' (*CD* III/2, 450–1). In this act God's time overcomes the discontinuity of temporal bondage and manifests 'real' temporal continuity.

Barth unambiguously asserts the 'real and therefore physical' resurrection of Jesus and thereby repudiates Bultmann. Barth's assertion is perhaps inconsistent with the thrust of his overall argument, for it has concentrated, certainly as regards time, upon the instantiation of the eternally real in time and the consequent transformation of time. In a manner corresponding with this affirmation of a physical resurrection Barth affirms that 'It is the Creator of all reality distinct from Himself who, taking flesh of our flesh, also took time, at the heart of what we think we know as time' (*CD* III/2, 455). Because of the creative temporal condescension of God, the philosophical denial of the reality of time may be abandoned in the face of the fact that 'God himself took time and thus treated it as something real' (loc. cit.). This 'making real' is a fulfilment applicable to all time through the properties of 'eternal time'. Barth now makes his crucial claim for the reality of the time of Jesus and he recognizes the dangers of granting the force of his own 'analogical' derivation of all realities (including that of time) from the divine prototype. Without the identity of Jesus' time with our own he becomes a mere function of divinity, a gnostic figure vouchsafed to man in the seamless receptacle of his own time.

... the time of Jesus is also a time like all other times; that it occurred once and once for all; that it had beginning, duration and end; that it was contemporary for some, future for others, and for others again, e.g. for us, past. *Only a docetic attitude to Jesus can deny that His being in time also means what being in time means for us all* [my emphasis]. Our recognition of His true humanity depends on an acceptance of this proposition. Even the recognition of His true deity, implying as it does the identity between His time and God's, does not rule out this simple meaning of His being in time. On the contrary, it includes it. (*CD* III/2, 463).

Barth has moved with utter consistency along the path of analogical derivation. The reality of the divine denies, subverts, and supersedes the reality of the mundane. Having thus severed all but a single thread connecting his theological system to the world of the commonplace Barth has now to retract and defend the reality of Jesus Christ. Can Barth give a positive answer to any of his implicit questions? Can Jesus' being in time mean what it means for us all? Barth's ambiguity is here quintessentially expressed, for his answer is affirmative, yet immediately qualified by the 'inclusion' of such time by the divine time. We are aware, however, that the divine time draws mundane fallen time into a synthesis of logically distinct temporal categories of dubious origin. The dialectic is resolved upwards in every context we have so far examined and Barth's defence of the resurrection time against the 'docetic' charge is groundless in view of his own arguments that we have examined at length. We must grant him the logic of his own theological position and allow the utter priority of the divine, and the analogical derivation therefrom. By this we allow ourselves insight into the dialectic of reality and unreality that suffuses the whole *Church Dogmatics* once the systematic completeness of the *circulus veritatis Dei* is unbroken by any arbitrary inconsistency on Barth's part.

The concluding passages of 'Jesus, Lord of Time' contain the application of the fulfilment of time posited in the life, death, and above all, the resurrection of Jesus Christ. In this Barth presents an elaborate interpretation of the axis of eternity and time as the distinctive feature of time of Jesus in 'the removal of the limitations of its yesterday, to-day and tomorrow of its once, now

and then' (*CD* III/2, 464). Above all, Barth attempts an
exposition of Revelation I:8 in terms of the temporal
transcendence he has elaborated (see *CD* III/2, 465). Jesus' time is
always simultaneously present and therefore he is the Alpha and
Omega, the beginning and the ending, and so on. After the
attempted repudiation of ambiguity apparent in Barth's
conception of the resurrection, the dialectic of eternity and time
as a conceptual juxtaposition of duration and contemporaneity
over against succession and division, becomes once more
dominant. On the basis of the divine supra-temporality, the
parousia and the resurrection, which are for us separate, are for
Christ one. Having descended inconsistently to the single point of
unambiguous identity of Christ's time with human time in the
resurrection, Barth ascends once again into the structural logic of
the *Church Dogmatics*, constituted by the dogma of God's being
in act, that is, the dynamic 'Now' of the divine eternity.

On a schematic and structural level, having re-established this
central affirmation of the divine simultaneity, Barth in exploring
its more concrete application commences with a devastating
return to the epistemological and ontological impossibility of any
knowledge of time, apart from that posited in revelation. In an
exposition strongly reminiscent of Augustine's critical reflections
in the *Confessions* and the *Contra Academicos*, Barth rehearses the
sceptical arguments concerning the ungraspability of the 'Now',
that lies between future and past. The present is the time between
the times that is 'no time at all, no duration, no series of
moments, but only the boundary between past and future,
which is never stationary, but always shifts further ahead'
(*CD* III/2, 514). Out of this flux of 'infinite succession of
moments, or rather constant shiftings of the boundary' stem the
attempts to gain the illusory knowledge of metaphysics and the
creation in such poetic expression as that of Hölderlin. Over
against this 'flight' the 'I am . . . which is, and which was, and
which is to come, the Almighty presents itself' (*CD* III/1, 516).
In the being of Jesus Christ a protest is made against the
'perverted and disturbed reality' of man. God has 'come to our
rescue, and therefore to the defence of our true creaturely
nature against the unnatural condition into which it had fallen'
(*CD* III/2, 518).

It is well to recall at this point that Barth has previously affirmed the need for man to live in such a 'fallen' time and there is little evidence of an appreciation of the inconceivability of existence in the divine 'I am' of eternity as the basis of human experience and subjectivity, that is, of subjectivity in a present without the division of before and after. What would it mean for a man to experience the eternity in which God is said to subsist in Barth's exposition? Is the use of the axis of eternity and time, thus understood, an adequate or desirable ontological vehicle for the mediation of the divine-human relation in the broad sense in which it is employed by Barth? The peculiar objectivity of Barth's account and its shortcomings are demonstrated in his explicit denial, 'We do not know what time means for animals or plants, or for the rest of the universe' (*CD* III/2, 521). Only because man himself is in time may he 'conclude or suspect that time is the form of existence of everything created' (loc. cit.). The principle of knowing by analogy, exploited in the notion of *analogia fidei*, is thus applied in a more normal way to knowledge of the external world as a temporally conditioned world. Barth's denial of direct knowledge does little to lessen the danger of the intrinsically stultifying limitations of never moving beyond anthropology into discussion of cosmic realities. So it is that Barth closes any final gaps in his theory of time, through the full enclosure of human life within the limits of a time posited in the manifestation of God's revelation, Jesus Christ.

'Humanity is temporality. Temporality, as far as our observation and understanding go, is humanity' (*CD* III/2, 522). By the strict application of this equation, interpreted by the content of temporality (*Zeitlichkeit*), defined as 'that movement from the past through the present into the future', Barth eliminates any treatment of time outside what may be termed a structural phenomenological analysis. The denial of any correlation between human time and that conditioning the 'being of plants and animals in the rest of the universe' (*CD* III/2, 521), except by way of an inferred analogy, provides additional evidence for our analysis of the self-enclosed nature of Barth's theology. The reasons for this, and Barth's derivation of 'real' time prototypically from revelation have been outlined in this essay. Ostensibly, as we have seen, grace confirms, even establishes, nature. The fact that grace cannot coexist with but destroys nature in the act of confirming it constitutes the ambiguity of the doctrine of time in the *Church Dogmatics*. Does the time of Jesus Christ merely confirm (by the removal of illusion and misconception) or does it destroy and re-create time? Clearly in 'Man in his Time' Barth asserts both, but both based upon, and sustained by, the will of God and his purposes. Why, might a reader ask, should the original time which is recovered from its lost division and transitoriness be different from the 'time' posited in revelation?

Barth does not answer this, but proceeds to an explanation of 'sin' in temporal terms which now corresponds to the existential 'ought' constituted by the paramount 'is' of God's time. A 'pledge' of the 'reality' of time is given in God's time: there is no material, metaphysical, or even phenomenological change. The epistemology of faith is fulfilled in the presence of God, 'The fact that the living God is present makes our present not only real but weighty and therefore important', and in this is enclosed 'the mystery of the grateful response we now owe to Him and in consequence to our fellow men' (*CD* III/2, 531). 'We are sinners who have forfeited our time': by these words Barth places the reader once more before the dilemma evident in the early work. Time and eternity conflict and eternity confronts and overcomes time. Grace has consumed nature and regurgitates it in the form of a natural theology derived from revelation, but such reality as is mediated through revelation remains the knowledge of faith. The healing of time which comes by means of the ontological and temporal structure of the object of faith is immediately translated, at the moment of encounter, back into purely theological terms of a 'pledge' and 'graceful presence'. The theological circle is ultimately complete in that it subsumes a legitimate and irreducible duality, that of Creator and Creation, into a unified epistemology and ontology of the divine being, a Christology of hypostatic unity and noetic reception and a subsequent realization through the 'acknowledgement' of this dogmatic nexus.

At certain points an identity of revealed reality and natural reality is made (and only unambiguously so in the resurrection itself). Ultimately the only 'cashed-out' content of the fulfilment of time is 'a promise', 'For the eternal and gracious God, who is the boundary of our beginning, will surely guarantee the whole of our life, the span which we are given, and its final end' (*CD* III/2, 570). Everything *is* as it *was* except that now we are *sure* that it *is* on the basis of the divine promise. The futility of human temporal exertion is obvious, our yearning and striving in time give way to acceptance of the 'already accomplished and uninterrupted work' of the inner life of God given in 'content' and 'promise'. Contemplation of the theological circle in its perfection, complexity (and ambiguity) constitutes the true obedience of faith, the 'knowledge' gained in 'acknowledgement'.

The character of the doctrine of time in the *Church Dogmatics*, seen as the logic of the object of faith is confirmed in Barth's account of death (*CD* III/2, 589 ff.). Death happens to man and is 'extinction', but in Christ eternal life is promised in a manner corresponding with the entire vicariousness (and consequently, theological circularity) of Christ's activity. Death for mankind is, according to Barth, a 'sign' of the 'second death' suffered by Christ and so once more everything *appears* to change, but in reality remains as it is, except for the promise of the 'beyond' of Jesus Christ. Man is to live in hope in God for, 'the definitive prospect in which he rejoices is for him an authorisation and command to serve God in his allotted span with all the preliminary joy without which his joy in his end and new beginning with Him would be purely imaginary' (*CD* III/2, 640). Man is to affirm Jesus Christ as his 'beyond' in his life now, in the intentionality of faith. God's revelation, held for so long at one remove from the human condition by its own inner logic, finally tells us that the limitations we endure are those endured by Jesus Christ – such is the message of the Gospel.

IX *Conclusion*
In the foregoing essay I have attempted to lay bare the 'inner logic' of Barth's theology inasmuch as this structure is constituted by the doctrine of time. In ensuing sections Barth's doctrines of God, Christ, and creation have been analysed from the standpoint of their dependence upon a set of temporal conceptions bound up with the doctrine of the divine act in the eternal 'Now'. This has revealed something of the richness of Barth's synthetic drive in

reuniting impulses from many strands of the Christian tradition.
More negatively, we have seen the theology of time function as a
container within which the act of revelation in Jesus Christ is
confined. Wherever the content of revelation and its time draw
close to the reality common to humanity, ambiguity results
because the 'reality' of revelation must both affirm and deny,
recreate and annihilate at the same moment. This ambiguity is
consistent with the double-edged quality of much of Barth's talk
of man (does he mean men or the man Jesus?) and is based upon
the fundamental theological developments which led to the
adoption of the 'analogy of faith'. Ultimately the ambiguity must
disappear in the face of the overwhelming principle of the divine
act and its various (but strictly identical) manifestations.

The complexity of this paper stems from the fact that it has
proved necessary to prise apart Barth's 'spiral arguments' and
relate the *loci* widely dispersed in his thought together into a
single argument. We have encountered a profound theological
totalitarianism stemming from the application of the principle of
analogia fidei in a context bereft of any vestiges of natural theology
(and thus of natural reality or the natural order itself). The
consequence of the functional identity between this principle and
the doctrine of being and time that Barth employs is the
systematic exclusion of any dimension not immediately derivable
from his primal sources of reality. Such a monopoly demands the
re-creation of genuine plurality and categorical distinction *within*
the structure of the new reality whereby the discontinuity
between that reality and the reality normally external to it is
reproduced. Thus a new world appears within which the old
distinctions of transcendence and immanence are re-created.
Whereas in traditional theology the analogy of being was used as
a means of relation and differentiation between God and cosmos,
Barth's analogy of faith functions within the sphere of faith
alone. Time, instead of being or substance as such, becomes the
medium of relation and disrelation between God and man, but, as
we have seen, its efforts to escape from the confines of Barth's
system to posit and structure a reality other than God and his
revelation get no further than ambiguity, and ultimately fail,
once we perceive the logic of the theology of the *Church
Dogmatics.*

The theology of Karl Barth is (despite his own protestations) a reworking of metaphysical theology, albeit in 'biblical' guise. As such it has entranced some and driven others from the Christian fold. One major factor influencing in different ways both the devoted disciples and the disaffected has been the great intellectual offence offered by the assertion of a reality about which so much could be said at such length. As we have seen, this reality is a single one which brooks no rival or opposition. It either exists and demands submission in the 'acknowledgement' of faith or it cannot exist for those who refuse to grant its totalitarian demands.

Through a profound ontological exclusiveness Barth has attempted to preserve Christian theology from the indifference and hostility of a secular world. The triumphalist aggrandizement of his theology was made at the risk of a disjunction and alienation of his theology from natural reality. The disturbing irony of his efforts is that Barth achieved this alienation by skilled and energetic use of traditional Christian theological categories. His creation stands before us as a warning as to what may happen if the God of the orthodox Christian Gospel is prized apart from the structures of contemporary human life. The ontological dogma of the Incarnation loses its roots in the shared and public reality of the world in which we live; it hovers above us like a cathedral resting upon a cloud. Can such an intellectual presentation of Christianity be entered with anything short of total alienation and lack of personal and existential authenticity? Is such a theology not a merely perfect illustration of (say) the Marxist critique of religion as alienation of the self, but an alienation so profound and complete as to daunt those who might wish to form a judgement upon it in the name of Christianity itself? In almost Proustian manner Barth has re-created a lost world[31] whose demands are nothing less than total and unconditional submission, but whose precepts and potential for the promotion of the interpersonal life of the Body of Christ in the world would appear to be minimal without radical appreciation of its dangers and limitations.

---

[31] George Steiner regards Joseph Needham's *Science and Civilisation in China* as the only adequate sequel to *À la recherche du temps perdu* (see *In Bluebeard's Castle*, London, 1971, pp. 99–100). The *Church Dogmatics* might well qualify as a third 'prodigiously sustained, controlled flight of the creative intellect'.

Should we now in conclusion turn away from the theology of Karl Barth in dismay, or even disgust? I think not, for Barth's great gift to the Church is his quite magnificent grasp and representation of materials drawn from the Christian tradition. His work is, moreover, not merely the product of genius or perversity on his own part alone but a phenomenon which illustrates the logic of the disrelation of Christian theological categories and the reality of which they speak from our own culture. Barth was not responsible for this situation; he merely illustrates it and yet manages to conserve and pass on the tradition. To accept or reject Barth would be merely to succumb to the demands of his own theological error. His work lies before us, the stricken, glorious hulk of some great Dreadnought – our task is to dismember and salvage, to exploit what is usable, and to melt down and re-forge the rest into weapons for the continuing theological battle for the truth.

2

The Ideal and the Real in the Theology of Karl Barth (1980)

The theology of Karl Barth is the greatest monument to Christian thought that has been erected in this century. It persists; it resists reduction and remains a challenge for those who would seek to think theologically along lines dictated by fundamentally Christian theological presuppositions. In positive terms, Barth recovered and restated much of the truly basic content and conceptions of the Christian understanding of God and of his revelation in Jesus Christ, in whom the fulness of the Godhead is conceived to have dwelt bodily. Indeed by his rehabilitation of what Professor T. F. Torrance has called 'Classical christology', Barth posits the Word-became-flesh as the supreme *plenum* of reality itself, expressed in the most intimate ontological identity with the being of God in act. The divine act in Jesus Christ subsists in majestic power as the central core of the structure of the *Church Dogmatics* and forms the basis of Barth's overall theological derivation of true reality, the ultimately real, from within, rather than outside of theological presuppositions.

It is the precise nature and the consequences of such a derivation that are of considerable importance; because while Barth's *magnum opus* (and Christian theology *qua* theology) postulates a correspondence with the nature of the divine being, they have both undergone a profound dislocation from the structures characteristic of contemporary culture. The 'reality' of this latter is no simple or readily coherent scheme, but a complex of disparate and at times conflicting explanations comprising the

secularised perspective which sees no pressing need to resort to
final explanation and in fact largely excludes even the expectation
of such explanation. How then does the supremely positive
assertion embodied in the theology of Barth relate to a secularised
view of reality which has dispensed with transcendence and grants
no *Lebensraum* to revelation? Some might think that no relation is
in fact evident and that Christian theology has become the
ideology of a hard-core ecclesiastical rearguard or the projection
of the theologian's neurosis. I am taking it for granted in this
paper that such a dislocation of theology from the reality of
contemporary culture does seem to pertain and that although
individuals may conceive of their lives in relation to the God of
Christianity it is assumed that the mass of Western European
humanity admits of no such direct adherence and that the
dominant cultural forces are understood as likewise operating
autonomously. This may be taken for the purposes of the
following argument as the fruit, for good or ill, of the rise of the
modern scientific outlook and the Enlightenment as generally
understood.[1]

It is clear that some theologians have responded to the rise of
explanations competing with that of Christian theology by
retreating into a metaphysical reality at one remove from the
causal complexity of the physical world. Thus in terms of such a
second reality, neo-Thomism was an attempt to rebuild the world
of faith within categories inherited from a bygone age and so
thereby to construct a haven for the 'reality' of Christian theology.
Again in a much more complex way in Hegelian Christianity,
reality was reborn into a philosophical dialectic of profound
ambiguity whose final *denouement* is the extinction of the tension
of finite and infinite, indicated in theological terms by the death
of the Son of God; God's own self-extinction.[2] Both of these
theological recreations of Christianity existed in the shadow of
Kant, the latter in direct relation and immediate response. Both
tried to do what Kant had criticised as beyond human possibility,
namely to regrasp the infinite, a pretension precluded by the

[1] I would now (1990) have a far more differentiated approach to the analysis of
the theology/social reality relation. This record of a stage in emancipation retains
its validity.
[2] Cf. *Lectures on the Philosophy of Religion*, London 1895, vol. 3.

Kantian critique of human knowledge.[3] The sphere of metaphysical assertion, a refuge for theologians in retreat from the cosmos and humanity as newly understood, proved but a temporary resting-place from whence they were pursued by philosophical criticism.

It is not possible to explain briefly Barth's place in this situation in which there is, so to speak, no hiding place for Christian theological assertions. Briefly put, my view is that as a theologian Barth attempted to re-engage with the ontological core of Christian dogma without straying into the area of speculative inquiry into which theology had been cast and consequently subjected to devastating criticism. In other words, Barth's work consists in an attempt to rebuild Christian theology upon foundations in a reality free from reductive analysis.[4] One reality was to be confronted by another which did not derive its substance from the realm of the immanent but from the self-positing of God himself in Christ. So it is that the dogmatic assertion of Barth's *Church Dogmatics* appears in the form indicated in the opening words of this paper as the very self-explication of the divine being, a gigantic celestial tautology, the *circulus veritatis Dei*. God is known by God alone; he is the objective reality of such knowledge in his Word and its subjective possibility in the Holy Spirit; real knowledge is therefore acknowledgment.

Such a theological *essai*, so conceived as a presupposition-less system (apart from the single assertion of the divine reality in Jesus Christ) would, without further points of anchorage, appear as something of an intellectual monstrosity, even a quasi-gnostic *afflatus*. This quite clearly is not, *a priori*, the case, inasmuch as Barth is concerned ostensibly with Christian revelation, which is historical in its occurrence, and grounded in the man Jesus Christ.

[3] I presuppose in this paper the decisive importance of Kant's *Critique of Pure Reason* for modern theology, including that of Barth, whose comments upon Kantian significance for the theological undertaking in ch. 7 of *Protestant Theology in the Nineteenth Century*, London 1972, have an important bearing upon what follows.

[4] The work of both Ritschl and Schleiermacher is an analogous response to that of Barth in that they all, despite their different places in the history of post-Enlightenment theology, seek to reconstruct Christian theology without recourse to metaphysics as such.

Insofar as Barth adheres to the latter the danger of radical dehistorification and unreality is lessened, but not banished, because the implications of his position are more far-reaching and problematic than would at first appear. In order to concentrate attention upon the difficulties inherent in Barth's thoroughgoing adherence to revelation I propose only to outline first the factors which brought him to the point of asserting the reality of god in Jesus Christ upon its own distinct ontological basis and then, secondly, the inner theological development from late German Liberal Protestantism to dialecticism, and subsequently via Anselm, to the ontological and epistemological exclusiveness of the *Church Dogmatics*. I intend to focus attention upon the actual structure of reality as it is presented in Barth's major work and in particular to show how exactly its 'internal' and the 'external' aspects are related together. By 'internal' and 'external' is meant the centre and the periphery of the overall structure of Barth's theological re-presentation of reality. In practical terms this goal of presentation and analysis of the thought of Barth can only be achieved through the selection of an aspect which may be said legitimately to convey insight into the structure. It is my contention that the category of time presents just such an aspect; by examining Barth's use of 'time' one may establish with some precision the bounds of his theological creation and indicate the nature of the interaction between this and the reality lying outside the structure of the revealed. Time as a universal category enjoys, as Kant argued, an even more fundamental status than space. It conditions human knowledge with transcendental inevitability and constitutes a framework within the very structure of reality itself.[5] Its corresponding analysis is complex and multiform but the comprehensive universality of the category of time means that the reality of revelation must be temporal if it is to be a reality accessible to humanity. As will become apparent, an examination of Barth's attempt at rendering temporal the dogmatic core of his systematic theology exposes the intractable difficulties of a single theological starting-point in the act of God's self-revelation.

---

[5] Cf. *The Critique of Pure Reason*, tr. N. Kemp Smith, London 1929, Transcendental aesthetic, B46, A34, 'Time is the formal *a priori* condition of all appearances whatsoever'.

It is because of the universality of the category of time on the one hand, and on the other a correspondingly pervasive theological preoccupation with the concept of time on Barth's part, that we find ourselves in possession of a tool which allows us to make a complete and (in a thorough-going sense) *systematic* analysis of the structure of reality in the *Church Dogmatics.* Through such an analysis the consequences of Barth's exclusive commitment to the object of theology will become apparent but, it is to be feared, not transparently clear, because of a profound and pervasive ambiguity. We shall see that this ambiguity is the consequence of an attempt to recreate the duality of transcendence and immanence *within* the confines of Christology and the doctrine of God. The realities of God and Christ are so dominated by a particular theory of the knowledge of God, which is itself so one-sided in its emphasis, that the duality becomes a complex but essential monism of being. All categories shared by both realms, and in particular the contrast of infinite and finite being are transmuted and transposed, so that they become amenable to synthesis. All synthesis is made secondary and subordinate to the primal synthesis of divinity and humanity in the *unio hypostatica* (Cf. *CD* I/2, 161–3). The hypostatic union of the Chalcedonian Christological tradition becomes the ultimate key to all reality, including that of time. Time and its correlate, eternity, have the vital interpretative and testing function we have indicated, but a further factor adds even greater importance to their role in our investigation of Barth's thought.

The second fundamental factor stems from the intrinsic meaning that Barth attributes to the axis of eternity and time. The category of time can be said to constitute a surrogate for 'substance', as exploited in traditional theology. Time and its inescapable correlate eternity are not merely formal features but:

> According to the Bible it is not being as such, but that which endures, duration itself, which is the divine . . . Eternity is before and after, above and below being. Being does not include eternity but eternity includes being. The genuineness of being is examined and weighed and measured and tested by eternity. It is being or non-being according to its relation to eternity. (*CD* I/1, 610)

The formal determinant of what is or is not, the 'genuineness of being', is eternity itself; a reality which as 'God's time' is the prototypical basis of time. (*CD* II/1, 611) 'God is both the prototype and the foreordination of all being and therefore the prototype and foreordination of time.' The language of 'inclusion' indicates semantically what is happening upon a substantial and a formal level. The ontology of God (and this must mean God in Christ) contains being, and it will be seen that eternity likewise 'includes' (*einschliessen*) time. Being and time co-exist and it is precisely because of the mode of 'containment' presupposed, that we may speak of a dialectic of the 'ideal' and the 'real' in the *Church Dogmatics*. The reality of God and the reality of man likewise co-exist but in so doing the distinctiveness of both is sapped and supplanted by a dialectical tension between the prototypical and the 'ideal' on the one side, and the fallen type of the 'real' on the other. The concepts of time Barth employs indicate the nature and range of this ontological inclusion, and furthermore, give insight into the truly systematic exclusion of his theology from a wider reality.

　　Thus in outline what I am to argue is this: in Barth's theological theory of time there lies the key to a structure which contains serious flaws, that in their turn reflect the illusory security of a theology which unfolds itself apart from the natural order and which, in attempting to recreate everything, appears to find itself in possession of nothing. Inasmuch as this loss of the contingent takes place, it represents a failure to grasp what J. P. Segundo has called 'the dialectic of the real',[6] that is the acute contradictions of the human condition, as opposed to the mere laying hold of an involuted and ultimately stultifying dialogue between the divine and the divinely human. These are, it need hardly be said, serious doubts to voice about a theology which remains great but which must undergo criticism if it is to maintain its significance in the public and shared world of intellectual discourse.

　　The general comments made above indicate the direction in which the argument will proceed. Whilst basic criticism of Barth's temporal inclusion is the product of a fuller study of his thought on time[7] the particular problem encountered here may be seen as

---

[6] Segundo's critique of Western theology in *The Liberation of Theology*, (London 1977), is especially relevant to Barth's work, see 262.

[7] R. H. Roberts, *Eternity and Time in the Theology of Karl Barth*, (unpublished Ph.D. thesis, University of Edinburgh, 1975).

a development that carries forward ideas hinted at in Henri Bouillard's brief, but astute study, *The Knowledge of God.*[8] After indicating the misplaced nature of Barth's criticism of analogy of being with respect to the actual teaching of St. Thomas Aquinas, Bouillard points out that he 'departs from the ground of the classical problematic' and 'abandons the field of *structure,* or *meaning,* for that of *event.*[9] In other words the change from analogy of being to analogy of faith, *analogia fidei,* is not merely a change in the method of analogy but a change of context as well; a transition is made from being *qua* being to being *qua* event, and that means for Barth, to eternity. If, however, such a transition is made away from the careful qualification of the distinction between divine and human being (as is found in traditional doctrines of analogy) to the realm of being *qua* eternity and the 'analogy of faith' then are the problems the former theory was advanced to counter in any way evaded in the context of the latter? The logic of the eternal-temporal dialectic is as the relation which replaces the qualification characteristic of the analogy of being: and as such it has an immense burden to bear as will become evident.

In order to provide a minimal context to this analysis some very brief allusions must now be made to the development of Barth's thought. First, the transition from the dialectical theology of crisis to the *Church Dogmatics* proper can be legitimately seen as a continuation in temporal terms of a series of contrasting idealist resolutions of the antinomy of finite and infinite existence. Thus Barth's synthesis in the *Church Dogmatics* may be understood as the culmination of Hegelian and Kierkegaardian dialectical progression. Second, the escape from this speculative antinomy is hinted at in Barth's response to Kant, who conceded ground for the church theologian to create a biblical theology in the realm of faith, which correspondingly might not pretend to the status of knowledge.[10] Third, exploiting this autonomous sphere through

---

[8] Eng. tr. London 1969 of *La Connaissance de Dieu* (Paris 1967).
[9] Op.cit., 115.
[10] Again see Barth's remarks upon *Religion within the Limits of Reason Alone* in ch. 7 of *Protestant Theology in the Nineteenth Century* where he discusses the possibility that theology would 'stand on its own feet in relation to philosophy . . . recognising the point of departure for its method in revelation' p. 307.

his appropriation of Anselm, Barth devised a theological method, which by a certain 'noetic necessity', saw the nature of theological truth as self-posited and self-theological given.[11] Fourth, this Anselmic understanding of the inter-dependence of the object of faith and knowledge of that object was enlivened and inspired by the Hegelian 'rediscovery' of the doctrine of the Trinity as the being of God in act.[12] Fifth, these factors were fused with a structural and architectonic approach to theology as a systematic discipline centred upon such Christological conceptions as the hypostatic union in a manner suggested to Barth by his study of the Protestant scholastic theologians. These factors, among others, secured the essential autonomy, form and content of a theology which would arise Phoenix-like from the damp ashes of German Liberal Protestant theology.

One further important point must be made in explanation of the term *analogia fidei*, the 'analogy of faith', and this is the transition from the theology of crisis to the 'logology' of his mature work, the change from 'dialectic' to 'analogy'. Whereas in dialectical theology the essential structure of reality is contradiction, 'infinite qualitative distinction', and an unresolved and profoundly eschatological tension between time and eternity, finite and infinite, in the latter the essential structure has resolved itself into an overt theological primacy, the principle of *analogia fidei*, the so-called 'analogy of faith'. The analogy of faith is the derivation of the structure of theological truth from the object of faith itself:

> Dogmatics as an inquiry presupposes the ascertainability by man of the proper content of Christian language about God. It makes this presupposition because it believes, in the Church and with the Church, in Jesus Christ, as the revealing and reconciling approach of God to man. Language about God has the proper content, when it conforms to the essence of the Church, i.e. to Jesus Christ ... (*Rom.* 12:6) (*CD* I/1, 11)

Our task in this paper is the pursuit of the ramifications and consequences of this initial theological commitment for the universal category of time. The ontological reality of God dictates

---

[11] See *Fides Quarens Intellectum*, London 1960, 45–6.
[12] See Barth's comments upon Hegel in the relevant chapter of *Protestant Theology* esp. 414ff.

the epistemological principles to be employed in knowing God, for Barth has disposed of subjectivity ('existentialism' characteristic of the *Christliche Dogmatik* of 1927) and an objectivity related to the perceived structures and being of the external world (the basis of the tradition of *analogia entis*, the analogy of being). There is for a Barth an ontological and epistemological *Novum*, which is its primal theological originality transcends the commonplace framework of human expectations grounded in the contrast of subjectivity and objectivity, conceived as the points of derivation of human knowledge. The 'essence of the Church' (*Wesen der Kirche*) is '*actus purus*, divine action beginning with itself' (*CD* I/1, 44, Thomson) which is the source and means of its own insight.

The question that inevitably arises is this: if a *beginning* is made with *actus purus*, the 'pure act' of the divine being, then can an *end* be made anywhere else, can any movement be made to a point beyond or outside such a novelty as that presented in the 'event of personal approach'? This event takes place in the act of 'real proclamation', a context in which it appears as 'man's language about God on the basis of an indication by God Himself fundamentally transcending all human causation' (*CD* I/1, 101, Thomson). 'God with us has happened' and this event has happened as 'self-moved being in the stream of becoming . . . as completed event, fulfilled time in the sea of the incomplete and changeable and self-changing (*CD*, I/1, 116, Bromiley). The theological basis of the act of revelation is the doctrine of the Trinity, and so accordingly the temporal distribution of the event is secured entirely through God's own temporal extension, that is through his 'contingent contemporaneousness' (*kontingente Gleichzeitigkeit*).[13] In this way God's being and his time are co-posited in the event of revelation in a manner entirely congruous with the identity of being and eternity: this is the ground for asserting that 'time' for Barth functions in a way analogous to 'substance' in classical theologies. But it is the very concept of 'contingent contemporaneousness' which makes Barth's doctrine

[13] *CD* I/1, 149, Bromiley. The whole subsection 'The speech of God as the act of God' contains a first rehearsal of Barth's conception of the time of revelation as the comprehensive key to the continuity of identity the divine being in Christian theology.

of time thoroughly ambiguous. In making God's own being revealed in his act the exclusive (and in a special sense the inclusive) basis of his theology and thus of his account of reality as a whole, the historical contingency of the event has to be derived from the 'event' of revelation. This 'event' is of a peculiar kind in that as a divine act it is temporally transcendent on the basis of its 'contingent contemporaneity'. This is, quite literally, a 'temporal togetherness' which sets it apart from time as the condition of contingency and historicity in any normally accepted sense.

The 'Novum' of revelation, the original reality, is underived and independent, a manifestation of 'Godhead in the Bible' which 'means freedom, ontic and noetic autonomy' (*CD* I/I, 307, Bromiley). The Lordship of God, expressed in his freedom is godhead in his 'divine *ousia, essentia, natura* or *substantia* . . . The essence of God is the being of God as divine being' (*CD* I/I, 349, Bromiley). In the realm of a divine reciprocity *in aeternitas* Barth develops the trinitarian basis of revelation, and in conjunction with this the initial statement of the theological basis of the person of Christ. He, as the embodiment of the act of the divine being, likewise, according to Barth, represents to us the reality of both creation and redemption. In strict congruity with the principle of analogical derivation, to which allusion was made above, the time of God as presented in Jesus Christ is posited as the original source from which temporal reality, 'real time' will flow. In accordance with the principle of contingent contemporaneity, the act of God in Jesus Christ ('an act which surpasses the whole of actuality we have come to know as act') (*CD* II/I, 263) is given its temporal elasticity (its capacity for temporal comprehensiveness) by the concept of eternity itself, an eternity which does not deny, but in a peculiar sense, affirms time.

Whereas our main concern is with the problematic conceptual affirmation of time by eternity it is necessary to make a distinction between this and the far-reaching architectonic theological creativity of Barth's exposition. Thus with regard to eternity the argument runs upon two levels: the first is where Barth extrapolates the divine perfections as expressions of God's freedom in mutual and reciprocal realisation; and, on the second, with conceptual feet of clay Barth relates the vision of God's munificent plenitude to the context and locus of revelation, Jesus Christ. The actual structure of the interrelation of the two levels is exposed in the category of time. The eternal divine freedom demands the outward manifestation of God's love and lordship which in its turn 'requires and creates and therefore possesses what we call time' and consequently time is the 'form of creation in virtue of which it is definitely fitted to be a theatre for the acts of divine freedom' (*CD* II/1, 464–5). So Barth's transformed doctrine of attribution (now understood as the divine 'perfections') is combined with a Christologically-grounded doctrine of revelation and the divine being in *actus purus et singularis* which are in turn set in the context of a modal trinitarianism.

All this is, however, contained in turn within a framework which is conceived of as transcending the traditional metaphysical scheme of finite and infinite existence.[14] The uniqueness of the divine being precludes its identity with what Barth conceives of as the merely human rationalisation of cosmological alternatives, as presented in classical form in Kant's criticism of the antinomies of space and time.[15] Thus safeguarded, the transcendence of God is ostensibly placed above the vulgarity of philosophical criticism. Such an elevation immediately poses a question concerning the immanence of God and the accessibility of revelation to man who is bound to the sphere of conditioned existence. Barth's solution to this difficulty is by overcoming the conditioned and limited nature of man's temporal existence on the basis of the revealing source: eternity posits its own time. In the area of traditional analogical argument a relation of qualified likeness and unlikeness between eternal and temporal being would have to be advanced. Barth has to reconcile the 'real time' of revelation, that is eternity, with the reality of time as conceived of in the immanent sphere of conditioned human existence. As we shall see later this inevitable derivation is supplemented by an illicit logical parasitism, whereby the very proximity of 'real time' and time as it is commonly known is reflected in the inadequacy of Barth's

[14] For example, see *CD* II/1, 183ff., also 303–4.
[15] For example in the 'Transcendental Dialectic' of *The Critique of Pure Reason*, 384ff.

conceptual distinction between the two. The inter-relation of eternity and time becomes a dialectic of ideal and real, an interplay of conceptions operating within the theological and thus eternal-temporal circle of the divine being.

Thus whereas Barth denies the so-called analogy of being, which he interprets as postulating a common bond of being *qua* being between God and man, God and cosmos, and reasserts the being of God *qua* eternal, trinitarian, supremely *actual* being, the analogically common bond nevertheless emerges once more in the area where we would expect to find it. Given Barth's ontological shift from 'being' to eternity and his use of the temporal category as *the* ontological dimension, the relation he sought to eliminate of divine-human continuity re-appears. The ontological discreteness of God, although powerfully recast in temporal categories, cannot avoid the inevitable dilemma that all human language about God is derived from the logic of the human condition and cannot escape without cost into an 'inner logic' of God unrelated to, or finally distinct from the structures of human reality. This is but half the truth, for Barth does not leave his divine reality so detached but recreates the 'human' reality of immanence on the basis of the act of revelation within the realm of Christology (*CD* III/2, 43ff.). The theological circle is thus greatly extended so as to include both time and humanity, but it remains unbroken, even if, as we shall see, it remains inescapably ambiguous.

Given the remarks made above, which relate Barth's ontological shift from *analogia entis* as a constructive theological principle to a doctrine of being conceived in terms of *analogia fidei* and God's eternal existence in the divine act, extended and applied through 'contingent contemporaneity', it is now possible to see the significance of the detailed analysis that is to follow. Barth expounds the doctrine of the super-infinity of God which transcends the finite-infinite antithesis. On the basis of the freedom of God in his grace, 'infinity' as a divine 'perfection' implies no exclusion of finitude, because God is in himself one who in his 'whole action posits beginning and end, measure and limit, space and time.' Space remains undeveloped except in the context of the divine perfections and this is perhaps natural enough in the light of the role of containment that temporal categories play in delimiting the overall bonds of theological reality and in reconstructing natural reality upon the basis of revelation. This pattern of generating every aspect of reality from a basis in divinity is reflected in the axis of transition from eternity to time, a movement form divine 'infinite' into self-limitation and divine 'finitude'.

> God is certainly infinite, i.e. He has no basis which is not Himself and no standard or law which is not Himself. But he is also finite-without destroying, but in His infinity – in the fact that as love He is His own basis, goal, standard and law. (*CD* II/1, 468).

The concepts 'finite and 'infinite' remain indeterminate in this context, they act as signposts to the divine self-disclosure in limitation. In terms which allow concrete analysis of the reality of such self-revelation of God to take place, the temporal bond is crucially significant. The movement from infinitude to finitude is grounded upon God's own temporal potential. The being of God so understood becomes the basis of a natural theology of time, a natural theology built upon revelation.[16] God's time, that is his eternity, enjoys a temporal 'superiority' (*Uberlegenheit*) because 'in the basis of its being, everything does not exist in itself but in God, in His knowledge of its possibility and its actuality' (*CD* II/1, 559). It is upon this basis that the gulf between the realm of divine and human being will be bridged; it is here that the actual logic of the 'analogy' is inevitably exposed. God's 'concrete temporal centre' (*konkretes zeitliches Zentrum*) is the ground of the prototypical temporal dynamism (*CD* II/1, 605); its expression is in the 'One who was born in His own time as the fulfilment of all time', the crucified and risen Son of God and Son of Man. What is the time of God as it finds fulfilment in the divine act in Jesus Christ? What exactly is its structure and how does this structure expose the logic of the 'interface' between the realities of God and man, God and cosmos?

Barth's answers are presented in terms of a temporal consummation of the drive towards synthesis, as a self-conscious merging of the major theological traditions of biblical and philosophical theology. In brief it may be said that the Boethian

---

[16] Cf. T. F. Torrance, 'The problem of natural theology in the thought of Karl Barth', *Religious Studies* 6 (1970), 121–35.

conception of eternity, the *'Interminabilis vitae tota simul et perfecta possessio'* reveals itself as the correct key to the interpretation of biblical insight; so emerges a mutuality of biblical exegesis and dogmatic exposition. The Boethian notion of an eternity which simultaneously possesses endlessness in a *totum simul*, a moment of perfect recollection, has never, Barth argues, undergone its 'proper exploitation'.[17] So Barth synthesises themes from philosophical and biblical theology in a way which ostensibly enhances the value of both, but which nevertheless cannot escape from profound difficulties that attend the whole structure. In an important passage Barth elaborates:

> God's eternity, like His unity and constancy, is a quality of His freedom. It is the sovereignty and majesty of His love in so far as this has and is itself pure duration. The being is eternal in whose duration, beginning, succession and end are not three but one, not separate as a first, a second and a third occasion, but one simultaneous occasion as beginning, middle and end. Eternity is the simultaneity of beginning, middle and end, and to that extent it is pure duration. Eternity is God in the sense in which in Himself and in all things God is simultaneous, i.e., beginning and middle as well as end, without separation, distance or contradiction. Eternity is not, therefore, time, although time is certainly God's creation or, more correctly, a form of His creation. Time is distinguished from eternity by the fact that in it beginning, middle and end are distinct and even opposed as past, present and future. Eternity is just the duration which is lacking to time, as can be seen clearly at the middle point of time, in the temporal present and in its relationship to the past and the future. Eternity has and is the duration which is lacking to time. It has and is simultaneity. (*CD* II/1, 608)

So an alliance has been effected between the 'biblical' theme of God's freedom, sovereignty and majesty (expounded in the doctrine of God's perfections) and a conception of eternity, which though 'positive' in the Boethian presentation of a sense of temporal 'gathering', cannot disguise its Platonic and Augustinian overtones and origins and its ultimate roots in the Parmenidean

---

[17] Barth provides a truly majestic exposition of the Boethian *nunc stans* on 310ff. Cf. *CD* II/1 in which the 'theological concept of eternity must be set free from the Babylonian captivity of an abstract opposite to the concept of time' (op.cit., 611). The passage in which this conception occurs is Boethius' *The Consolation of Philosophy*, bk. V, ch. 6.

fragments.[18] The context of this synthesis, the so-called 'analogy of faith', suffused with a thoroughgoing actualism of the divine being-in-act, is in reality an actualised exemplarism, inasmuch as it postulates the prototypical derivation of time from eternity. This is the ontological framework, the context of the interface of the realms of divine and human being. The logic of the encounter is as follows: time has a 'beginning, middle and end distinct and opposed as past, present and future', whereas eternity, the *nunc stans*, the 'standing now', is 'just that duration which is lacking to time'; the latter 'has and is simultaneity' a duration expressed in the 'middle point of time', that is in Jesus Christ. Thus it is in the context of time that the doctrine of God, the Boethian *nunc stans* as the prototypical basis of time itself, and the revelation of God in Christ undergo mutual realisation. God's act in his being is his act in Jesus Christ; and as divine being is eternity, thus it is in the temporal logic that the very ontological core of the *Church Dogmatics* is exposed to view.

It is not surprising that as well as the elements alluded to above being present, a further parallel may be drawn, not merely with regard to the Augustinianism in Barth's theological presentation, but also with the temporal logic of Hegel. Indeed it might be said that it is in Barth's doctrine of time that we find an implicit acknowledgment of Hegel and without doubt grounds for detecting in the *Church Dogmatics* an explicit (even if unwelcome) idealism. Hegel's phrase, 'The true present is eternity'[19] precisely characterises Barth's own formulations but the latter is in a more difficult position insofar as he must maintain historicity and temporality as they are normally understood in the contingent sense *on the basis of eternity*. Time (upon which an ontological discontinuity must be built) is understood in nothing more or less

[18] H. Diels, *Fragmente der Vorsokratiker*, frag. B. 8, lines 5–6; *oude pot' ên oud' estai, epei nun estin homou pan hen, suneches*; ('Neither was nor will be; it is all simultaneously one'). This forms the basis of a conception developed and exploited by Plotinus (*Enneads* III), Augustine (*Confessions*, bk. XI, *City of God*, bk. XI) Boethius (*The Consolations of Philosophy*, bk. V, ch. 6 and by Aquinas (*Summa Theologica*, part I, qn. X). Initial guidance to the development of the Boethian conception conception taken up by Barth may be found in W. Kneale's article, 'Time and Eternity in Theology' *Proceedings of the Aristotelian Society* 51 (1961) 87–108.
[19] Cf. *The Philosophy of Nature*, London 1970, 78–86.

than the following terms: God's eternity is a simultaneity in which co-exist 'beginning, middle as well as end, without separation, distance or contradiction' and time as it is deprived of the distinct order of 'before' and 'after' conversely is 'distinguished from eternity by the fact that in it beginning, middle and end are distinct and even opposed as past present and future' (*CD* II/1, 608). On this basis eternity is said to have a constitutive role with regard to time, yet at the very instant of 'fulfilment' time ceases to be time in a recognisable sense the succession of events in time. It was an analogous distinction that was criticised in Hegel by the philosopher-logician Adolf Trendelenberg and taken up by Soren Kierkegaard in his analysis of 'the Moment'.[20] More ironically, Barth's position shows signs of a retreat on his part from the standpoint of his early thought in the dialectical theology of *Romans* to a Hegelian theme of synthesis and the inevitable suppression of the real distinction of immanence and transcendence in the name of a higher reality, a reality, needless to say, that Kierkegaard regarded as an illusion. Kierkegaard sought to reassert the role of 'movement' (κίηνσις) in the existential 'Moment' in which the transition from being to becoming is made in such a way as to preserve the atemporality of the eternal 'Moment' yet also the historicity of past moments of time in which the eternal had manifested itself. In other words, Barth's theological development represents a retreat to a Hegel-like posture when it is seen in the context of his early thought, especially in the second edition of *The Epistle to the Romans*. At this earlier stage of Barth's development the relation of eternity and time was of thorough-going *krisis* in the context of his appropriation of the 'infinite qualitative distinction between time and eternity'. Eternity overwhelmed time, for '. . . time is nothing by the standard of eternity' (*ER*, 43) but on the other hand eternity is equally 'nothing' in strictly temporal terms as:

> Between the past and the future – between the time – there is a "Moment" that is no moment in time. This "Moment" is the eternal Moment – the Now – when the past and the future stand still, when the former ceases its going and the latter its coming. (*ER,* 497)

[20] Cf. H. Diem, Kierkegaard's *Dialectic of Existence,* Edinburgh 1959, 30ff. for an illuminating account of Trendelenberg's criticism of Hegel regarding the latter's categorical reduction entailed by the synthesis in the dialectic.

Essentially what is found in the developed doctrine of time in the *Church Dogmatics* is a consistent attempt to re-temporalise the 'Moment', which in becoming the 'middle point' of time takes on temporal overtones. The temporality of the event of revelation is structured through *analogia fidei* but concretely expressed in the life of Jesus of Nazareth and above all in the 'forty days' of the Risen Lord. It is during this period that the hiddenness of God in Jesus Christ becomes explicit and putatively unambiguous: the temporality of God becomes the temporality of man. Whilst the temporal structure and conceptions that have been outlined in this paper are consistently expressed in other areas in the *Church Dogmatics*, for example in creation and in election, it is in the realisation of the Incarnation in the resurrection that the validity of Barth's theological theory of time can be tested.

In general, the interaction of time and eternity (the logic of ontological discontinuity) is the positing of God's temporality in which present, past and future co-exist without 'opposition or competition or conflict', that is in *duration* without *division*. This conceptual parasitism, the dialectical derivation of two realities from the single conception of a temporal event (which logically demands both durational and divisional dimensions) is supremely expressed in the Incarnation. The Incarnation conceived in the Christological structure of *enhypostasis* and *anhypostasis* is based upon the 'completed event' of the *egeneto* (*CD* I/2, 163), which as such is the expression of the divine act, the '*actus purus et singularis*'. The temporal comprehensiveness of the contingent contemporaneity of the time of God is displayed in a manner strictly parallel to the consummation of Christology, for 'the event of Easter Day and the resurrection appearances during the forty days was the mediation, the infallible mediation as unequivocally disclosed in a new act of God, of the perception that God was in Christ' (*CD* IV/1, 301). In its theological dimensions Barth's exposition is both consistent and relatively unproblematic given an acceptance of Chalcedonian Christology, but as regards time itself, difficulties are apparent.

> The resurrection of Jesus Christ tells us . . . that as the Crucified "He lives and reigns to all eternity" (Luther), that as the One was was, having been buried, He is not of the past, He did not continue to be enclosed in the limits of time between His birth and death . . . He became and is Lord of all time. (*CD* IV/1, 313)

On the basis of God's undivided past, present and future 'our' separated and non-contemporaneous past, present and future are subject to a 'removal of limitations' (*CD* III/2, 464). In conformity with the doctrine of hypostatic unity Jesus' time is both three-dimensional (and thus human) but also contemporaneous (and thus divine) for in the 'forty days the presence of God in the presence of the man Jesus was no longer a paradox' but 'the total, final, irrevocable and eternal manifestation of God Himself' (*CD* III/2, 449). Barth then develops his exposition upon the basis of an exegesis of Revelation 1:8, 'I am the Alpha and Omega, saith the Lord God, which is and which was and which is to come, the Almighty' (R.V.), of which he makes the following:

> I am all this simultaneously. I, the same, am; I was as the same; and I will come again as the same. My time is always simultaneously present, past and future. (*CD* III/2, 465)

Such positive statements of the Boethian notion as Barth makes in the context of Christology are theologically comprehensible in the light of his fundamental assumptions, but what are the consequences for time of his application of the Christological doctrine of *anhypostasis* and *enhypostasis*? Given the *en*hypostatic derivation of time (that is 'real time') from God's revelation in act, and the corresponding *an*hypostatic relation of this time to the vulgar time of the historical order as we know it, can Barth then legitimately claim that the forty days of resurrection time is more than ambiguously present in our time? In other words can 'time', used as the ontological medium of the analogy of faith and God's eternal being, be part and parcel of the temporal historical sphere of commonplace existence, when it is qualified by the doctrine of hypostatic unity? Is there not here an acute danger of a temporal docetism parallel to a docetic view of Christ's humanity as conceived in Chalcedonian Christology?[21] The time of Christ remains grounded within the theological circle in such a way that we are to *regard* it as fully temporal as Barth demands; but it is nevertheless not in *substantial* coinherence with our time. Christ's time in the forty days *seems* to be in our time,

---

[21] See *CD* I/2, 163, Christ's humanity subsists by virtue of its divine mode of being *alone*, it has no existence of its own.

but the movement that Barth has made to identify eternity (and therefore time) with being completes the effective encapsulation of revelation in its own time. Barth's own unease is apparent and the 'attitude' he calls for is immediately subverted by a return to the language of 'inclusion', as we see in the following passage.

> ... the time of Jesus is also a time like all other times; that is occurred once and once for all; that it had beginning, duration and end; that it was contemporary for some, future for others, and for others again, e.g. for us past. Only a docetic attitude to Jesus can deny that his being in time also means what being in time means for us all. Our acceptance of His true humanity depends on an acceptance of this proposition. Even the acceptance of His true deity, implying as it does an identity between his time and God's, does not rule out this simple means of His being in time. On the contrary it includes it. (*CD* III/2, 463)

Given Barth's basic presuppositions and his consistent adherence to them, upon what basis (other than that of mere assertion) may he assert the identity between God's time and what 'being in time means for us all'? In addition, Barth's arguments against the reality of time (in which he rehearses traditional sceptical arguments based upon the transitoriness of the present) mean that the congruence of the time of God in Jesus Christ with our own time is only tenable as regards the time of the humanity of Jesus Christ, which is itself posited on the basis of the divinity of the Word acting hypostatically. In other words, on what authority may Barth breach the circumference of his own theological circle? It is not an entry into time that confronts us but the closest contiguity, a contiguity that manifests itself as ambiguity, but not in a full identity. As he intimates, 'only a docetic attitude to Jesus can deny that His being in time means what being in time means for us all', but can Barth do any more than recognise this? He has no substantial grounds for the identity he seeks to assert and this is confirmed by the relapse back once again into the language of 'inclusion'.

In the light of these comments can we not perceive a certain irony in T. F. Torrance's comment that 'Barth rightly insists that in the knowledge of God we cannot raise questions as to its reality from some position outside of it?'[22] Barth's own utter consistency

---

[22] Space, Time and Incarnation (London 1969), 54.

entails the consequence that *all* questions about reality have to be asked and answered within the realm of the knowledge of God. We can see that the theological structure of the *Church Dogmatics*, developed in terms of the identity of being and time reflects in a very precise way such commitment. Indeed has not the structure of Barth's thought, based upon the explication of a single related and exclusive set of presuppositions, led inevitably to the necessity of the total recreation of 'reality' upon a strictly theological foundation? In doing this such a 'reality' becomes the realm of ambiguity, an inner dialectic of prototypical ideal and Christological 'real' extended upon the plane of 'God's time'. This time of God is a temporal 'fulfilment' which abrogates time as it is seen in the logic of the 'before' and 'after' of events. Thus the very 'extension' of the act of God's being in revelation endangers the reality of actual temporal extension, that is if an emphasis is laid upon the logical contrast drawn between eternity and time. The danger of an ontological 'implosion' or collapse is held off by the asserted historicity of the event of revelation; but the exclusivity of Barth's starting-point in revelation precludes a more than merely formal temporal extension of a highly Pickwickian kind. If Barth is honoured with an interpretation based upon the consistency of his own presuppositions then the logic of theological self-inclusion and circularity must be allowed to stand.

Why, it might well be asked, should such a harsh and reductive approach be taken to Barth's work. First, the harshness is and should be a reflection of the urgency of a situation in which Christianity and Christian theology find themselves in acute danger of accepting the dilemma of reduction into pure secularity or withdrawal into the illusory security of a *disciplina arcani*. Secondly, our apparent reduction of Barth is not illegitimate in that we are merely demanding consistent reflection of those principles he himself regarded as fundamental. The principle of *analogia fidei* applied to a doctrine of God who reveals himself with utter exclusivity in his act in Jesus Christ leads to a dangerous and ambiguous recreation of reality as the structure and receptacle of revelation itself. The logic of such containment is the form of the doctrine of time, which is itself the vehicle of the divine being, (indeed the very manifestation of its substance), as we saw at the outset of these remarks. The consequences of Barth's conception of *analogia fidei* when seen in the context of his ontological transformation of traditional methods in dogmatic theology are extremely serious. In wider terms we have observed how in one major contemporary theologian the alienation of the natural order and its attempted recreation as a natural theology based upon revelation, presents in a particular way the general isolation of Christian theology from the realm of commonplace secular reality. Such an alienation is nothing less than a comprehensive theological disaster which must itself be understood before adequate rectification can be made. It may then prove possible to reassert a fuller conception of the distinctions implied by the transcendence of God and to recover for the world of public and shared intellectual discourse a theology ensnared in its own comprehensive and consistent logic, the logic of self-isolation.

3

Karl Barth on the Trinity
(1980)

In their Preface to the retranslation of volume I/1 of Barth's *Church Dogmatics* G. W. Bromiley and T. F. Torrance draw attention to the earlier translator's comment, that this work contains 'undoubtedly the greatest treatise on the Trinity since the Reformation'. Whereas the late Professor G. T. Thomson only referred back to the Reformation, Bromiley and Torrance go further, and make the tentative claim that it is only with Augustine that we meet the equal of Barth. The basis of such a grandiose assertion is not merely that of extent or intellectual complexity, but is, according to Barth's commentators, the overall redirection of theology that his doctrine of the Trinity is said to have achieved. Barth's undoubted redirection of theological interest to the doctrine of the Trinity was, and is, of global theological importance, inasmuch as it presents a challenge to the fundamental and persistent denigration of the Trinity, as a mere problematical implication of biblical evidence. Besides this, Barth sought to reform Christian theological endeavour between, and apart from, the Scylla of the anthropological and subjective starting-point of modernistic Protestantism and the Charybdis of Roman Catholic medieval thought, purportedly with its shared notion of being, participated in by both man and God. In other words, the Trinity itself is the authentic power-house of theology from which radiates the true energy of Christian revelation. Indeed, in the words of the Preface, 'the doctrine of the Trinity itself belongs to the very basis of the Christian faith and

constitutes the fundamental grammar of dogmatic theory.'
(*CD* I/1, ix, Bromiley)[1]

It is important to distinguish between what Barth sets out to
achieve, and claims made on behalf of his work by others. What
shall be attempted in this brief study is to show first how Barth
develops his doctrine of the Trinity in volume I/1 of the *Church
Dogmatics*, and then, second, how this basis underlies the vast
structure of the whole work. On this basis it is possible to advance
some tentative comments upon the overall nature and
consequences of this presentation of the doctrine of the Trinity.

At the outset a basic contrast may be drawn between the so-
called father of modern theology, Friedrich Schleiermacher, who
places the doctrine of the Trinity in an appendix to *The Christian
Faith*,[2] and Barth, who begins with this conception. The
difference of placement is no mere formal characteristic, because
for the former the Trinity is an incidental rationalisation of the
Christian experience of God, whereas for the latter the Trinity is
utterly fundamental; indeed the very distinctiveness of
Christianity is constituted by this datum (*CD* I/1, 301).[3] Barth's
arrival at this starting-point was not sudden or arbitrary, and his
development may be studied elsewhere. In essence, however, he
moved from the Protestant Liberalism characteristic of nineteenth
century German thought (epitomised by Adolf von Harnack,
Barth's own teacher in the early years of this century) to the so-
called 'dialectical theology' of the second edition of his
commentary upon the Epistle to the Romans.[4] In this latter work
Barth systematically destroyed the theological basis of any easy
accommodation between Christianity and contemporary culture
by the exploitation of a radical disjunction between the divine and
human spheres of being. The 'infinite qualitative distinction'
between eternity and time, infinite and finite existence, which
Barth borrowed from Kierkegaard, was interpreted in such a way
that crisis and paradox displaced mediation and synthesis. The

[1] In this paper reference is to the earlier translation (1936) by G. T. Thomson
unless otherwise indicated.
[2] *The Christian Faith* (Edinburgh 1928), 738–751.
[3] The doctrine of the Trinity fundamentally distinguishes 'the Christian
doctrine of God as Christian'.
[4] *The Epistle to the Romans* (London, 1933). Translation of the 1922 second,
rewritten edition.

divine realm confronted and overwhelmed the human. God's Word came as the annihilator of any human pretension based upon any immanent theological point of contact between God and man. The annihilation was so complete as to threaten the whole of theology with its own reduction. The possibility of positive relation essential to both a stable Christology and doctrine of creation was threatened by the total nature of the crisis of confrontation. In the period between the second edition of *Romans* and the first volume of the *Church Dogmatics* Barth explored the possibility of new theological starting-points and so the latter in its positive aspects is the culmination of a dramatic series of developments.[5]

Positively, Barth combined his interpretation of Anselm's theological method in the *Proslogion*, the notion of 'faith seeking understanding' and that God himself provides a rational authentication of language about him in the 'analogy of faith' with the structural method of Protestant scholasticism and its uninhibited exploitation of systematically related theological *loci* or points of focus. These two sets of factors allow Barth to extrapolate from fundamental theological data on the assumption that there is in fact a single truth (albeit multiplied in appearance), which provides the basis of all such so-called analogical derivation. In other words, there is no speculative exploration made in the hope of locating and isolating theological truth. On the contrary, God has acted, acts and will continue to act in Jesus Christ. God's act in Jesus Christ is not therefore a surmise but is the primal ontological datum apart from which any talk of Christianity or revelation is at best misleading and at worst a damnable perversion. God's act is Jesus Christ is not merely the exclusive source of the knowledge of God but also supremely inclusive, for in this the Trinity of God is revealed and along with it the total theological potential of Christian dogma. To be more explicit, it may with justice be said that the act of God in Jesus Christ unites the Godward and trinitarian dimension of the divine being with the expression of that being towards man and in history in the doctrines of creation and reconciliation. The doctrine of the Trinity is, in Barth's theology, the divine being in revealing action: God is in Trinity insofar as he is in Jesus Christ.

[5] See T. F. Torrance *Karl Barth, The Development of his Early Theology* 1910–31 (London, 1962) ch. 1 and 2.

How then does Barth understand and explicate the Trinity as the 'immediate implicate of revelation'? The initial presupposition is that the 'proper content of Christian language about God' is ascertainable by man and that, in consequence 'language about God has the proper content, when it conforms to the essence of the Church, i.e. to Jesus Christ' according to what Barth terms the 'analogy of faith'.[6] Jesus Christ, the 'proper content' of Christian language about God and thus Christian theology, is not to be developed by the extrapolation of the propositions contained either in Holy Scripture (as in a Protestant biblicism) or in a 'deposit of faith' (the truths consigned to the Catholic Church by the Apostles) but by an explication of the actual contemporaneity of God in Christ. The Trinity is consequent upon the reality of God in Christ, the 'essence of the Church'; it is the 'possibility' that rests upon the presupposition that God in Christ approaches us in a uniquely distinctive and irreducible way.

What then does this fundamental datum of the 'essence of the Church' consist in? It is not anything that the Church possesses, just as it was not anything possessed by Bible or tradition. It is, Barth argues, a 'pure act', an utterly original (and, therefore, underived) divine action, which has its own basis and is essentially self-explanatory. Knowledge of it is not speculative but an acknowledgment of a given which is independent of all human causation and truly autonomous. The occasion of this divine act is the Church's proclamation in which, in accordance with Reformation principles, the essential sacramental medium is the preached Word of God. God objectifies himself according to his own grace and will in his language, in a manner analogically parallel to Christ's own assumption of human flesh. As with Christ, so with the Word of God; the analogy becomes an identity, for revelation is, has been and will be the Person of Jesus Christ. In asserting that revelation is, the statement is made and repeated that 'The Word became flesh and dwelt among us'.[7] This carries with it the inescapable implication that 'we are asserting

---

[6] *CD* I.I, 11 (Bromiley). See also H. Bouillard, *The Knowledge of God* (London, 1969), for a critique of Barth's conception of the 'analogy of faith'.

[7] John I.14 is Barth's scriptural *Leitmotif* in the great early volumes of the *Church Dogmatics*.

something that is to be grounded only within the Trinity; namely, by the will of the Father, by the mission of the Son and of the Holy Spirit, by the eternal decree of the Triune God' (*CD* I/1, 134). Thus it is that revelation is an immediate implication of the Trinity itself. God is in his revelation; the implication is mutual and complementary for there is, according to Barth, no hidden abyssmal God apart from his revelation in Jesus Christ and correspondingly no revelation of God that does not express God in his fullness.

The mystery of God's uncreated reality in the Word is a veiling of God in which he unveils himself. This is the dialectic of the worldliness of the transcendent Word that presents itself in an irresolvable tension that demands acknowledgment and resists reductive explanation. The general principle of the worldliness of the Word incarnate, which has replaced the utter disjunction of divine and human existence characteristic of dialectical theology as such, is supplemented by a further 'analogy' which provides the initial step in translating the argument from the doctrine of the Word to that of the Trinity, 'the doctrine of the three-in-oneness of God'. The doctrine of the Trinity has no analogy other than that of the threefold form of the Word of God (preached, written and revealed), and the analysis of the concept of revelation yields the doctrine of the Trinity. The content of the 'original reality' or revelation is the 'analytical judgment' that 'God reveals Himself as Lord'. Revelation is not argued towards, but is a self-grounded and self-authenticated fact which occurs on the basis of God's sovereign freedom. From this 'fact' of the free lordship of God that happens in revelation there may take place the analytical (indeed it might be said near-tautologous) derivation of the truth that 'Godhead in the Bible means freedom, ontic and noetic independence' (*CD* I/1, 352).

Repudiating decisively the Augustinian attempt to isolate traces of the Trinity in the created world because of his desire to safeguard completely the absolute primal uniqueness of the revelation of God, Barth proceeds towards what he conceives of as the legitimate 'interpretation' (as opposed to the 'illustration') of revelation. The only veridical trace of revelation is that of God's Word (and not those expressed in the Augustinian psychology of memory, thought and will, for example) in which there is the triply one voice of Father, Son and Spirit speaking in his revelation, in Holy Scripture and in proclamation. This is the exclusive basis of our knowledge of the Trinity.

There is a profoundly rhapsodic quality to Barth's argument; the fundamental nature of revelation and thus God's own making accessible of himself makes it inevitable that the logical path from the realm of immanence to that of transcendence is incomplete precisely because of the nature of the subject in question. Once it has been made clear that God has in reality acted (and acts) in the way he did (and does) then the inner logic of his nature unfolds strictly upon its own terms, as an exegesis of the events of revelation witnessed to in Holy Scripture. For Barth it may then be said that the Trinity creates its own evidence and all other 'evidence' is of necessity misleading and perversely false.

The Trinity, as the 'possibility' lying behind the 'reality' of revelation, is now explicated in the context of the 'analytical' sphere of the trinitarian act of God in revelation, an act which supremely expresses the three-in-oneness. It is the point of derivation of the doctrine of the Trinity in the single (yet temporally extended and recurrent) act of God in revelation which dictates the fundamental commitment to the principle of unity in the trinitarian thought of the *Church Dogmatics*. Such a point of unity is also taken by many critics of Barth as an indication of a pervasive Christomonism in his scheme. The complete and comprehensive source of the knowledge of God in his revelation in Christ and the derivation of the dogmatic structure from this 'fact' has been regarded as a principle which obscures and reduces the reality and importance of these other items on the Christian theological agenda. The claim made by Barth is that the Trinity is not a merely formal explanation of revelation but its ontological enabling, the real possibility behind the revealed reality. This potentially reductive criticism of Barth must be borne in mind as the explicit logic of the Trinity is unfolded, for it is possible that here is encountered a source not only of Barth's 'Christomonist' tendency but also of the heavy emphasis he places upon the unity of God's 'ways of being' in the Father, Son and Holy Spirit.

The exposition of the trinitarian being of God in Father, Son and Holy Spirit that Barth provides is in terms of three 'modes' or 'ways of being', which indicate a threefold repetition and mutuality that is so complete as to allow a complete 'involution' and 'convolution' of these 'modes' in a 'single act' of revelation, for all God's operation, as we are bound to conceive it on the basis of his revelation, is a single act, occurring simultaneously and unitedly in all his three modes of existence. Indeed, Barth argues, from 'creation, past revelation and reconciliation, to the redemption to come it holds good, that He who acts here is the Father and the Son and the Spirit' (*CD* I/1, 430). God is fully trinitarian but any such assertion is subordinated to the demands of singularity posited in the act of revelation, in which the eternal antecedence of God in Trinity is given temporal realisation in this 'single act'.

A certain tension in Barth's trinitarian thought is apparent at this point, for despite his reciprocal exposition of the oneness in threeness (indicated by a reference to Luther's exposition of the baptism of Jesus in which Father, Son and Holy Spirit participate) the emphasis upon unity is predominant. This predominance is apparent in the explicative motifs that have been encountered earlier, the threefold Word of God, for example, in which the analogy of the Trinity of God is this single recurrent principle. Now it is reinforced by the description of the manifestation of God in Trinity as Revealer, Revelation and Revealedness. In other words the distinctiveness of divine function upon which meaningful distinction-in-unity of the 'modes' relies (Barth shrinks from the word 'person' as implying an anthropomorphism) is subsumed into moments in the act of revelation. This is to some extent a reductive account in that one functional category becomes the medium both of unity and ostensibly of distinction also. Again it must be noted that it is the biblical witness to the 'veiling, unveiling and impartation of God' that gives 'cause to speak of a threefold otherness of the one God' in the first place (*CD* I/1, 431). The function of the Trinity is revelation; content of revelation is the disclosure of the Lordship of the one God.

The reciprocity and co-equality of God's 'ways of being' so heavily stressed by Barth is a dogmatic conception that finds its consummate expression in the assertion that the 'Church doctrine of the Trinity is a self-enclosed circle' (*CD* I/1, 436). Here what has been 'analytical judgment' becomes, as 'self-enclosed circle', an explicit presentation of the celestial tautology that tells us that the Revealer is God. The potential weakness of this conception stems not solely from the fact (Barth admits) that such extreme reciprocity is not admitted by the New Testament itself, but also from a further tendency of this trinitarian act to encircle and absorb not only the 'moments' of God's revelation as Father, Son and Holy Spirit (*CD* I/1, 437) and the events of the New Testament, but beyond this, the whole scheme of creation, incarnation and reconciliation, that is, reality as a whole.

> And this Lord can be our God. He can meet us and unite us to Himself, because He is God in these three modes of existence as Father, Son, and Spirit, because creation, reconciliation, redemption, the entire being, language, and action in which He wills to be our God, is grounded and typified in His own essence, in His Godness itself. As Father, Son, and Spirit God is, so to speak, ours in advance. (*CD* I/1, 440).

The grounding and typifying of such diverse realities in the essence of God, in his 'Godness itself', is an indication that the doctrine of the Trinity as the explication of the divine 'possibility' that underlies the 'reality' of revelation is no mere abstraction but bound up intimately with the total logic of Barth's presentation of reality as such in the *Church Dogmatics*. It is not by a mere chance that this assertion of the inclusiveness of the divine prototypicality is associated with a radical denigration of our own existence, for it is 'held by Him, and only by Him, over the abyss of non-existence' (*CD* I/1, 446). Our existence, Barth continues, is 'real so far as He wills and posits it a real existence'. This negative strain in Barth's thought leads to an overall ambiguity in the presentation of reality as we know it on the mundane level and raises problems that can only be hinted at here. In positive terms the prototypical potential of the trinitarian divine being is expressed initially in Barth's exposition of the Fatherhood of God. The importance of this exposition is that it provides, within the confines of Barth's trinitarian framework, the detailed theological rationale for the inclusion (albeit prototypically) of all truly real reality, both created and recreated. The prototypical potential of Barth's doctrine of God in Trinity is of an extent determined by the temporal structure and extension of the single act of the divine being in revelation. The temporal inclusion which correlates with the prototypical capacity of the divine being has consequences which are extremely far-reaching. The centrality of the act of revelation and its temporal extension provides the prototypical basis, through its eternal status, of the whole temporal order of reality.

The trinitarian explanation of the divine being is part and parcel of a comprehensive structure which dominates and conditions the explicit theology of the Trinity. Such a theme as that of the Fatherhood of God is not only an exposition of divine personhood in reciprocal relation but also the theological link relating Trinity to creation in the sphere of prototypical antecedence. From God's own Fatherhood of Jesus Christ may be derived prototypically not only fatherhood in general but the fact of creation itself, 'it is again as this Eternal Father, and not in any other way, that he reveals himself as the Creator' (*CD* I/1, 12).

Unfortunately, just as the outward limits of the doctrine of the Trinity imply an inclusion of the totality of reality (and this is especially clear with regard to time and human nature as the human nature of Jesus Christ) so inwardly such an inclusion has a corresponding compression and implicit categorial reduction. The derivation of creation and createdness from the equation of Creator and Father in the context of the Trinity means that once more the latter does not remain so much a mystery transcending human rationality as an ontological battle-ground whose strife is muted by a suppression of incompatibles. Effectively all the tensions of the antithesis of created and uncreated being and of immanence and transcendence are translated into the area of the doctrine of the Trinity, precisely because the act of revelation is the direct correlate of the Trinity and vice versa. This act is the dialectical interplay of divine being and worldly mask in revelation. The absolute identity of act and Trinity, of three-in-oneness, means that an ontological compression has to take place and evidence of this is apparent in the implications of the equation of Fatherhood and Creatorhood that Barth presents.

In the first part of this brief outline of Barth's doctrine of the Trinity the dangers of his method of grounding and deriving this conception from the 'single act' of the divine being have become apparent. In crude but not inaccurate terms it may be said that Barth effectively inverts the Hegelian doctrine of the

Trinity.[8] Hegel resolves the Trinity into the historical process, God dies in Christ, history moves towards its spiritual and intellectual consummation. Barth, in positing the contingent historical order upon the basis of the putative contingency and historicity of God, attempts to recreate the natural order but by doing so effects a resolution and extinction of that order in the trinitarian abyss of the divine being. This is the primary significance of Barth's doctrine of the Trinity which is no mere theological excursion of some originality but a structured reinterpretation of reality as a whole *within* the confines of fundamental dogma.

It is only upon the basis of the realisation of the global ontological and epistemological role of Barth's doctrine of the Trinity as the ostensible explication of God's act of revelation that the reader may proceed without misconceptions to examine the burgeoning theological ornamentation of his work. Thus the exposition of the trinitarian 'modes' as stated initially in the Niceano-Constantinopolitan Creed that Barth then proceeds to develop must be understood and appreciated with caution. Without such caution a certain mystification may well overcome the reader as he becomes gradually enmeshed in the implications of Barth's basic theological method whilst he conceives of himself as engaged in mere doctrinal analysis. It is consequently necessary to analyse Barth's thought on at least two levels. The first of these has involved a critical appreciation of some of the reasons for the basic monism, or trend towards unity in the doctrine of the Trinity in the *Church Dogmatics*, which stems primarily from the mode of its generation and derivation in the so-called single act of revelation. Given this analysis, the second level concerns the actual dogmatic outworking of the doctrine in the architectonic structures of the *Church Dogmatics*. The former may not ultimately be divorced from the latter level for they are methodologically interwoven. Exploration of the trinitarian development extending from the genetic revelatory core outwards in the doctrines of election, the Incarnation, Christology, creation and reconciliation reveals progressively both the strength and

---

[8] Such as it is expounded in *The Lectures on the Philosophy of Religion*, in particular volume III, to which Barth refers in his article on Hegel in *Protestant Theology in the Nineteenth Century* (London, 1972), 384–421.

underlying weakness of Barth's doctrine of the Trinity. With enormous energy the doctrine of the Trinity is propounded in all these contexts inasmuch as Father, Son and Holy Spirit manifest themselves, but the unity thus achieved is matched by the dispersal of the initial difficulties throughout the system.

In the latter stages of the exposition of the doctrine of the Trinity found in volume I/1 Barth provides a first schematic statement of the three different modes or ways of being. Here the essential scriptural reference of the exposition comes to the fore and Barth finds and exploits ample evidence for the fundamental work of the trinitarian revelation of God as Lord, Yahweh and Kyrios, in Old and New Testaments respectively. In specific terms, it is in the life, death and resurrection of Jesus Christ that God as Father, Creator, and free, holy God is revealed. God's own capacity for such a revelation depends upon his being what he is in revelation antecedently in himself. The events of the life of Jesus Christ are the *sole* medium of revelation and in virtue of the trinitarian capacity in antecedence and reciprocity the *completeness* of revelation of Father, Creator and Lord is guaranteed. The exclusiveness of revelation in Jesus Christ depends absolutely upon the fullest form of trinitarian inclusiveness. Revelation is the *Novum* (a really new unveiling of mystery) because 'Jesus did not so much re-proclaim the familiar word "Creator" and interpret it by the likewise unfamiliar name of Father, but he revealed the unfamiliar Father, his Father, and thereby, and first thereby and only thereby that and what the Creator is, and that He as such is our Father' (*CD* I/1, 449). The fullest unity and integration of the doctrine of the Trinity is essential, if the fullness of revelation in God's act in Jesus Christ is to be preserved, given that no evidence in the cosmos, human life or even Holy Scripture can be taken as the basis of trinitarian inference, apart from the peculiar mode of trinitarian deduction made possible by entry into the 'self-enclosed circle' of the doctrine of the Trinity, a circle that becomes a reality in Jesus of Nazareth, and in him alone, uniquely and exclusively. This reality is one of 'mutual and reciprocal reflection', for as Barth argues, 'We cannot call God the Father, without the Son and the Spirit, and we cannot call the Son Saviour or the Spirit Comforter, without implying the Father in both cases' (*CD* I/1, 453).

The unity in trinity of the divine action is sustained by Barth's exploitation of traditional dogmatic conception of 'appropriation' and 'communion' which relate the modes of existence. There must be mutual interpenetration and communion without mutual extinction or reduction to a 'neutral, undifferentiated fourth'. God's being both inwardly and outwardly is a work, an act which is distinctively trinitarian and yet indivisible through the mutuality of attribution. Yet, despite this indivisibility and mutuality of appropriation that the inner distinctions of the Trinity secure, Barth asserts the peculiar and apposite nature of certain statements applicable to this or that mode of existence of the Trinity. God the Father, Son and Holy Spirit are what they are both in mutuality *and* distinctiveness. Whether Barth's reunification of the immanent and economic doctrines of the Trinity (that is God in Trinity in himself and in revelation, respectively) can be sustained without some of the dangers alluded to in this short account is open to doubt. At this point not merely Barth's understanding of the Trinity is called into question, but the whole Western tradition. Since Augustine this has relied upon a 'filioquist' and Christologically-conditioned extrapolation of the doctrine of the Trinity expressed in both ecclesiology and spirituality which has tended towards distortion, even the disintegration of the trinitarian framework.

This fragmentation can be seen in many contexts, especially in the history of the doctrine of the Church which has, in Catholic traditions, focused upon the Christologically-dominated motif of the prolonged Christ, the extended Incarnation as the basis of the Church and Christian life, and in Protestant thought, upon God's death in the man Jesus Christ, and subsequent to this act upon the Holy Spirit as the primal instrument in the historical perpetuation of Christ in the Church. The point of focus of piety has thus shifted uneasily from the primal unity of God to Christ, from Father to Son and even to Spirit. This unease is expressed in recent controversy because without an adequate doctrine of the Trinity, and awareness of the need for it, the orientation of Christian worship and theological understanding alights upon one aspect and interpets the whole in the light of one mode.

The difficulties in Barth's doctrine of the Trinity must not be allowed to obscure the fact that in the *Church Dogmatics* he draws this conception back into the realm of theological import and thereby he challenges an environment interpreted largely through the monocular anti-dogmatic and anti-trinitarian perspective of the practitioners of the historical-critical method. His treatment of the Trinity is grandiose, yet as has been seen it is genetically suspect, largely because the mode of derivation is affected by the difficulties in generating any doctrine of revelation in the present age. Nevertheless despite these problems which find expression in deep tensions, distortions and ambiguities throughout the *Church Dogmatics*, Barth forces the theologically-concerned reader to consider fundamental questions. Is there a God to whom the New Testament witnesses? Has he revealed himself in Jesus Christ and does he continue to reveal himself in the Church in concert with the Holy Spirit or are we, in the words of T. F. Torrance, left with a mere word-play and the arbitrary theological jottings of the primitive churches? For Barth, if God is, then he is God in Trinity and not otherwise. His arguments are imperfect and incomplete, but they are worthy of the most serious attention, because without doubt they point the reader to crucial questions and re-open a level of discussion gradually excluded and subdued in the history of modern theology. The painful dilemma that faces us is this: without the Trinity there would appear to be no basis for the unity and continuity of Christianity with the tradition of Israel and its monotheism with the consequence that we might revert to Judaism and dispense finally with the divinity of Christ.[9] With the doctrine of the Trinity in its Barthian form the danger of an inward reduction into a Christological exclusivity seems to be held off by assertion alone. Clearly the former is only acceptable if unconditional surrender is the order of the day, and the latter must therefore be regarded as provisionally important even as Barth would wish it to be. Barth should be taken seriously because he re-engaged with the doctrine of the Trinity; but he must be understood in order to be surpassed.

---

[9] This was written at the time of the 'Myth of God Incarnate' controversy, I had Don Cupitt in mind.

4

The Reception of the Theology of Karl Barth in the Anglo-Saxon World: History, Typology and Prospect (1986)

Introduction

There is a real sense in which an investigation of the 'reception' of the theology of Karl Barth[1] would demand an examination of virtually the whole of the Christian (certainly the Protestant) theology of the twentieth century, besides mastery of the very considerable body of material written by Barth and published both during his lifetime and in the posthumous *Nachlass*. Our limiting strategy in the face of this complex and extensive requirement will be as follows: first, we shall articulate what can be understood as the 'problem' of the reception of the theology of Karl Barth; second, in elucidation of the origins of that reception, we shall examine its history in Britain and North America, using as the primary but not exclusive focus of attention the immediate interface of tradition to be found in the contemporary journals; third, on this historical basis we shall examine the theological assimilation of Barth in the period of the Second World War, using a 'typology' to represent the range and diversity in the

[1] This essay is an expanded and revised version of a paper entitled 'Die Aufnahme der Theologie Karl Barths im angelsächsischen Bereich: Geschichte – Typologie – Ausblick' delivered on 16 April 1986 at the Evangelische Akademie Tutzing, West Germany in the context of *Theologie zwischen den Zeiten Symposium zum 100. Geburtstag von Karl Barth* and published in *Evangelische Theologie* vol. 46 (1986), pp. 369–393. My friend and Durham colleague Dr. Ann Loades read and commented freely on both drafts – I am deeply grateful.

manifestation of Barth's influence; fourth, in conclusion, we will find ourselves in a position to venture both the hypotheses that there has not in fact been a consistent, comprehensive 'reception' of Barth's work which goes 'through' rather than 'around' it, and, beyond this, to suggest what might be the necessary conditions for an adequate reception of the latter.

Professor S. W. Sykes argued in 1979 that at the very least the study of Barth posed some considerable puzzles and it is to this problematic dimension in the delayed and often distorted mediation of Barth's thought to which we first turn our attention.[2] There were, as will become apparent, conditioning factors in the German, British and North American contexts which influenced the nature and timing of the impact of the early Barth as embodied in the 'dialectical theology' and the 'theology of crisis'. Whilst the latter were not readily distinguishable from each other in the early years after the First World War, the 'dialectical' mode proved virtually unassimilable into the Anglo-Saxon sphere of theology, whereas the 'theology of crisis' could, under certain conditions, prove more socially translatable in a suitably modified form. The differences lie more in the perception rather than the substance of the theology developed under the influence of the early Barth. This period has, therefore, to be seen in historical terms. The later absorption and transmutation of Barth's theology is, however, best understood in terms of a 'typology'[3] which reflects the stage and mode of interjection of alien ideas into a variety of contexts within each national setting. At this juncture our approach is sociological in inspiration and operates on the assumption that theological

[2] The present contribution is in effect a specific sequel to S. W. Sykes', 'The Study of Karl Barth' and my own 'Karl Barth's Doctrine of Time: its Nature and Implications' in S. W. Sykes (ed.), *Karl Barth Studies of his Theological Method* (Oxford, 1979), pp. 1–16 and 88–146. I have focused my attention upon the Protestant reception of Barth; the Roman Catholic reception in the Anglo-Saxon world has in effect taken place after the Second World War and lies outside the major thrust of the argument in this paper. See E. Lamirande, 'The Impact of Karl Barth on the Catholic Church in the last half century' in H. M. Rumscheidt (ed.), *Footnotes to a Theology The Karl Barth Colloquium of 1972* (Waterloo, 1974), pp. 112–141.

[3] The word 'typology' is used here in order to avoid the imagery of 'left' and 'right', the theological application of which was justly criticised by the American

reflection is at least in part a function of such particular contexts. Our conclusions take up and move beyond the position established earlier and contain the assertion that an adequate Anglo-Saxon 'reception' of Barth would have, in the developed Hegelian sense, to be both a dialectical mediation and a multi-disciplinary exploration of a cultural phenomenon which was in the final analysis an expression of power. What we are to undertake is, in effect, the narrative presentation of an encounter of cultures, followed by a 'deconstruction' of the subsequent assimilations into a typology of responses; and then, in conclusion, we venture an outline of the conditions of recapitulation and reconstruction of an episode that is of both historical interest and continuing contemporary importance.

The historical situation with which we are concerned, which involves the interaction and interpenetration of different cultural traditions, was early expressed by Barth's great English advocate Sir Edwyn Hoskyns in 1936, and his words written to Barth himself crystallise both something of the challenge and the inspiration of the following inquiry:

> We are separated by the very real barrier of a different language, a different political tradition, a different quality of piety and impiety, a different structure even of theological and untheological heritage. And you well know that there are still wider divergences lying behind all these things. . . . And yet, however different the background and texture of human thought and behaviour may be, the problem of faith is the same problem, the problems of theology are the same problems, – and the answer

---

theologian Claude Welch in 'On Theological Typology', *Theology Today*, vol. 22, 1965/6, pp. 176–189. Welch wrote that, 'Responsible theological analysis of any whole period or scene requires not only a plurality of categories, but a variety of kinds of categories of interpretation', p. 185. Thus whilst it might be apt to describe the interpretation of Barth in germanophone Europe in terms of an analogy with the followers of Hegel, that is with 'Left-' and 'Right-wing' Barthians, this would be misleading in relation to the reception of Barth in the English-speaking world in which a political interpretation of theology is both recent and relatively under-developed. Methodologically, I therefore draw upon insights afforded by the sociologist J. W. Beckford in *Cult Controversies: The Societal Response to the New Religious Movements* (London, 1985), in which he examines comparatively the modes of interaction between religious groups and the distinctive societal contexts to which they address themselves.

is the same answer. To have recognised this is to have apprehended the situation in which theologians stand together and side by side.[4]

Ultimately, then, the following essay is directed towards a re-conception, drawing upon the deepest impulses of Barth's inheritance, of the pursuit of theology as *ministerium verbi divini.* This (as Barth himself recognised in his preface to the Hoskyns' translation of *The Epistle to the Romans*) is a summons to conflict, such was and is the price of the apprehension of truth.[5]

I   *The Problem of Barth's reception in the Anglo-Saxon world*

In his survey of the study of Barth by the English reader, Stephen Sykes drew eclectically upon British and American material, noting the preference for the more accessible Emil Brunner and the tendency of the English to fumble their way towards Barth through the medium of popular and semi-popular works. It is not difficult, as Sykes shows, to find indications of the ignorance, exasperation and perplexity that characterised the attitude towards Barth on the part of leading English theologians such as J. K. Mozley, Charles Gore, W. R. Matthews and William Temple, besides lesser figures. By contrast, in Scotland Sykes noted the warmer (yet not uncritical) reception of Barth on the part of H. R. Mackintosh, and the brothers John and Donald Baillie, which was followed by the monumental labours of T. F. Torrance, whose commitment to Barth was massive and consistent. In addition, Sykes referred to the growth of 'Biblical theology' in Britain and North America and to the ambivalent effects of a close acquaintance with Barth. Sykes' conclusion, that the English reader's approach to Barth was in danger of predetermination by powerful, contextually-related factors, still stands as a general historical observation. The Sykes' symposium of 1979 was directed towards the comparative analysis of Barth's methods so as to provide modes of access to a huge and intimidating oeuvre. These earlier conclusions deserve repetition because they summarise factors behind which it is our intention to penetrate, along the lines indicated earlier. Sykes maintained that these included:

---

[4] 'A letter from England' in E. Wolf (ed.), *Theologische Aufsätze Karl Barth zum 50 Geburtstag* (Munich, 1936), pp. 525–7.
[5] Cited by Hoskyns, in Wolf (ed.), p. 525.

a tradition of amateurish comment on Barth, based largely on the negative impact made by some of his early works; a willingness to use the term 'Barthian' or 'Barthianism' to characterise certain presuppositions which are supposed to run counter to a long tradition of Anglo-Saxon theology; a powerful counter-movement of approval of Barth, which sees him as standing in the select company of the unquestionable geniuses of the history of Christian theology, and a legacy of disillusionment among those who once would have counted themselves as disciples of Barth. At the very least the study of Barth poses some considerable puzzles.[6]

Our concern is not to demonstrate the inadequacies of these responses by opening up comparisons with the German and mainland European reception of Barth, but to concentrate upon the patterns of reception in particular English-language contexts, which through their distinct differences provide a way of penetrating into the processes whereby any system of theological ideas can be socially and culturally translated. From such a closer knowledge and understanding of the 'puzzles' attending the 'study of Barth' we may then in turn generate ideas capable of wider constructive use and application.

II   *The Reception of the Theology of Karl Barth in the English-speaking world: an historical outline*

(i)   *Britain*

The emergence of Karl Barth from the obscurity of his Safenwil pastorate into a central position in German theological life was intimately associated with his reflection upon and theological response to the First World War. The precise character and the interpretation of Barth's response to this and other political events throughout his life as a practising theologian is a matter of some dispute that awaits the (eventual) publication in full of the early writings in the *Nachlass*. Correspondingly, the Great War had a marked influence upon the reception of Barth's theology in both Britain and North America, a process which was itself determined by the different characteristics of these contexts. As T. A. Langford has argued in his study of English theology in the immediate pre-war period, the Great War accelerated social and

---

[6] Sykes, op.cit., p. 12–13.

cultural changes which were already taking place.[7] Its effects upon
organised religion were catastrophic; in particular, residual belief
in Providence and trust in authority were dramatically weakened.
Theological reflection upon the experience of war, with its degree
of random suffering and mechanised slaughter, new to the
generation that entered the ranks in 1914, was relatively rare; such
figures as G. A. Studdert-Kennedy[8] and P. T. Forsyth[9] were
exceptional inasmuch as they confronted the implications of the
destruction of the remnants of traditional theodicy in the popular
mind. The 'war-theology' of the Established Church, notoriously
expressed in the Bishop of London, Winnington-Ingram's
declaration that 'this is a straight fight between the mailed fist and
the nailed hand' further compromised a religion already deeply
divided in terms of class structure.

More significant from the standpoint of the reception of Barth
was the aftermath of the war; it was only an exceptional figure like
Hensley Henson who could remark, "After the war men must face
again the old questions which perplexed them before, but which
the strain of the crisis drove from mind ... The traditional
theology will be again seen to be plainly inadequate to express the
truth of religion as they must needs perceive it."[10] Otherwise, it is
a sense of an ecclesiastical and theological as-you-were, a return
not only to pre-war *questions*, but also their old *answers*, as though
nothing had happened, which pervaded the theological
discussions of the ensuing decade. In this, the 'roaring twenties'
and the era of Weimar culture in Germany, there took place a
decisive (even if only semi-conscious) step on the part of
theologians away from the wider social consensus. A class
isolation, the pursuit of theology and Church leadership as an

[7] Thomas A. Langford, *In Search of Foundations: English Theology 1900–1920*
(New York, 1969).

[8] G. A. Studdert-Kennedy, *The Hardest Part* (London, 1918). It is, however,
important to recall that others of those who experienced the Western Front at
first hand could come up with very different views from those of Studdert-
Kennedy and Dick Sheppard, whom Bernard Shaw referred to as 'shell-
shocked chaplains'. Relevantly, see Charles Raven's strictures on Barth, note 42
below.

[9] P. T. Forsyth, *The Justification of God* (London, 1916). Forsyth is often
regarded as a pre-Barthian 'Barthian'.

[10] Cited by Langford (1969), op.cit., p. 252.

élite activity,[11] had previously existed; but this was exacerbated by the historic discontinuity of the War, a factor which Barth (admittedly as a Swiss-German non-combatant) recognised theologically, but which was, if we are to believe the literary evidence, largely suppressed and circumvented in Britain. Thus the long-standing and difficult relationship between German and British theology stemming, so far as England was concerned from the early nineteenth century, was characterised by even greater alienation as the shock of conflict turned infrequent interlocutors into enemies. Not only this, but the very experience of the war itself, the source of a profound psychic wound, was afterwards repressed. This repression was not confined to theologians and Churchmen, but was characteristic of a decimated generation whose experience only surfaced in literary terms after the lapse of a decade in, for example, the autobiographies of Robert Graves and Siegfried Sassoon.[12] Nevertheless, the sublimation of grief did provide a context for the formal enactment of established religion, as Owen Chadwick has shown in his account of the origins of the Armistice Day and the erection of the Cenotaph.[13] All in all, the Great War must be accounted as a decisive event in the gradual marginalisation of religious belief in English society.[14] As David Carradine has written:

> At a mere general level, the established Church, concerned, like all Christianity, with explaining the significance of death in this world and life in the next – seemed unable to cope when

[11] The formal expression of this retrenchment can be seen in T. S. Eliot's *Idea of a Christian Society* (London, 1939), in which the consequences of secularisation are rationalised along lines which preserve the ideological dominance within a residual consensus of the priestly-hierarchical and lay expert Christian élites, that is in a 'clerisy'.

[12] Robert Graves, *Goodbye to All That* (London, 1929); Siegfried Sassoon, *Memories of an Infantry Officer* (London, 1930); and, from a woman's standpoint, Vera Brittain's *Testament of Youth* (London, 1933), are representative of a generation.

[13] O. Chadwick, 'Armistice Day', *Theology*, vol. 79, (1976); see further A. Wilkinson, *The Church of England and the First World War* (London, 1978).

[14] The displacement of religious concerns as the correlate of secularisation is documented by, for example, Terry Eagleton in 'The Rise of English' in *Literary Theory An Introduction* (Oxford, 1983), pp. 17–53. The early proponents of the serious study of English literature associated with the Cambridge School of I. A. Richards and then F. R. and Q. D. Leavis saw this taking over the human and social space vacated by formal religious belief and practice.

confronted with so much mortality and grief . . . But to neither the soldier at the front nor to the bereaved at home, baffled and numbed by the cataclysmic events in which they were caught up, could the Church offer plausible explanation or abiding comfort.[15]

The German theological response to the First World War is reported thoroughly in Karl Hammer's study[16] of German 'war-theology' and this provides clear parallels with British patriotic exploitation and distortions of religious belief.[17] The consequences of defeat for German society and the churches, both Protestant and Roman Catholic, were even more dramatic, as Klaus Scholder has shown;[18] this was not so much because of a failure of theodicy in the face of hideous suffering, but a result of the unashamed commitment of both groupings to the cause of German political and cultural imperialism. Barth's place in the universal social, cultural and religious regrouping that took place in the Weimar Republic following the revolution of 1919 is unique. He cannot be identified with any of the established parties within the German churches, but his activities both as regards the *Wirkungsgeschichte* of the *Römerbriefe* and in the circle associated with the journal *Zwischen den Zeiten* (1923–1933) have to be understood against this background.

British attitudes towards Germany in the immediate post- and inter-war period can be traced through the occasional reports and comments upon the German situation and upon the relationship between German and British theology that appeared on an irregular basis.[19] The only concerted effort at actual contact and

[15] 'War and Death, Grief and Mourning in Modern Britain' in Joachim Weley (ed.), *Mirrors of Mortality: Studies in the Social History of Death* (London, 1981), pp. 218–9.
[16] Karl Hammer, *Deutsche Kriegstheologie 1870–1914*, (Munich, 1971).
[17] There would appear to be, so far as regards the aesthetic assimilation of the experience of the First World War, no Allied equivalent to the extraordinary 'war-mysticism' classically expressed by Ernst Jünger in his book *In Stahlgewittern* (1920) and *Der Kampf als inneres Erlebnis* (1922).
[18] Klaus Scholder, *Die Kirchen und das Dritte Reich* (Munich, 1977), vol. I, ch. 1, provides a fascinating account of this ecclesiastical disarray which was the religious correlate of the social disorder and the threat of cultural nihilism that followed in the aftermath of Germany's defeat.
[19] Indications of attitudes between the world wars may be drawn from: H. Weinel, 'The present state of religious life in Germany and its most important tendencies', *Hibbert Journal*, vol. XXII (1923/4), pp. 260–279 (contains a very

organised *rapprochement* in the first decade after the War was through three theological conferences held at Canterbury in 1927, at the Wartburg in 1928 and again at Chichester in 1931, the proceedings of which[20] reflect explicitly neither the experience of the Great War nor the influence of Karl Barth, whose name is conspicuously absent. For evidence of attitudes during this period we select the remarks of one well-informed and influential figure, later Editorial Secretary of SPCK, W. K. Lowther Clarke, who was one of the minority of contributors to British theological journals with first-hand knowledge of German publications. That such an important Anglican educationalist could write in the following terms about Germans and Germany, besides England, at the end of the decade after the Great War is itself a comment not only upon the ancestral resistance to things German traceable at least to the time of Coleridge, but also upon the social

early reference to Barth's *Römerbrief*); G. Hubener, 'The present mind of German Universities', *Hibbert Journal*, vol. XXIII (1924/5), pp. 65–71; W. K. Lowther Clarke, 'New movements in German thought', *Theology*, vol. XI (1925), pp. 227–8; idem, 'Some recent German books', Theology, vol. XI (1925), pp. 295–7; Willy Schuster, 'Present-day religious movements in Germany', *Church Quarterly Review*, vol. 103 (1926/7), pp. 135–163; W. K. Lowther Clarke, 'A German Survey of British theology', *Theology*, vol. XVI (1928), pp. 284–5; F. Gavin, 'Contemporary Religion in Germany', *Theology*, vol. XIX (1929), pp. 272–282; R. J. C. Gutteridge, 'German Protestantism and the Hitler regime', *Theology*, vol. XXVII (1933), pp. 243–264; A. C. Bouquet, 'A Note on the situation in Germany', *Theology*, vol. XXX (1935), pp. 362–3; E. M. Moulder, 'Germanic Faith Movements, their origins, principles and attitude towards Christianity', *Theology*, vol. XXXIII (1936), pp. 336–348; E. Quinn, 'The Religion of National Socialism', *Hibbert Journal*, vol. XXXVI (1937/8), pp. 441–450; W. K. Lowther Clarke, 'A German Catholic Manifesto', *Theology*, vol. XXXVII (1938), pp. 300–2; H. P. Kingdon, 'Church and State in Germany', *Theology*, vol. XXXVIII (1939), pp. 140–7; anon., 'A Visit To Germany', *Theology*, vol. XXXIX, (1939), pp. 296–9; F. H. Heinemann, 'The Unstable Mind of the German Nation', *Hibbert Journal*, vol. XXXVIII (1939/40), pp. 217–229; A. C. Bouquet, 'Rosenberg's new Nordic Religion', *Theology*, vol. XL (1940), pp. 179–189; R. H. Fuller in *Theology*, vol. XLI (1940), pp. 219–226, 268–276; H. Obendiek, 'Protestant Theology in Germany during the past fifty years', *Scottish Journal of Theology*, vol. 5 (1952), pp. 249–266.
[20] For a detailed contemporary account see *Theology*, vol. XIV (1927), pp. 247–295; vol. XVII (1928), pp. 182–260; and vol. XXII (1931), pp. 301–346. The collective volume *Mysterium Christi. Christological Studies by British and German theologians* (London, 1931), edited by A. Deissmann and G. K. A. Bell, embodied the full fruits of these theological encounters. N. P. Williams in reviewing this volume in *Theology*, vol. XXII (1931), pp. 45–8, could remark that the 'religious and theological situation in post-war Germany is still somewhat of a mystery' to those with pre-war acquaintance with that country.

standpoint of the writer in the context of English class structure. Thus in 1928, shortly after the General Strike of 1926 Lowther Clarke could assert that:

> The German is an individualist. His conception of religion is withdrawal into himself. His loyalties are to his party or school. The Englishman, on the contrary, is imbued with the team spirit. . . . Co-operation is the keynote of modern England. The fraternal relations of the religious bodies are remarkable. So is the general loyalty to the Government, the ethical strain which leads an Englishman constantly 'to do (something for someone)', the mutual confidence which inspires social relations, and the absence of friction in political and business life.

On the basis of this somewhat biased and complacent vision of contemporary English society, Lowther Clarke then proceeded to characterise the contrasting mind-sets of the two nations through an informal venture into the sphere of socio-linguistics:

> The difference between the two nations is shown best in the use of common words. The Englishman goes 'to see' his friend, the German 'to speak' to him, 'to hear' him. 'Seeing' is the dominant category with the English. Picture papers, for example, are far more developed than in Germany. The Anglican Church exemplifies the national characteristic in its emphasising of the Incarnation. 'Whereas I was blind, *now I see*' is a favourite text in England, hardly noticed in Germany.[21]

Obviously much might, but will not be said here about the relation of Anglican theology to class-factors in its formulation and perception of social reality. In mitigation, it can be said that the Anglican dalliance with socialism in such influential figures as Charles Gore and William Temple lacks none of the convolutions characteristic of Barth's own engagement. Lowther Clarke then concluded his peroration on the English social virtues, with the remark that:

> Finally, and this is most striking, the Englishman *remembers*. He dates everything as pre-war, war, and post-war. The German has almost forgotten the war. Probably for this very reason, that he can forget, he is the better philosopher and psychologist, and the better understands the universal values of history.[22]

[21] Lowther Clarke (1928), op.cit., p. 285.
[22] Lowther Clarke (1928), ibid.

It is not our purpose to comment definitively upon the broader adequacy of these observations. The last comment does suggest, however, a smouldering inner awareness, represented above all, in both public and private, by the word 'remembrance' and its cognates. The reports surveyed suggest that there was a basic but limited understanding of the German situation available to the informed British theological readership of the time.

Our concern is to grasp something of the intellectual and affective milieu into which Barth's theological renovation might be introduced, although the reports surveyed would suggest that there was an at least basic understanding of the German situation from the late 1920's onwards.[23] There is in general a repetitious assimilation of Barth's influence upon German theology and Church life under the terms of a renewal of 'revelation' and 'transcendence', together with some later awareness of his role in the German Church struggle. The general sense that Barth was somehow an axiomatically central figure comes into British consciousness, it can plausibly be argued, only with the post-war appropriation of the *Church Dogmatics*, which, apart from a limited group of distinguished exceptions remained a relatively closed reality in England, but a pervasive source of theological renewal in Scotland, which had, as regards the core of Barth's theology some sense of the reality of the 'real present' of the Word of God in the central act of preaching within Presbyterianism.

The reception of the theology of Karl Barth in Britain may be divided into three main phases, which, although they overlap to some degree, are relatable to the publication of major works in translation and to changes in the wider perception of Barth as a

[23] Relevant material is contained in A. Keller, 'The Theology of Crisis I' *The Expositor*, 9th series, vol. III, no. 3 (March 1925), pp. 164–75 and 'The Theology of Crisis II', op.cit., vol. III, no. 4 (April 1925), pp. 245–60; J. McConnachie, 'The Teaching of Karl Barth: a new positive movement in German theology', *Hibbert Journal*, vol. XXV (1926/7), pp. 385–400; H. R. Mackintosh, 'Leaders of Theological Thought. Karl Barth', *Expository Times*, vol. 39, (1927/8), pp. 536–540; J. H. Morrison, 'The Barthian School I. An Appreciation', *Expository Times*, vol. 43 (1931/2), pp. 314–7; N. W. Porteus, 'The Barthian School II. The Theology of Karl Barth', *Expository Times*, vol. 43 (1931/2), pp. 341–6; A. J. MacDonald, 'The Message and Theology of Barth and Brunner', *Theology*, vol. XXIV (1932), pp. 197–207, 252–258, 324–332; M. Chaning-Pearce, 'The Theology of Crisis I-III', *Hibbert Journal*, vol. XXXII (1933/4), pp. 101–174, 437–449; R. W. Stewart, 'The Theology of Crisis. A Criticism', *Hibbert Journal*, vol. XXXII (1933/4), pp. 450–454.

theologian that can be detected in the literature. The first phase of Barth's reception extends from the earliest references in the immediate post First World War period up until the publication of E. C. Hoskyns' translation of the second *Römerbrief* in 1933; the second consists in the reception of the latter (probably as regards British theology the single most important theological act of cultural translation in the first half of the twentieth century); third, finally, the post-war period from 1946. This latter is a rather more arbitrary dating which relates to the end of the Second World War and to the general realisation that a new era was about to begin, in which, so far as theology was concerned, Barth's mature work would henceforth appear in a sustained flow largely under Scottish inspiration and direction. In 1947 Barth became as it were an 'ordinary theologian' and associated with him a considerable secondary literature then arose commenting in detail upon many aspects of his work. Whether, however, the former or the latter stages constitute an adequate 'reception' is, as Sykes suggested in his 1979 introduction, open to question.

The high points of the early reception of Barth's theology were marked by the translation of *Das Wort Gottes und die Theologie* by Douglas Horton published in 1928[24] and the translation by E. C. Hoskyns of the second *Römerbrief* published in 1933.[25] Earlier, Adolf Keller had pioneered the presentation of Barth's theology, seeing it as the expression of dialectical method standing beyond the dogmatic and critical alternatives, presenting the cross as 'the last obscurity in which human history ends' and, paradoxically, 'the new Life which can be faced only through Death, (Keller, 1925b, p. 249) in a revival of the Reformation doctrine of justification by faith. The nascent dialectical theology movement, perceived as a 'small but extremely aggressive group of younger theologians' (Keller, 1925b, p. 254) was presented by Keller as tripartite: Barth the exegete; Gogarten the philosopher; and Brunner the systematician. The 'theology of crisis' defied objective appraisal, for it rightly discriminated between the 'aims of the transcendent God' and the 'elements of a worldly culture' (Keller, 1925b, p. 255). Whereas, however, Keller perceptively remarked upon the questionable character of the dialectic as a

---

[24] D. Horton (tr.), *The Word of God and the Word of Man* (London, 1928).
[25] E. C. Hoskyns (tr.), *The Epistle to the Romans* (Oxford, 1933).

foundation for future theological construction, he did not see it destined to 'take the place of any other theology' (Keller, 1925b, p. 260). John McConnachie, a faithful populariser of Barth's work, understood something of the distinctive importance of the commentary on Romans as 'an erratic block among commentaries' and he would appear to be the first to have pointed to the affinity between Barth and P. T. Forsyth (McConnachie, 1926/7, p. 388). Barth's conceptions of the transcendence of God, his focus upon the Word of God and the 'radical and cosmological dualism which rules his whole system' (McConnachie, 1926/7, p. 392) are recorded, but, clearly following Keller's lead, McConnachie perceived some drawbacks: a religious and ethical pessimism; an absence of all verification in experience; an inadequate place given over to Christian nurture and education; and an unresolved understanding of the relation between the historical Jesus and the risen Christ. It was a theology that 'attracts and repels us; it attracts by its lofty daring, and spirituality, it repels by a certain want of heart' (McConnachie, 1926/7, p. 400).

Here we see developing those tendencies within the journals, which, broadly speaking, corresponded with the reactions recoverable from the theological works of the time; but it is clear from an early stage that enthusiasm for Barth's work (as opposed to mere curiosity) was primarily a Scottish attribute. J. H. Morrison, N. Porteus, H. K. MacKintosh, J. McConnachie and (presumably) A. J. MacDonald were all Scots and it would seem apparent that Barth's revivification of the reality of the Word of God as the existential core of the human encounter with the divine corresponded with their expectations. Thus Morrison asserted that 'The Barthian message . . . is a tremendous onslaught on the modern world-spirit by men whose whole souls are captivated by the word of God' (Morrison, 1931/2, p. 314) and that 'One explanation alone is adequate – God is speaking to these men; the Eternal has broken in upon them' (Morrison, 1931/2, p. 315). The 'autopistic Word encountered in crisis, reversion to Reformation insights, the new trembling before the Word of God, all fitted the 'Barthian school to act as a wholesome tonic to our Age'; it could even 'help bring back authority to the preacher's message and a revival of evangelical religion' (Morrison, 1931/2, p.317). Also pertinent is Norman Porteus' early observation of that consistent tendency to adapt Barth to a context of faded, yet revitalisable tradition. Indeed Porteus, a distinguished Old Testament scholar, saw the younger Barth's extreme view of sin as a symptom of an 'early confused stage in his thinking' (Morrison, 1931/2, p. 342) and thereby lent his weight to a tendency amongst those (a minority) sympathetic towards Barth to 'normalise' his teaching. This process of 'normalisation' became the easier as the distance in Barth's own work from the early dialectical extremity seemed to grow greater in both time and actual content.

H. R. MacKintosh, however, resisted this tendency either to drain away or to apologise for the extremity perceived in Barth's teaching. With characteristically judicious learning and caution he situated it in a wider context putting a different interpretation upon Barth's most famous book, the commentary on Romans: 'It exhibits not a trace of purely historical interest or philological precision; it seeks only to pierce the historical transparency and reach what is spiritual, super-historical transcendent, to make everything present and urgent, to hear what God is saying to men today out of the Epistle.' (MacKintosh, 1927/8, p. 537). MacKintosh was able to circumvent questions as to the validity of Barth's views in relation to the norms of tradition and formulate an agnostic and provisional judgement: 'Barth is important and memorable, if not for his solutions, at least for the cardinal questions he compels us to encounter' (MacKintosh, 1927/8, p. 540). In a slightly later contribution, A. J. MacDonald decisively rejected aspects of the standard semi-popular introductions to Barth by R. Birch Hoyle[26] and J. McConnachie,[27] which were the first substantial studies to be directed at an English-speaking readership.

MacDonald was one of the first to articulate the genetic either/ or that has persisted in subsequent discussion. Either: did Barth's theology arise out of the crisis of War and of post-war Europe?; or, as MacDonald trenchantly maintained, was the origin of the Barthian system to be found in his dissatisfaction with the state of theology and theological teaching? On this latter basis MacDonald could assimilate Barth's theology into a functional confrontation with features of a purportedly common situation:

[26] R. Birch Hoyle, *The Teaching of Karl Barth: an Exposition* (London, 1930).
[27] J. McConnachie, *The Significance of Karl Barth* (London, 1931).

Consequently Karl Barth's message is vastly more than a mere apocalyptic response to the challenge of crisis. In its origin it is not a theology of crisis, in the narrow sense, at all. It is the proclamation of a return to the radical content of all true religion, and the enunciation of the radical need of every religious teacher.[28]

This process of assimilation continued inasmuch as MacDonald could generalise Barth's theology into a broad 'challenge to the over-emphasis laid upon immanental theology in our day' (MacDonald, 1932, p. 201). MacDonald, a now forgotten figure, is remarkable for his attempt here to grapple not merely with the early works of Barth but with the *Christliche Dogmatik* of 1927, which he treated in parallel with Brunner's *Der Mittler* (also published originally in 1927). In essence, MacDonald detected in the first *Dogmatik* a trenchant reassertion of the doctrine of the Incarnation in terms that resisted excessive immanentism and which culminated in a restatement of the Resurrection. Barth's work in effect underwent a forceful 'normalisation' in the interests of contingent local needs: in particular this is the case with regard to the residual and uncritical incarnationalism within English Anglicanism. Finally, writing in a perceptive but wholly non-committal manner, M. Chaning-Pearce (from Ripon Hall, Oxford) did succeed in putting a really fundamental question to the 'theology of crisis', one which is, I believe, still important: was it 'one among the many despairing reactions and atavisms of which our modernity has of late been so prodigal . . . or is this a re-affirmation of a reality, a real Christianity, to which we have grown blind?' (Chaning-Pearce, 1933/4, p. 449). This writer was one of the few from within the theological teaching body as a whole to grasp something of the importance of Barth's work and of the growing peculiarity of theological statements in the contemporary socio-cultural matrix. Chaning-Pearce drew out an important parallel between the theology of crisis and the dominant literary figure of T. S. Eliot:[29]

[28] MacDonald (1932), op.cit., p. 200.
[29] An exploration of the conflicting ideologies of Eliot's literary journal *Criterion* and the Leavis's 'post-Christian' *Scrutiny* seen in their historical context might cast considerable light upon the nature and limits of the social translation of theology in English culture. For an account of the period written from a Marxist standpoint see Francis Mulhern, *The Moment of 'Scrutiny'* (London, 1979).

Thus theology offers to our crisis only the 'Word of God', not the
word of the Bible, but in Mr T. S. Eliot's phrase, 'the Word
without a word', the absolute word of God veiled in the relative
word of man. It is an audacious thought, this of a 'Word of God'
unguaranteed by any human authority, of church or book or man,
guaranteed only by a God Who is hidden from men's eyes,
comprehensible only by His Spirit dwelling with the soul, by faith
alone – *sola fide*. Faith in church or book or man is a little thing
beside this all-surrendering, all-risking faith, this veritable 'leap
into the dark'.[30]

This is one of the single most astute remarks to emerge so far
within a theological tradition apparently lacking the desire or the
ability to confront a complex social reality. The general reactions
to Barth of repudiation and disdain, or of a 'normalisation'
through assimilation back into the norms of tradition of the
context of reception itself, which we have illustrated above, were
confronted in passing by Chaning-Pearce's altogether more
sophisticated articulation of the central dilemma of Barth's
thought as it informed the dialectical theology of crisis. This was
a fitting, if isolated, introduction to the second phase of the
British reception associated with the translation of the *Römerbrief*,
which, after the delay of a decade, put a crucial work into the
hands of the English-reading theological public. It is, however,
more typical that R. W. Stewart, immediately following Chaning-
Pearce, could voice the following sentiments:

> Barth's commentary on Romans is one of the longest books in
> existence, and almost impossibly difficult in style, and it was
> hardly printed off before it was all rewritten. May we not smile at
> the length and turgidity of a book that deals particularly with
> religion as revelation? May we not be amused at the incessant
> italics and jingling repetitions of catchwords that Barthians
> confuse with penetrating thought and arresting statement?[31]

Here, indeed, is a stygian lack of comprehension: Hoskyns' light
could scarcely have striven to penetrate a deeper darkness.

Until the publication of the translation of the second *Römerbrief*
by Edwyn Clement Hoskyns (1884–1937) in 1933, the British
response to Barth was largely occasional and indirect; even the

---

[30] Chaning-Pearce (1934), op.cit., pp. 449–50.
[31] Stewart (1934), op.cit., p. 454.

appearance of *The Word of God and the Word of Man* in 1928 was relatively insignificant in comparison. E. C. Hoskyns, however, inaugurated the second, direct, phase in the mediation of Barth. Hoskyns (and his associate Francis Noel Davey) were central figures in Cambridge theology early in the inter-war period.[32] In the face of considerable opposition from other Faculty members, Hoskyns' name became inescapably linked with that of Barth; although as one contemporary commentator was to claim, he 'was never a Barthian,[33] Hoskyns' first published references to Barth appeared in a 1928 review of the German translation of Th. L. Haitjema's *Karl Barths 'Kritische Theologie'*[34], in which he recognised a 'new method of approach, a new point of view, in thinking about God, Christ, men, faith and grace' (Hoskyns, 1928, p. 201) as distinct from scholasticism, intellectualism or mysticism. There was, so Hoskyns argued, 'no Barthian theology, no Barthian psychological experience' (Hoskyns, 1928, p. 202). Hoskyns, as an Anglo-Catholic resistant to the excesses of his co-religionists, saw Barth and Maritain as 'moving along the same lines'; yet whilst the latter might understand the former, 'Barth has as yet shewn no glimmering of a perception of the significance by which men like Maritain are moved and redeemed' (Hoskyns, 1929, p. 204).

Hoskyns' attempt to forge a contemporary *via media* does not concern us here. What is more important is that his translation of the second *Römerbrief* was received with acclamation, and had a profound influence, epitomised by the distinguished New Testament theologian, C. K. Barrett, who later wrote: 'Barth's commentary . . . I read as an undergraduate. If in those days, and since, I remained, and have continued to be a Christian, I owe the fact in large measure to that book, and to those in Cambridge

[32] Their lives (both tinged with tragedy) are outlined by Gordon S. Wakefield in biographical sketches in *Crucifixion-Resurrection The Pattern of the Theology and Ethics of the New Testament* (London, 1981).

[33] J. O. Cobham, cited in the Editorial, *Theology*, vol. XXXVII (July 1938), p.1, maintained after Hoskyns' death that: 'Hoskyns was never a Barthian. That, I am sure, wants saying. But at a time when his own work on the New Testament was forcing him away from Catholic Modernism he discovered Barth as someone who supplied him with a language through which to express what he himself was discovering from the New Testament. And the Barth he appreciated was the Barth of the Römerbrief, not the Barth of the Dogmatik.'

[34] E. C. Hoskyns, *JTS*, vol. 29 (1928), pp. 201–204.

who introduced it to me.'[35] Above all, for Hoskyns, 'Barth's claim
to be heard rests, and rests only, upon a decision as to whether
what Barth finds in the Scripture is really there or not'.[36] That,
and his championing of Barth's text, 'the product of a severe
wrestling with the Scriptures', have to be understood within the
framework of a specific strategy within English theology that led
to the creation of a powerful, but relatively short-lived 'Biblical
theology' which must be understood as the most distinctive, even
if indirect, fruit of the English response to Barth.

Here indeed was a parting of the ways between the distinctive
English and Scottish appropriations of Barth. Through Hoskyns
and his collaborators and pupils, most notably in Cambridge,
there emerged a movement which, whilst not exclusively
attributable to Barth's influence, can be seen as the positive
product of the impact of dialectical theology in England. The
early, relatively superficial absorption of Barth in Scotland
reviewed by McConnachie in 1936[37] was later to give way to the
only development of a sustained theology influenced by the later
Barth, that of T. F. Torrance. In England, the Scots, but English-

---

[35] C. K. Barrett, *A Commentary on the Epistle to the Romans* (London, 1957). See
also the reviews by S. Cave, *JTS*, vol. 34 (1933), pp. 413–416; W. K. Lowther
Clarke, *Theology*, vol. XXVI (1933), pp. iii–112; C. S. Nye, *Church Quarterly
Review*, vol. 117 (1933/34), pp. 359–361; J. K. Mozley, *Theology*, vol. XXIX, (1934),
pp. 368–372; and post-war re-reviews by D. M. MacKinnon, *Theology*, vol. 65
(1962), pp. 3–7; R. S. Barbour, *Expository Times*, vol. 90 (1978/9), pp. 264–268. It
is high time that Hoskyns' translation underwent contemporary re-appraisal of a
more far-reaching character.
[36] Review of R. Birch Hoyle, op.cit., in *JTS*, vol. 33 (1932), p. 205. Hoskyns'
claims on behalf of *The Epistle to the Romans* contrast strongly with the
contemporary consensus that it was not, in any straightforward sense, a
commentary illuminating the text of Romans. Further to this the elderly
A. C. Cochrane applies the Christological analogy to the enigma of Barth's
personality in recalling 'The Karl Barth I knew', in H. M. Rumscheidt (ed.),
op.cit., pp. 142–148.
[37] See J. McConnachie, 'Der Einfluss Karl Barths in Schottland und England',
Theologische Aufsätze Karl Barth sum 50 Geburtstag (Munich, 1936), pp. 529–570,
provides (560) a delightful comment: 'Barth ist ganz und gar ein deutscher
Theologe mit deutscher Mentalität. Der britische Geist und insbesondere der
englische ist praktisch, unmittelbar, ungeduldig. Paradoxe schätzt er nicht und
möchte auf einfache Fragen einfache Antworten. Er ist ganz und gar ein
vermittelnder Geist und ist nicht sehr heimisch im Lande der eigentlichen
(dogmatischen) Theologie. Die Barthsche Dialektik in der Auslegung seiner
jugendlichen Anhänger erscheint vielen als ein produkt etwas ungewöhnlicher
Windungen des deutschen Gehirns.'

educated philosopher-theologian D. M. MacKinnon, again writing under the influence of Hoskyns, attempted to recast Barth's early dialectic in two short, extremely interesting, but also neglected and problematic works, written in the early stages of the Second World War.[38]

In summary, it is then possible to see in the periods prior to and after the publication of Hoskyns' translation of Barth's second *Römerbrief* some evidence of an indigenous reaction to Barth's work. The secondary mediations were inconclusive, and Brunner's more accessible and well-translated works gained a readier acceptance. In positive terms, however, Barth's influence in England can be discerned most directly and significantly in E. C. Hoskyns himself, who was inspired by it to produce a translation which gave considerable impetus to the Biblical theology 'movement' (or rather a *tendency* with diverse strands) in which many leading theological thinkers participated. MacKinnon's daring but abortive expedition into Barth's dialectical rhetoric would seem to be a near exception in a context generally speaking inimical to such a mode of thought. The general tendencies exhibited in the material available from the period could thus be encapsulated in the slogan: 'from dialectic to normality', reflecting the changing perception of Barth's theology from the publication of Hoskyns' *The Epistle to the Romans* through to the growing realization that Barth himself had altered his outlook very considerably. Thus whilst Hoskyns' translation acquainted readers with the key work in Barth's early development its appropriation was attended with a simultaneous dismissal of its continuing relevance. So in an important review Sidney Cave could quietly blunt the edge of the *Römerbrief* by

[38] Numbers 2 and 7 in the *Signposts* series: *God the Living and the True* and *The Church of God* (London, 1940). It is interesting to note G. S. Wakefield's remarks on the political background of this series, op.cit., p. 62 in the light of MacKinnon's commentary. On the texts, see ch. 5 below. The position we take up with regard to both Barth and MacKinnon is an implicit rejection of A. McGrath's assertions that 'dialectical theology is an aspect of the history of Christian thought, rather than a contemporary theological force' and that it is 'difficult for the modern scholar to appreciate the full force of this violent work when it broke upon an unprepared theological world', *The Making of Modern German Christology* (Oxford, 1986), p. 95. McGrath continues a time-honoured, but misleading, English tradition when he refers to the *Römerbrief* as 'a work of prophecy rather than theology', ibid.

reduction to its original context and the application of the 'normalisation' hypothesis. Thus, 'it would be futile to judge of this book as if it were a conventional "scholarly" commentary on St. Paul' for the book was 'significant, not as a contribution to the study of St. Paul, but as the fountainhead of that Barthian movement which, whether it attract or repel, had become of decisive importance in the Continental Protestant Christianity' (Cave, 1933, pp. 412–3). Aware of Barth's work up to and including volume I of the *Kirchliche Dogmatik*, Cave could then go further and assert that Barth had admitted that 'faith is experience and an act of recognition. This takes the sting out of what seemed to some of us the gravest error of Barth's earlier theology', thus (and this is a key phrase) 'Barth's theology is today less distinctive because more true' (Cave, 1933, p. 414). Whilst Barth's 'shrill and passionate' stridency 'saved many German Christians from complete despair ... most of us', Cave concluded, 'prefer to hear a quieter voice, but in spite of its violence and, indeed, perverseness this is a book to read and study' (Cave, 1933, p. 416). Safely distanced, Barth's work had become an interesting temporary aberration of youth, the prelude to a return to traditional norms. Apparently the way was then opened to a full reception of the emergent *Church Dogmatics*; this was not, however, to be the case, at least in England.

The general features of the theological mediation of Barth's thought were decisively influenced by Hoskyns' translation of the second *Römerbrief*. Following 1933, during the period of Barth's struggle in Bonn and then his more distant participation in the German Church conflict there were reports in the journals that allowed at least as glimpse into these events.[39] On a theological level, however, there was no substantial reaction to the emergent volumes of the *Kirchliche Dogmatik*: the torch was to pass from the faltering hands of English theologians into those of those who, rightly or wrongly, saw in Barth's work epochal significance. In the post-war period, the third phase of the British appropriation, the Scottish thelogian T. F. Torrance and his collaborators worked with energy and zeal rendering Barth's magnum opus into

---

[39] See, for example, the notice of the publication of *Theological Existence To-day!* in *Expository Times*, vol. 45 (1933/4), pp. 145–147. Regular brief reports on Barth's political interventions followed.

English. Later, to aid this act of translation, Torrance produced a
notable introduction which both set Barth's oeuvre in context and
expanded its wider theological significance. The nature of the
English reception was, however, effectively summed up by
F. W. Camfield in 1947 when he presented Barth as an 'ordinary
theologian'.[40] As an early (but prematurely deceased) co-worker
with Torrance, Camfield showed how, despite the relative
indifference within English university theology[41] Barth's work
nevertheless appealed to some parish clergy, but as early as 1934
H. C. Rouse had asserted that the 'Barthian movement in
England is a spent force' (Rouse, 1934/5 p. 17) with its place in the
popular mind supplanted by the Oxford Group Movement. We
note too the view of Raven that 'Barthianism' was a 'noble but
demonstrably one-sided and therefore sub-Christian theology',[42]
and O. C. Quick's unanswered question: 'And yet how far is it
true that the theology of crisis is but a gesture of intellectual
impatience after all?'[43] As a Baptist free from the securities of
establishment, Rouse looked in vain for a full critical evaluation of
Barth. M. Chaning-Pearce wrote once again upon Barth in 1936

[40] F. W. Camfield's characterisation of Barth as 'ordinary theologian' (as
opposed to a disregardable 'prophet') comes at the end of chapter 1 of *Reformation
Old and New A Tribute to Karl Barth* (London, 1947), p.29.

[41] A number of contributions are worthy of note: J. D. Smart, 'Karl Barth and
Other-Worldliness', *Expository Times*, vol. 45 (1933/4), pp. 525–526; H. C. Rouse,
'The Barthian Challenge to Christian Thought', *Baptist Quarterly*, vol. NSVII
(1934/5), pp. 256–263; A. Farrer, review of G. T. Thompson's translation of *The
Doctrine of the Word of God* and *God in Action, Theology*, vol. XXXIII (1936),
pp. 370–373; J. S. Boys Smith, 'The Sovereignty of God and the dignity of man',
Hibbert Journal, vol. XXXV (1936/7), pp. 205–212; M. Chaning-Pearce 'Karl
Barth as a post-war prophet', *Hibbert Journal*, vol. XXXV (1936/7), pp. 365–379;
Lindsay Dewar, review of *The Doctrine of the World of God, Church Quarterly
Review*, vol. 124 (1937), pp. 174–176; Daniel Jenkins, 'Mr. Demant and Karl
Barth', *Theology*, vol. XXXIX (1939), pp. 412–420; H. P. Kingdon, 'Church and
State in Germany', *Theology*, vol. XXXVIII (1939), pp. 140–147.

[42] *Jesus and the Gospel of Love* (London, 1931), p. 57. This comment scarcely
does justice to the bitterness of Raven's feelings about Barth in the context of
Cambridge theology. See *The Gospel and the Church A Study of Distortion and its
Remedy* (London, 1939), pp. 219–221.

[43] O. C. Quick honestly admitted his inability to read Barth in the original and
his dependence upon the translation of *The Word of God and the Word of Man*
(1928) and the introductions to Barthianism by Birch Hoyle and Brunner. His
comments in *The God of Faith and the Chaos of Thought* (London, 1931), pp. 96ff.
and *The Gospel of Divine Action* (London, 1933), pp. 104ff. nevertheless cast
interesting light upon the sharp conflict over Barth between Hoskyns and
Streeter, likewise in the Cambridge Faculty.

and could report that the 'first fury is now spent' as regard the 'thunders of Barthian theology' which had not succeeded in troubling the 'placid provincialism of English theological thought' (Chaning-Pearce, 1936/7, p. 365). Barth's transcendentalism was not, he concluded, a 'theology which can minister to the mind and conscience of the twentieth century' despite its timeliness in the context of modernism.[44] In 1939 Daniel Jenkins could comment with exasperation that 'the small group of faithful followers of Karl Barth in this country have begun almost to despair of his ever being understood by the mass of English theological writers' (Jenkins, 1939, p. 412). By any standards the reception of Barth in Britain, and in particular England, could not be regarded as a success. It was, as we have seen, partial, fragmented, delayed, and in the final analysis effectively redeemed only by the pioneering and substantial work of E. C. Hoskyns and the growth of the 'biblical theology' movement, and then later by T. F. Torrance's monumental labours.

It has been our intention in this first section of the essay to indicate, primarily through exhumation of the theological journals, how Barth's theology was received in British theology. We conclude by referring to a remarkable article written by R. Cant in 1946 in which the watershed between the period of reception of Hoskyns' translation of the *Römerbrief* and the modern period of Barth's role as a 'normal theologian' is represented with admirable clarity.[45] Assisting, as he saw it, at the deathbed of liberalism, Cant regarded the legacy of Barth as ambiguous: 'beneath all the things which repel and exasperate us he is saying something to me of quite ultimate importance' (Cant, 1946, p. 152). The Church of England then stood between Neo-Calvinist Barthianism and Neo-Thomist Scholasticism. Between these contrasting (yet formally similar) movements 'Biblical theology', inseparably linked with Hoskyns,[46] might, he thought,

[44] As in his earlier article, Chaning-Pearce again illuminated the affinity between Barth and T. S. Eliot: 'Mr Eliot's St. Thomas seems to incarnate the Barthian "word" in modern drama'. op.cit., pp. 370–1.

[45] R. Cant 'Recent Tendencies in theological writing', *Church Quarterly Review*, vol. 142, 1946, pp. 149–175.

[46] Cant placed under this influence Noel Davey, Michael Ramsey, R. V. G. Tasker, J. O. Cobham, Charles Smyth, besides C. H. Dodd together with Lionel Thornton and A. G. Herbert, op.cit., pp. 163–4.

form the basis of a *via media*. Described by some as a 'kind of theological Fascism' and by others as the 'flight from reason' the Biblical theology movement, the distinctive culmination of the initial reception of Barth in Britain, awaited re-integration into the world of modern philosophy and science; and for the latter Cant turned in expectation to F. L. Cross, A. M. Farrer and Donald MacKinnon. Whether in fact the post-war and more recent history of British theology constitutes such a progression is open to doubt: despite heroic and isolated exceptions (Donald MacKinnon springs to mind) an eclectic pluralism has diluted the effective pursuit of any well-structured *via media*. It is this characteristic, a fissiparous breakdown of strands into mere threads, underlaid by a prolonged crisis of 'authority' that has, in reality, given the post-war era in England its main features. Consequently the variegations that have emerged draw, on occasion, upon Barth, and these we outline in our 'typology' below. In overall terms the English tendency to respond in a belated way to winds of doctrine blowing both from the continent and then, increasingly in recent years, from across the Atlantic, impeded any readily sequential or narrative description of the reception of Barth's work. The story, such as it is, is one of episodes, temporary fixities in a constantly altering picture without truly paradigmatic, constructive thinking; above all, it is characterised by tentative and exploratory ventures, quintessentially represented by the 'radical theology' and the emergence of the individual, publicity-conscious theologian enjoying the transient universality of self-projection in a media-culture. In other words, post-war British theology has largely been through a period of decline marked by pluralism, internal fragmentation and progressive loss of nerve in the face of secularisation.

(ii)   *United States*
The religious history of North America is long and complex, involving the transposed developments of many European traditions: Puritan, Anglican, Presbyterian, Revivalist, Catholic, Jewish, Evangelical, besides the indigenous phenomena of the Black Churches and the growth of Liberal Theology within the last two decades. For the purposes of comparison we focus our attention on the American experience of the First World War and

its effects upon the perception of Germany and its theology within which context the reception of the theology of Barth has to be understood.

If Germany's social and cultural crisis took place in the immediate aftermath of the First World War, and Britain's reaction was one of repressed trauma, then, as the distinguished historian S. E. Ahlstrom has remarked;

> For Americans World War I was 'over there' – a long, long way from Times Square. On the home front only a very few seemed to comprehend the tragic dimensions of the holocaust. During the twenties their numbers increased as participants and observers began to expose the reality and its aftermath. But only with the coming of the Great Depression did a fairly wide range of thinkers begin to see that bourgeois civilization was deep in crisis. And not until a quarter century after that did the idea of a 'post-Christian' world begin to dawn on the popular consciousness.[47]

Ahlstrom traces the career of the concept, inherited from the Puritan sense of divine mission, of the 'Manifest Destiny' of America, from the nineteenth century into the First World War, an event which endangered the heavy dependence of American cultural development upon Germany. Attitudes changed suddenly with the advent of violent chauvinism; in the word of the influential preacher Randolph H. McKim:

> It is God who had summoned us to this war . . . This conflict is indeed a crusade. The greatest in history – the holiest. It is in the profoundest and truest sense a Holy War . . . Yes, it is Christ, the King of Righteousness, who calls us to grapple in deadly strife with this unholy and blasphemous power.[48]

With the signing of the Armistice the way lay open, so President Wilson believed, for America to bring civilised values back to a

---

[47] *A Religious History of the American People* (New Haven, 1972), p. 877. In addition for the general American background see: R. T. Handy, *A History of the Churches in the United States and Canada* (Oxford, 1976), esp. ch. XII; R. T. Handy, *A Christian America: Protestant Hope and Historical Realities* (New York 1971); and W. S. Hudson, *Religion in America An Historical Account of the development of American religious Life* (New York, 1965), writes of the 'abortive' theological revival in the complex aftermath of the assimilation of Barth (pp. 380–1); M. E. Marty, *Righteous Empire: The Protestant Experience in America* (New York 1970). The crisis of the Civil War had its effect upon the role of religion in American society; but that trauma lies well before our period.

[48] Cited by Ahlstrom, op.cit., p. 884.

self-mutilated and war-torn Europe (and, indeed, to the world). It is in this context that the interface between European and American theology must be understood; this was a setting fraught, above all, with acute ethnic problems of national identity and racked by internal denominational dissension, besides theological disagreements between Fundamentalists, Liberals and the proponents of the Social Gospel. The relation of American religion, especially Protestantism, to the American market-led economy and the ideology of free enterprise, put the professional practitioners of religion in a very different position from Europeans, be they German or British. American religion had (and has) to meet the needs of its practitioners or it will, put crudely, fail with literal rather than metaphorical bankruptcy. Again the fundamental crisis of the economic 'Crash' and the Depression had a profound effect upon the relative success (in terms of adherence) of different denominations. There was serious questioning of the alliance of Christian churches with the ideology of capitalist development. In none of this could it easily be said that an awareness of a profound crisis existed of the kind that had allowed the 'theology of crisis' to take root and flourish in post-First World War Germany.[49]

The American perception of Germany as reflected in the theological journals was exceptionally well-served by two articles by Richard Lempp published in 1910[50] and 1921[51] in the *Harvard Theological Review*. Richard Lempp studied at the Harvard Divinity School in 1908–1909 and then returned to the Stift in Tübingen before a pastorate and then service as a war chaplain.

---

[49] As Ahlstrom puts it: 'To most Americans of the 1920's, the notion of "crisis" and "despair" could arise only in the frightened and diseased minds of those who stalked the remote European ruins, the world of yesterday – or in the minds of expatriate intellectuals who preferred the ruins to the world of Cal Coolidge', op.cit., p. 937.

[50] R. Lempp, 'Present religious conditions in Germany', *Harvard Theological Review*, vol. 3 (1910), pp. 85–124.

[51] 'Church and religion in Germany', *Harvard Theological Review*, vol. 14 (1921), pp. 30–52. In addition, see Gustav Kruger, 'The "Theology of Crisis" remarks on a recent movement in German theology', *Harvard Theological Review*, vol. 19 (1929), pp. 227–258; E. Krebs, 'Changes in German Thought', *Anglican Theological Review*, vol. 10 (1927/8), pp. 230–237; J. S. Bixler, 'Men and Tendencies in German Religious Thought', *Harvard Theological Review*, vol. 23 (1930), p. 1–18; W. Pauck, 'National Socialism and Christianity: can they be reconciled?, *Journal of Religion*, vol. 20 (1940), pp. 15–32.

His first article conveys a vivid first-hand impression of German church life prior to the First World War and his account is remarkable for its sensitivity to political, cultural and sociological aspects of a complex situation. Despite the inter-dependence of religion and culture Lempp saw in 1910 a constant antagonism between them. The stability of the population, the uniformity and centralised control of church life and a low level of lay involvement, a profound commitment to Lutheran piety and an exaltation of the Word of God in forms of worship and a detestation of 'Roman servitude' were characteristic of German Protestantism. Bismarck and Luther were both held in enthusiastic esteem as genuine German heroes. Lempp saw the need for a correction of Lutheran apolitical religion of the heart, especially in the face of secularisation which reduced the function of the church into a 'mere institution for preaching and teaching' which was bound 'to be dissolved into state and general culture' (Lempp, 1910, p. 91). There was, furthermore, acute class division: 'The differences of class and education are so great in Germany that the classes scarcely understand one another. They speak different languages, and therefore the new ideal of parish life can never be fully realized' (Lempp, 1910, pp. 92–3). The new ideal of reconciling classes as an important part of education through fellowship was thus to be frustrated. Most helpful was the *'Innere Mission'* movement which attempted to revivify Christian commitment through voluntary associations outside the moribund parish system. In theological terms Lempp distinguished four organized parties in the German churches: the genuine Liberals (*Protestantenverein*); the 'friends of the *Christliche Welt*' who, working originally under the influence of Ritschl stood for theological freedom but believed that conservative and modern theology could coexist in the unity of the Spirit in one church; a 'middle party' (*Evangelische Vereinigung*); and, finally, the orthodox 'Positive Union' with a huge ministerial, but small professorial following. In this context Lempp considered that the *Christliche Welt* performed an heroic, mediatory role. In this tense situation the 'missionary' activities of English and American denominations were distinctly unwelcome. Rome, the eternal troublemaker, meddled in politics and rejected art and science, and since the syllabus of 1864 'condemns the foundation of all modern culture as impious errors' (Lempp, 1910, p. 99).

Lempp saw no way out of the pre-war impasse. 'How this increasing antagonism, which divides and hampers Germany in almost all questions of inner politics, science, art and social work, is to develop and to be overcome, it is impossible to know' (Lempp, 1910, p. 100). Crucial in this situation was the role of the state which was then conceived in terms different to both Britain and America:

> The old liberal conception of the state as merely the protector of law and order, and of the free development of the individual, is completely gone in Germany; the German states, by their traditions and historical development, have taken into their hands all the tasks of culture, provision for education, health, science, art, industry, agriculture, the care of the sick, the poor, and the old, schools, post offices, railroads, banks. But if the government so promotes all culture, shall it leave the most important part of it, religion, to individuals?[52]

Given the ancestral and contemporary tensions, and threats of division, the state was the best protection of freedom within the church, and, Lempp concluded, 'the state and the church alike have at present many good reasons for maintaining the union' (Lempp, 1910, p. 103). Yet it was on the cultural level that Lempp feared most for the main political groupings: conservatives; liberals; ultramontanes; and socialists or social democrats; all differed not merely politically but represented 'different practical principles . . . different philosophies, ideals, views of life'. Indeed, he concluded that it was 'a great calamity that the different groups of the German population have almost nothing in common' (Lempp, 1910, p. 104). There were, unfortunately, no heroes whom the whole nation honoured (as might be the case with Washington or Lincoln). The split in cultural allegiance between educated and lower classes (who accepted 'as gospels' Strauss' *Life of Jesus* and Haeckel's *Riddle of the Universe*) was fundamental and Lempp rightly located the distinction between revisionist social democracy and orthodox Marxism as one of fateful importance. Ultimately, Lempp believed that ancestral tendencies would win through: 'The German working man is much more of a philosopher

[52] Lempp (1910), op.cit., p. 101.

and a politician, and in the end he will have to recognise the shallowness of materialism' (Lempp, 1910, p. 113).

Out of this cultural flux of competing groups and tendencies Lempp depicted the emergence of a pluralism (to him realistically recognised, but profoundly unwelcome) comprised under the term 'liberalism'. Thus since its origins in the eighteenth century a culture independent of the church had arisen, imbuing all educated Germans and including within its broad ambit classicism, romanticism, naturalism and impressionism. One element, so Lempp argued, seemed to be common to all the tendencies of the then modern culture: 'the purely negative characteristic of Anti-supernaturalism' (Lempp, 1910, p. 115), a tendency shared both by the classical idealist and later realist phases in German culture. With the vanishing of religion from the minds of the representatives of the highest modern culture so art took the place of religion. Since, however, the turn of the century faith in the security of secular culture had been shaken and displaced by a 'new spirit' of neo-romanticism, or mysticism, or symbolism, which was not seemingly a 'definite new type of culture' but a 'great striving, – but this striving we may fairly call religious' (Lempp, 1910, p. 118). The supreme ruler of this new cultural era, Nietzsche,[53] was still, despite the immense literature about him, the 'unsolved riddle for Germany' (Lempp, 1910, pp. 118–19). As the new Messiah, attributing decadence to the lies of Christian religion and morality, preaching that 'God is dead, sin never existed, truth we do not want, the will of the few to be mighty is alone God and truth and righteousness', Nietzsche had been taken up by those who 'preached brutal immorality with provoking frankness' (Lempp, 1910, p. 119). Lempp thought that there was possibly a more positive interpretation of Nietzsche's ideas: 'He saw that there is only one problem in life, the problem of the soul; and his whole life was one great longing after true idealism in contrast to realism and naturalism, his whole thinking was a seeking after God, after holiness, after eternal life.[54]

[53] Nietzsche's luminary role was expressed by Alfred Kubin with devastating clarity in 1910: 'Er ist wirklich – unser Christus' R. F. Krummel (ed.), *Nietzsche und der deutsche Geist* (Berlin, 1983), p. 416.
[54] Lempp (1910), ibid. We do not here question the adequacy of this interpretation of Nietzsche, but merely reiterate it.

It is this characterisation of the contemporary state of German culture as racked by a longing and striving for forms of self-transcendence that forms the background to the astounding success of Harnack's *What is Christianity?*, and, at a non-theological level to the host of writers who all treated religious questions. The cult of Goethe, of Tolstoi, of Ibsen, besides 'Teutonic' and other 'religions' was symptomatic of the crisis of post-naturalistic thought: 'The age is disgusted with mere realistic culture, and is characterised by religious longing, but this longing has not yet found a definite satisfaction.'[55] So far as Christianity was concerned there was a demand for decision: orthodoxy would not do because (since Spinoza) the 'older supernaturalism is gone for ever' and any reneging upon this would involve the stultification of all modern culture. If, on the other hand, Christianity (owing to its ethical concepts of sin and salvation) retains a 'relative dualism' then neither immanent idealism nor naturalism would be compatible with it. Thus, if the then contemporary religious longings were to find their answer in the Christian religion, then modern thinking would have to admit the possibility of transcendence and the validity of the yearning for 'eternal values, for a deeper reality and a higher aim of life than this mere immediate world and its happiness can offer' (Lempp, 1910, p. 121). Without such an understanding 'modern culture and the Christian church will separate for all time,'; and so, Lempp argued, 'a new conception of transcendence of God, of salvation, can settle it' (Lempp, 1910, p. 122). Following the breakdown of Hegelianism in mid-century and the abortive efforts of Ritschl, the prospects of a readily apparent 'saviour' had faded; but after the rise of a neo-Kantian 'critical idealism' and its religious interpretation by Rudolf Eucken there was still an unsatisfied demand for the 'final solution of the antagonism between religion and culture' (Lempp, 1910, p. 124). Thus Lempp still saw as 'the problem of the transcendental life in us men, the problem of sin and of regeneration by the saving grace of God, who is himself the personal embodiment of the transcendental world' (Lempp, 1910, p. 123).

[55] Lempp (1910), op.cit., p. 120–121. There is, significantly, no mention of Kierkegaard at this juncture.

We have dwelt at some considerable length upon Richard Lempp's pre-war description of the situation in Germany because it is probably the best informed first hand contemporary account in English to be found, which was accessible to American theological readers. Correspondingly, the second report published in 1921 on 'Church and religion in Germany' voiced with passion the social consequences of the policy of the victors which embodied the demand for crippling reparation and the desire for vengeance excoriated by Keynes.[56] Lempp, writing under protest and only as a favour to his pre-war friends, was frank:

> Americans can have little idea of the terrible sufferings of my country, or of the hopelessness of the future which the peace of Versailles has set before us; nor can they easily imagine the mood of the nation which, after gigantic achievements and the most heroic endurance, has at last been broken in body and spirit by the force of hunger that its enemies saw fit to employ as an instrument of war. If, after the slaughter of the innocents, the representatives of Herod had inquired of the good people of Bethlehem concerning the outlook for religion in the period of reconstruction then beginning, they would hardly have elicited a dispassionate reply.[57]

There then followed an extensive and informed analysis of the (relatively contained) effects of the revolution of November 11, 1918 upon the separation of Church and State, a policy pursued by the socialists according to the Erfurt Programme of 1891, which, along Marxist lines, maintained that 'Religion is a private matter'. The church had, however, not split along class divisions, but all activity was certainly undermined by the financial crisis. Whilst the church had proved too strong to be overwhelmed by the cultural forces Lempp had reported in 1910, the split within socialist ranks had clearly helped the church, in that the moderates, whilst not sympathetic, were not hostile to it as the hard-line communists were. Socialist excesses had, in fact, reinforced the position of the churches, but Lempp saw the key to the situation in a working class hardened against the Christian religion and teetering on the brink of outright Bolshevism:

[56] See the classic critique by J. M. Keynes, *The Economic Consequences of the Peace* (London, 1919).

[57] Lempp (1921), op.cit., pp. 30–1.

Either we shall overcome the fanatical mutual distrust of the classes in Germany, and in particular free the working class from its materialist delusion and hostility to religion, which, I am convinced, is possible only through an awakening of the spirit of the love of Jesus in both upper and lower classes; or else Germany like Russia will perish together with its churches and its working class. Whether the 'Volkskirche' in its traditional form will ever be able to win back the workingmen in Germany must be regarded as doubtful. Rather we may hope that in the distress which all of us, and not least our workingmen, are now facing, a prophet may rise from the working class itself, to preach the Gospel of Christ in a new tongue and devise new forms of fellowship for a re-awakened Christian faith.[58]

Seen with hindsight this passage is fraught with ambiguities and unconscious ironies; from the standpoint of an inquiry into the reception of Barth's thought, the desire noted in 1910 is now given more urgent social embodiment:

The idea that only a new spirit of devotion, sacrifice and sincerity can save us from the Russian chaos, that our external culture must give way to a new inwardness, is widely prevalent among educated men and women.[59]

In this situation, theoretical idealism, what we might term an insatiable appetite for transcendence, was then in reality being sated by the 'new idealisms' of Christian Science and the theosophy of Rudolf Steiner. Whilst Steiner could claim he was engaged in a 'common struggle with the churches against the great enemy of all civilisation, materialism', this was likely, so far as Lempp was concerned, to draw people away from genuine religion towards abstruse and empty speculation:

On the other hand, not a few people of education eagerly await the rise of some new prophet, some creative genius, who, amid the present confusion of thought and the crumbling of foundation, shall point a new way and proclaim the old gospel in new language. May the bitter and fearful period which by the will of God we face, and which threatens to surpass in incalculable misery all that has been experienced in the past, raise up for us such a man! Assuredly he would prove a blessing, not only in Germany,

---

[58] Lempp (1921), op.cit., p. 50.
[59] Lempp (1921), ibid.

but likewise to other nations, which are beset with the same confusion and cherish the same longing for new ideas and a new spiritual leader.[60]

Whether or not we are to regard the appearance of Karl Barth and the flowering of the 'theology of crisis' as the Messianic answer to this call for a 'new prophet' is a matter open to discussion. What is indisputable is that the ground for such an intervention could not have been better prepared: Karl Barth was, in the fullest Nietzschian sense, *zeitgemäss*, that is, timely.

As we indicated earlier, the material available concerned with the earliest reception of the theology of Karl Barth in the American context is not prolific, for the conditions did not yet exist in which the message of 'crisis' couched in dialectical terms would readily generate interest and take root. The reports upon the German situation up until 1930 were, however, increasingly supplemented by a flow of articles[61] which focus more precisely upon the influence of Barth, who was regarded as a central figure of fundamental importance by G. Krüger as early as March 1926. Krüger singled out for his audience at a Union Theological Seminary a 'movement which seems most characteristic of the present situation, and which is likely to command the interest if not the assent of American theologians', that is, a 'Theology of Crisis' (Krüger, 1929, p. 230). Indeed, Krüger himself claimed that the subject had not hitherto been treated in English and thus appended a bibliography. This established the pattern of the North American reception which was, in essence, better informed

[60] Lempp (1921), op.cit., p. 52.
[61] See in the period 1926–1940: G. G. Kullmann, 'Karl Barth and the Barthian movement', *Anglican Theological Review*, vol. 10 (1927/8), pp. 116–134; H. Offermann, 'The Theology of Karl Barth: an orientation', *Lutheran Church Quarterly*, vol. 2 (1929), pp. 271–288; W. L. Wood, 'Karl Barth, prophet and theologian', *Anglican Theological Review*, vol. 14 (1932), pp. 13–33; L. H. Awes, 'The Theology of crisis and the problem of evil', *Lutheran Church Quarterly*, vol. 5 (1932), pp. 25–35; J. S. Bixler, 'Appraisal of Barth', *Journal of Religion*, vol. 14, (1934), pp. 226–7; K. H. A. Rest, 'The Theology of crisis and the crisis of capitalism' *Journal of Religion*, vol. 14 (1934), pp. 183–193; Th. Engelder, 'The Principles and Teachings of the Dialectical Theology', *Concordia Theological Monthly*, vol. 7 (1936), pp. 81–94, 241–252, 329–339, 401–411; W. N. Pittenger, 'Some trends in American theology', *Theology*, vol. XXXVIII (1939), pp. 65–69, and 'America and the "New" Theology', *Theology*, vol. 40 (1940), pp. 305–309; P. Lehmann, 'Barth and Brunner: the dilemma of the protestant mind', *Journal of Religion*, vol. 20 (1940), pp. 124–140.

than the British (and particularly the English) response. German theologians had strong connections with American institutions which permitted them to lecture in the U.S.A.; this was and remained almost impossible under British conditions. Consequently the North American mediation of information based on primary sources was more detailed, faster in arriving, and more adequately contextualised in relation to recent theological developments. Thus it was that Krüger could set the scene for the rise of dialectical theology with references to Ritschl (the 'Bismarck' of German theology), Troeltsch, and his own mentor, Harnack. This tradition had issued in historicist modernism, that is, in Troeltsch's terms 'the systematic historicising of all our thoughts about man, his culture, and his values' (Krüger, 1929, p. 230). Again writing with a lack of inhibition and passionate sensitivity entirely absent in the British sources Krüger described the conditions giving rise to a result against the dominant historicist 'seats of Satan':

> Then came the war, and with it a reaction. Students of theology, and those who still looked forward to that vocation, *were* summoned to the field of battle. They fought and bled for honor, home and country. And they came back, with hearts stirred with longing, and with a veritable hunger for religion. They had experienced the infinite, the unspeakable; the heights of enthusiasm and the depths of dejection, the tremendous and the trivial, the sublime and the hideous, things to confirm their faith and things to provoke despair. Their souls were alive with a new impulse to deliver mankind from the demon of hatred. Consciously or unconsciously, they recoiled from that mechanical civilization whose horrible excrescences they had constantly witnessed during the dolorous years of war, and to whose disastrous effects they had themselves been forced to contribute. Had they really gone to war for such a civilisation? and in the name of religion?[62]

The war had achieved nothing but destruction and devastation, ruined real culture, and brought about the 'suicide of Europe' and the 'decay of the West', a perception given 'scientific rendering' in

[62] Krüger (1929), op.cit., p. 231. This passage again expresses that ambivalent attitude to the War, that of both the 'sublime and the hideous', which is not, we venture to suggest, characteristic of the British experience as reflected in the literature of the time. See note 17 above with reference to E. Jünger.

the work of Oswald Spengler. Young students emerging from this experience were like Goethe's Faust, they 'longed for revelation', yet:

> Instead of reviving, this historicism repelled them; instead of refreshing, it chilled them. That purely relative appraisement of every event in history which went hand in hand with it was as dust to souls thirsting for the absolute.[63]

The 'science' of critical study of Old and New Testaments, Church history and doctrine, and the systematic elaboration of the faith in dogmatics and ethics culminated in the utter futility of the attempt to reconcile modern civilization with 'living religion'. All this 'might conceivably have happened without the war, but the decisive factor was certainly the war' (Krüger, 1929, p. 232). Most interestingly, Krüger drew a parallel between the aftermath of the First World War and of the Thirty-Years War which had led to the Pietist reversal of theological work after confessional sterility which had hardened into its opposite in the Enlightenment: 'Here God the supramundane, not man the intramundane, is the measure of all things' (Krüger, 1929, p. 233) to whom our duty it is to surrender and before whom man, his culture, and his values are as nothing.

Krüger had witnessed Friedrich Gogarten's intervention at the Wartburg conference of 1920 which, so he had claimed, owed its stimulus to Barth's 'great book on Paul's Epistle to the Romans' upon which in turn the influence of Kierkegaard and Tertullian was apparent. Both Gogarten and Barth thus saw that 'Religion is not the soul of culture; it is the *crisis*, that is, the doom, of culture' (Krüger, 1929, p. 236). In such a situation judgement is as it were being passed every moment. Barth's dialecticism, the interpenetration of affirmation and negation in a method which though 'lucid', 'animated' and 'fascinating' tended to defeat the critic: 'Dialectics are very difficult to deal with' (Krüger, 1929, p. 238). Granted this difficulty Krüger recognised a fundamental problem: what was to become of a theology as a university science when it regarded religion as the 'crisis of culture'? In Barth's lecture of 1922 'The Word of God and Theology' he saw a possible answer to this question and consequently recommended

---

[63] Krüger, op.cit., p. 232.

the translation of the whole volume of essays in which it had appeared.

Horton's later translation of the collection *The Word of God and the Word of Man* and its publication in 1928 was a milestone in the American reception which then in consequence thoroughly absorbed the triad of the 'dogmatic', the 'critical', and the 'dialectical' paths towards understanding divine immanence in the 'Word of God'. This pattern reappears frequently in the American literature as this provided a convenient programmatic representation of Barth's strategy that could fit into the orthodox-liberal divide. As, however, in Britain, the 'dialectical' path nevertheless presented difficulties for America. The paradox of 'The word of God' as at once 'the necessary and the impossible task of theology' could not remain a stark methodological proposal within the given structures and context of assimilation. It is precisely at this point that Brunner's own 'normalisation' of the dialectical method proved the more easily assimilable approach. Krüger saw the theology of crisis, when interpreted in a more extensive historical setting than the aftermath of the War, as the replacement of the 'idealistic conception or interpretation of the Bible' with that of the Reformers (Krüger, 1929, p. 251). Perceptively, Krüger detected in dialectical theology 'the best weapon for putting to flight "historicism" and replacing its relativity with a new absolutism' (Krüger, 1929, p. 253), that is an absolutism of the Word which could result in a pessimistic, triumphant rhetoric and excessive narrowing of vision.

The tradition of publishing first-hand accounts of developments in German theology continued throughout the 1920's with articles by E. Krebs (1927/8), G. G. Kullmann (1927/8), and H. Offermann (1929) who whilst often repetitive do nonetheless display an awareness of the gradual transformation of Barth's outlook. Notably Offermann commented at length upon the *Christliche Dogmatik* of 1927 and saw it as the heart of a theology which could be taken as the basis for the correction of misperception of the early (and always seemingly problematic) work. In essence, the dialectical method reappeared as the stumbling block to many informed readers and apparently a major cause of misapprehension. In addition, however, Barth's use of language, his emergence as the 'preaching dogmatician'

(Offermann, 1929, p. 283) provoked a range of accusations, not least that of being a pure transcendentalist and a *Calvinus redivivus*, strangely recasting the theology of the latter. In the American literature the observation of the apparent, gradual estrangement of Barth himself from his dialectical phase and the emergence of the strongly systematic thrust of the *Christliche Dogmatik* in 1927 and then the *Kirchliche Dogmatik* proper from 1932 onwards provided the opportunity for commentators to relate Barth's later work to their own presuppositions without excessive compromise. Barth was thus assimilable into given critical expectations once the dialectical origin had been distanced. As in Britain so in North America a process of 'normalisation' took place which did not necessarily lead to an uncritical response to Barth, but one which in North America was conducted primarily in terms of national structures and theological norms. Thus in 1929 Offermann could regard the 'dialectical method' as the greatest obstacle in the way of understanding Barth's theology, fraught as such method was with contradictions, paradoxes and antitheses. Yet the diversity of the second stage of reception, seen as the products of the initial assimilation, display a range of divergence which cannot be accounted for as the product of the extraordinary comprehensiveness of Barth's theology as tied to the emergence of volumes of the *Church Dogmatics* in translation. We suggest that the diversity of responses was also influenced by the more interesting and indeed profound problem: as to the nature of the relation of Barth's theology as a whole to modernity. Was, and indeed in what sense was Barth's theology 'contemporary' (in the German sense of *zeitgemäss*)? In 1929 Offermann's comment that: 'Barth himself is a modern theologian, and in many respects he is ultra-modern' (Offermann, 1930, p. 285) poses a problem of continuing, even revived importance, in the present context of a 'post-modernity'.

It is clear that the initial North American reception of the theology of Karl Barth was better informed and more fully reported than in Britain. For different reasons the initial impact of dialectical theology in the United States was delayed. In Britain the experience of the Great War reinforced an already existing tendency to repel and repress things German (that is outside definite Germanophile circles); whereas, by contrast, although the higher education system and North American culture owed much to Germany, the absence of real 'crisis' in the United States until the economic collapse of 1929 insulated all but a coterie of intellectuals from the kind of sensibility that could absorb dialectical theology as something more than a function of a distant and alien context. Thus in 1930, J. S. Bixler expressed this distancing in a way that both put Barth in context and seemingly saw in him a wider utility, given the spreading crisis:

> Barth's real achievement is his success in making the theocentric emphasis in Germany at a time when defeat and resolution threatened to lead the chaos, and in warding off all pessimism as to human life by pointing to the real of the eternal.[64]

In general terms in the 1930's Barth was assimilated into the role of 'prophet' and the more accessible Brunner into that of the 'Melancthonian interpreter of Barth' (V. Ferm, 1930, p. 322). There was in effect a hiatus; Barth's early dialectical work did not take immediate root as it was not socially translatable into either the British or North American contexts until such time as Barth himself had seemingly passed beyond the dialectic into systematic work. Meanwhile Brunner, whose dogmatic work had been written in the twenties and rapidly translated[65] became the effective representative, although not the acknowledged leader, of the dialectical movement. As a 'corrective' to the clergy and preaching, Barth was acceptable in 1932 to W. L. Wood inasmuch as he brought a 'hopeful expectancy' in the 'twilight of a civilization' (Wood, 1932, pp. 31–2). In the same year, however, the Lutheran, L. H. Awes regarded the Barthians as 'hopeless pessimists' unable to grapple with the real achievement underlying the ideal of 'progress'. Here we find one of the first expressions in the journal literature of the indigenous transformation of the abstract theology of *crisis* (as opposed to 'dialectic') into 'realism'. Apocalyptic promise was insufficient and,

---

[64] J. S. Bixler (1930), op.cit., p. 9.
[65] Thus, for example, Brunner's direct experience of the United States and the services of Olive Wyon, his translator, put him before a wide public. Indispensable for the illumination of Barth and Brunner's influence upon the Niebuhr's 'theological realism' is Hans W. Frei, 'Niebuhr's theological background' in Paul Ramsey (ed.), *Faith and Ethics The Theology of H. Richard Niebuhr* (New York, 1957).

Instead of a metaphysical relation in God and forgiveness in the abstract, the problem appears rather to be the achievement of an uncompromising realism in dealing with the facts of life and a readiness to compromise with those laws of life which express the way of God and which, as experience teaches us, make for more harmonious and meaningful human living.[66]

This is, in effect, an early affirmation of the Niebuhrian approach which tamed the excesses of 'dialectical theology' (admitted under the term of 'crisis') whilst retaining some of its critical content. Opinions varied as to the success of the translation of 'Barthianism' into American religious thought. Adolf Keller, in a translation of his major work on Barth published in 1933, could write: 'Barthianism is threatened with the peril of being translated too well into American life and thought. ... Only through rationalizing, through intellectual simplification and adaptation, does the worked abstraction of Barthian thought become comprehensible to the empirical, more naive American thinking'.[67] John MacConnachie put it even more bluntly in the same year: 'In America the theology of the Word ... can hardly be said to have reached the stage of understanding criticism.'[68]

From this time onwards until the later assimilation of the *Church Dogmatics* proper it is not possible to detect a consistent or highly-developed direct response to Barth in the North American literature. Th. Engelder, writing in 1936 and clearly a confessional Lutheran, exemplified the reductive approach to Barth's influence which, isolated from Brunner, was seen as having progressively less power and could, in any event be subsumed into a 'repristination of the soul of Calvinism' (Engelder, 1936, p. 86). Conversely, however, Norman Pittenger reviewed the situation in 1939 in terms which indicate a far greater effect when seen in conjunction with social circumstances:

It is no exaggeration to say that within the last decade (or perhaps even less) the entire spirit of American theology has changed. In a

[66] L. H. Awes (1932), op.cit., p. 34.
[67] A. Keller, *Karl Barth and Christian Unity* (New York, 1933), p. 202.
[68] J. McConnachie, *The Barthian Theology and the Man of Today* (New York 1933), p. 320. J. S. Bixler (1934) cites Keller and McConnachie in his short 'Appraisals of Barth', op.cit., pp. 226–7.

sense this fact is a reflection of a profound change which has come over the mentality of the American people as they have faced an economic and social situation almost unparalleled in their history.[69]

The Protestant denominations, other than the Episcopalians, had swung from an 'ultra-liberalism' through to an 'ultra-conservatism of a neo-Barthian type'. The American equivalent of *via media* consisted in a 'realistic theology' with its re-emphasis upon radical doctrines of human nature, the Incarnation and the Atonement. This loosely allied movement led by Reinhold Niebuhr, H. P. van Deusen, W. M. Horton and Paul Tillich was influenced by Brunner, Heim and the translations of Kierkegaard, besides Barth. The extremities of liberalism, orthodoxy and the new 'realistic theology' all subsisted, however, in an increasingly pluralistic context as other continental (and even English) influences were drawn in. The specific influence of Barth, related in the post-war era to the emergence of the *Church Dogmatics* and attendant theological controversies spilling over from Europe, cannot, however, be readily integrated into the relatively narrow conception of initial 'reception' employed in this paper. Barth's voice was but one amongst many. 'Neo-Orthodoxy', the major Protestant theology from the late 1930's to the late 1950's, owed much but not all to Karl Barth. As a movement affirming the unity and authority of the Bible, the uniqueness of the Christian revelation, the deity of Christ, the sinfulness of humanity and, the strength and transcendence of God's power, Neo-Orthodoxy may be considered the most impressive indigenous assimilation of the theology of crisis.[70] Its exegetical correlate 'Biblical Theology' became evident in both Britain and North America and grew in forms related to the respective contexts.[71] Henceforward Barth's

---

[69] W. N. Pittenger (1939), op.cit., p. 65.

[70] See D. W. Ferm, *Contemporary American Theologies: A Critical Survey* (New York 1981), pp. 13–20.

[71] See F. N. Davey, 'Biblical Theology' in *Theology*, vol. XXXVIII (1939), pp. 166–176; Alan Richardson, 'The Nature of the Biblical Theology', *Theology*, vol. 39 (1939), pp. 166–176; Alan Richardson, 'Biblical Theology and the Modern Mood', *Theology*, vol. 40 (1940), pp. 244–252; James Barr, 'Trends and prospects in biblical theology', *Journal of Theological Studies*, vol. NS25 (1974), pp. 265–282; Henning Graf Reventlow, 'The Anglo-Saxon "Biblical Theology Movement"' in *Problems of Biblical Theology in the Twentieth Century* (London, 1986), pp. 1–9. The latter contains comprehensive bibliographical information.

influence was integral to the various strands and episodes in post-war American theology. As a means of containing the scale and complexity of the emergent situation it is necessary to turn at this point from the history of the immediate 'reception' to a typology of responses which indicates the extraordinary variety of phenomena attributable in different ways to Barth as aspects of the complex matrix of post-Second World War Anglo-Saxon theology.

In a postlude to our appreciation of the initial reception of Barth's thought and in particular its initial impact is it worth noticing the observations of two historians of the era. First, S. E. Ahlstrom (1972) remarks that:

> All considered, there are many reasons for regarding Neo-Orthodoxy as an ambiguous prelude to the theological radicalism of the 1960's. Yet the interest in traditional doctrine which the movement stimulated – especially when Karl Barth was being heeded – did undeniably lead to a revival of supernaturalistic ways of thinking. And because they ignored many intellectual difficulties, Neo-Orthodox theologians have been justifiably accused of putting down only a very thin sheet of dogmatic asphalt over the problems created by modern critical thought.[72]

Writing a decade later D. W. Ferm sharpens this perspective, arguing that after an intellectual hegemony of three decades within Protestant theology, Neo-Orthodoxy collapsed, mainly because it maintained a 'leap of faith' into a 'supernatural order which forever remained beyond the reach of human initiative' (Ferm, 1981, p. 19). This option was rejected by the modern believer as inconsistent with the modern world view. Moreover, Ferm argues, the problem of evil takes on a form insuperable in terms of repristinated orthodoxy:

> The suggested answer to this problem, which led in part to the birth of neo-orthodoxy, was precisely the opposite from the solution which provoked its death. The origins of a neo-orthodoxy lay in part in liberalism's neglect of the evil dimension of human nature. Human beings had to be saved from their worst selves. Since they appeared unable to save themselves, they turned to a transcendent God for salvation. Now, however, neo-orthodoxy died in part because this same evil dimension made it

[72] Ahlstrom (1972), op.cit., p. 947.

impossible for human beings to believe in a loving, parental God who would permit such evil as the Holocaust and Hiroshima to happen. Human beings now sought salvation within themselves.[73]

It is plausible, in the light of the evidence we have educed, to argue that a transition into individualistic scepticism with corresponding secularised substitutes for 'salvation' happened earlier in Britain than in North America, but this is a complex and wide-ranging issue. Neither Ahlstrom nor Ferm in commenting upon the fate of Neo-Orthodoxy are particularly illuminating at this juncture. Indeed the necessary socio-cultural elucidation of the role of Barth's theology *as a whole* (or indeed the comparable roles of other theologies) in the social matrices of Europe and North America is relatively uncharted intellectual territory. Thus how the 'early' and the 'later' Barth so function is not necessarily identical: eschatologically-informed theological rhetoric, and, conversely, the 'inner logic' of an ecclesially-bound dogmatics may have distinct modes of social insertion yet fully to be explored and understood.

On the basis of our argument thus far we have observed processes of theological 'normalisation' taking place, in which a relatively alien 'dialectical' pattern of theological thought only became assimilable as and when its extreme characteristics either corresponded with analogous forms of social and cultural disruption as 'crisis' or, alternatively, the dialecticism itself actually waned in intensity and itself changed. In reality, both processes took place in the settings we have described. For a variety of reasons the historical, cultural and social circumstances of each context dictated the pattern of reception and 'normalisation'. Theological and non-theological evaluations of this reception may well differ and such distinctions call into question fundamental issues it is not here our purpose to explore at length.

(iii)   *Canada and Australasia*
It would smack of condescension to assimilate the reception of Barth's theology in Canada with that which occurred in the

---

[73] D. W. Ferm (1981), op.cit., p. 20.

United States. Inevitably, however, the relationship was close and
R. T. Handy in his standard history isolated but a single figure,
W. W. Bryden of Knox College as a significant Canadian
interpreter of Barth (Handy, 1976, p. 409). In the period following
Barth's death, the founding of the very active Karl Barth Society
of North America and the work of H. M. Rumscheidt indicates a
notable community of interests, despite resurgent post-war
Canadian nationalism. This finds effective expression in the
Canadian Journal of Theology, which has, however, consistently
reported on developments in Barthian theology. Both in Canada
and in Australia denominational conflict and the absence, well
into the post-Second World War period, of a powerful
indigenous theological tradition has impeded the growth of an
original reception of the theology of Barth. The growth of distinct
national cultural identities in the sphere of theology has been
more obvious in Canada, rather than in Australia which is highly
secularised outside (from a historical standpoint) the powerful
ethnically-based denominational traditions (modified by the
function of the Uniting Church) and this has made theological
innovation problematic.[74] A few gifted and often isolated
individuals have attempted to move beyond these limits into a
wider theological world than that of arid internal conflict and,
amongst these, a pattern of emigration is notable.[75]

All in all, the most powerful and important Anglo-Saxon
receptions of the theology of Karl Barth have been in Britain and
the United States. It is upon the basis of the later, diffused and
consequential reception that the following typology is based and
this conveys a response which goes well beyond the relatively

[74] See G. Stuart Watts, 'Theological Thought in Australia', *Theology*, vol. 39
(1939), pp. 309–312; and the only account of the influence of Barth published in
Australia I have been able to locate is by R. Swanton, 'Scottish Theology and Karl
Barth', *Reformed Theological Review*, vol. 33 (1974), pp. 17–25 which takes the
ethnic line indicated by the title. Conditions in Australia were poignantly
described by G. Stuart Watts as characterised by 'party spirit' and the inability of
many Australian churchmen to 'consider theories on their own merits apart from
the person who prefers them', in 'Theological Thought in Australia', *Theology*,
vol. 39 (1939), pp. 309–312.
[75] The unpublished doctoral thesis of my late friend, the saintly Australian
theologian William G. Wakefield, *Turning to God in the Theology of Karl Barth*
(Ph.D, Edinburgh, 1975) was an attempt to develop a theology of conversion
applicable in Australasia.

narrow confines of the theology of crisis and its transmutation
over time into the mediating positions of 'biblical theology' and
the complex development of 'Neo-Orthodoxy'.

III   *A Typology of Anglo-Saxon Responses to Barth*
It has been our purpose to indicate how the initial reception of the
theology of Karl Barth in the Anglo-Saxon world was related both
to the internal self-perceptions and as it were to the external
relations of the social and cultural milieux into which the
distinctive ideas of dialectical and 'crisis' theology were introduced.
Although a comprehensive history of what then followed in both
the British and North American settings has yet to be written, our
initial survey is directed at depiction of the means by which an
alien mode of thought was, by processes both on Barth's part and
as a result of influences in the social context, brought to the point
of 'normality' and ready assimilation. This latter stage, which was
reached just after the Second World War in Britain and just
before in North America, is relatively easy to relate in historical
terms. It was immediately followed by the discussion of the issues
raised by Bultmann's demand for a demythologisation of the
Gospel; from that point on, the remaining stability of the Neo-
Orthodox position with all its variants was in principle
endangered and awaited the sudden and drastic *aggiorniomento* of
Protestantism itself in the 1960's. Once Barth had become in
F. W. Camfield's words, 'an ordinary theologian' the reception of
his work becomes a process broadly relatable to the translation of
the succeeding volumes of the *Church Dogmatics*, which
continues into recent and continuing discussion. The typology of
responses now proposed is linked in broad chronological terms to
the assimilation of the *Church Dogmatics*, and represents stages,
each of which tends to develop into a partial and semi-
autonomous development, that does not in itself represent an
interpretation of the *whole* of Barth's work, nor necessarily a
consistently developed *aspect* of it. They are, in effect, growths
within Anglo-Saxon theology stimulated, rather than consistently
moulded by the intervention of Barth's theology. In this the
Anglo-Saxon reception differs in some respects from the German
and mainland European receptions. In fairly comprehensive
terms we may isolate the following types of response, which do

not exhaust the modes of influence of Barth's theology, but at least indicate its range and potency, albeit often indirect.

(i) Dialectical Assimilation

The foregoing historical survey indicated that the 'dialectical' dimension of the 'theology of crisis' was for Anglo-Saxon observers problematic to the point of being effectively unassimilable. It would nevertheless be possible to see some of the early work of D. M. MacKinnon, and to a lesser extent that of A. Vidler[76] and Daniel Jenkins[77] as the partial exceptions proving this rule. In general, however, the dialectical mode of thought would seem alien to the English theological mind. In post-war terms, the American R. W. Jenson's provocative book, *God after God*,[78] is a systematic reworking of major theses of Barth's mature theology on the basis of the 'rediscovery' of the early dialectical Barth of the *Römerbrief.* Despite these exceptions it is plausible to argue that the effective reception of Barth's theology in Anglo-Saxony has depended in the first instance on the extinction of the nihilistic, Germanic stranger and his replacement with the recognisable and respectable dogmatician of the last thirty years of Barth's life.

(ii) Barth and the critique of religion

From early on the critique of religion embodied in Barth's contribution to the theology of crisis was recognised,[79] and later formalised, as regards world religions, by the Dutch missiologist Hendrik Kraemer, whose books, The *Christian Message in a Non-Christian World*[80] and *Religion and the Christian Faith*[81] had a powerful influence upon attitudes in the English-speaking world until their transformation in the course of the last twenty years.[82] On

[76] A. Vidler, *The Gospel of God and the Authority of the Church* (London, 1937).

[77] S. Jenkins, *The Nature of Catholicity* (London, 1942), and *The Gift of Ministry* (London, 1947). In the latter Jenkins saw through Barth the recovery of 'authentic criteria of the theological judgment', p. 12.

[78] R. W. Jenson, *God after God – The God of the Future and the God of the Past seen in the Work of Karl Barth* (Indianapolis, 1969).

[79] See, for example, W. Pauck 'Barth's Religious criticism of religion', *Journal of Religion*, vol. 8 (1928), pp. 453–474, a well-informed account.

[80] H. Kraemer (London, 1938).

[81] H. Kraemer (London, 1946).

[82] The continued development and modification of this line of argument can be seen in Bishop Leslie Newbigin's *The Open Secret* (London, 1979), and his autobiography *Unfinished Agenda* (London, 1985).

a more local level the separation of 'religion' and the 'Christian faith' has helped widen, with mutually disastrous consequences, the gulf in the tertiary sector between 'religious studies' and 'theology'. Recent theological polarisation in the United States reflects this growing disjuncture as it is embodied in the Hartford (1975) and Boston (1976) Declarations, respectively.[83]

(iii) *Individual Inspirational Assimilation*
Whilst many distinguished figures within the 'Biblical theology' and 'Neo-Orthodox' tradition owe much to Barth in a variety of ways, there are a number of independent minds who have consistently drawn on and commented upon Barth. In Britain, the first most obvious example is D. M. MacKinnon, who after his 'dialectical' phase under Hoskyns' influence, continued to defend the ontological uniqueness of the Incarnation and the *Novum* of revelation and sought to combat the intellectual downgrading of English theology.[84] Another, very different, example is W. A. Whitehouse whose acute comments[85] upon the whole series of Barth's texts appearing in the post-war period were of a consistently high quality. The only major Barthian systematic theology to emerge in Britain is that of T. F. Torrance, but this is so distinctive as to merit separate treatment as an 'orthodox' Barthianism. In North America, Paul Lehmann stands out as a parallel figure, an individual powerfully influenced by Barth whose fidelity remains steadfast despite the changes and pluralistic diversity of his environment.[86] For these individuals Barth's thought would appear, in different ways, to have helped

[83] Texts published in *Theology Today*, vol. 31 (1975), pp. 94–7 and vol. 32 (1976), pp. 101–4, respectively.
[84] See D. M. MacKinnon whose sympathies were apparent in 1941: 'I incline somewhat in a Barthian direction myself' in 'Revelation and Social Justice' in *Malvern 1941 The Life of the Church and the Order of Society* (London, 1941), p. 89, and his continued modified Barthian emphasis in 'Philosophy and Christology' in G. W. Roberts, D. E. Smucker (eds.), *The Borderlands of Theology* (London, 1968), pp. 68–9.
[85] See A. L. Loades (ed.), *The Authority of Grace – Essays in Response to Karl Barth* (Edinburgh, 1981), in which these contributions are conveniently assembled.
[86] See, for example, P. Lehmann in 'Karl Barth and the future of theology', *Religious Studies*, vol. 6 (1970), pp. 105–120, where he provides a valuable contextualisation of Barth's work in the post-war context and its varied contributions to the types of its assimilation.

sustain commitment to the strangeness and distinctiveness of Christianity. None, apart from Torrance, produced a fully developed position, and all have pursued the path of critical self-distancing from the majority views of their time.

(iv) *Biblical theology*

Without doubt the theology of crisis with its emphasis upon the central, biblically-witnessed events of revelation inspired and lent impetus to the renewed study and interpretation of the Bible. The actual work evident within the amorphous 'Biblical theology' movement is diverse, produced by such British figures as Hoskyns and Davy, besides A. M. Ramsey[87] and A. M. Farrer, through to the Americans Brevard Childs and G. E. Wright. The different strategies implicit in the claims to biblical authority in this movement and beyond were reviewed by D. M. Kelsey in 1975.[88] The methods of exegesis employed in such monuments to this Biblical re-engagement as the Kittel *Wörterbuch*, besides other individual works, were subjected to destructive attack by the Old Testament scholar James Barr.[89] This was not so much a *direct* assault upon Barth (although this happened *en passant*) as the expression of one aspect of a renewal of critical methods over against the systematising tendencies of the Biblical theology movement, which, through the insights of redaction criticism and a sharpened sense of historical discontinuity, made textually problematic the assertion of any inner conceptual unity. The exegetical crisis should not, of course, be divorced from wider, contextual factors which were predisposed towards the denigration of all residual authority, biblical or otherwise. In Britain perhaps the most durable reflection of Barth's influence upon biblical theology is in his inspirational role, as we saw earlier, in the lives of biblical scholars, such as C. K. Barrett,

[87] A. M. Ramsey, *The Gospel and the Catholic Church* (London, 1936), is an early example of the English Biblical theology genre but no direct attribution to the influence of Barth is here in question (verbal communication with the author); Ramsey does, however, imply the influence of F. N. Davey and A. M. Farrer in the preface, p. viii.

[88] *The Uses of Scripture in Recent Theology* (London, 1975), in which extensive reference is made to Barth's impression upon the proponents of 'Biblical theology'.

[89] See *The Semantics of Biblical Language* (Oxford, 1961), and *Biblical Words for Time* (London, 1962, 1969²).

who recounted a specific debt. Interestingly, his longstanding Durham colleague, C. E. B. Cranfield, also acknowledged his indebtedness, but to the later dogmatic, not the dialectical Barth.[90]

(v) Neo-Orthodoxy and 'Orthodox' Barthianism

The influence of dialectical and 'crisis' theology and then the later more systematic theology of Barth upon 'Neo-Orthodoxy' is complex and manysided, although it contains distinct, isolable features. Such is the importance of Neo-Orthodoxy that it can be seen as a dominant force in the context which eventually broke down in the 1960's with the advent of radical secular theology and the 'death of God' school. Within Neo-Orthodoxy there have been theologians who can in more specific terms be regarded as 'orthodox' Barthians; they found in Barth a satisfactory and indeed normative interpretation and restatement of tradition in the broadest sense. Amongst these must certainly count F. W. Camfield, T. H. L. Parker,[91] H. Hartwell,[92] G. W. Bromiley and above all, Thomas Forsyth Torrance.[93] Thus within the ambit of 'Barthianism', the less than flattering epithet used to denote theologians and others influenced by

[90] Cranfield comments upon the influence of the *Römerbrief* in the introduction to his monumental study, *The Epistle to the Romans* (Edinburgh, 1975): 'The publication of Barth's first commentary on Romans . . ., came just after the war – though, as far as the English-speaking world was concerned, its action was somewhat delayed, since the translation made by Hoskyns (made from the sixth German edition which was very different from that of 1919) did not reappear until 1933. Of its importance as a turning-point in the history of theology there can be no doubt, and Barrett was certainly right to say that 'to read it must be reckoned an essential part of a theological education' *The Expository Times*, vol. 65 (1953–4), p. 177; but, while it rendered the Church, and can still render it, a much-needed service, it has very serious deficiencies as an exposition of Romans, and to take it for one's main aid in studying the epistle would be to demonstrate one's failure to learn from Barth's maturer thinking and one's lack of an essential element in theological seriousness, a sense of humour.' pp. 41–2.

[91] T. H. L. Parker, editor of *Essays in Christology for Karl Barth* (London, 1956).

[92] Hartwell's basic textbook, *The Theology of Karl Barth: An Introduction* (London, 1969), remained for many years the only comprehensive English presentation of the *Church Dogmatics*. It is essentially a skilled paraphrase of the 'ordinary' Barth.

[93] T. F. Torrance, *Karl Barth An Introduction to his Early Theology 1910–1931* (London, 1962), is as yet unsuperceded in English.

both Barth and Brunner, Torrance and his associates have been consistent in their support of Barth.[94] The mediation of Barth's theology in the English-speaking world owes much to both Bromiley and Torrance, editors of the translation of the *Church Dogmatics*. Thus Torrance's conception of revelation is advanced in a way that leaves the reader in no doubt as to the significance of Barth:

> Barth found his theology thrust back more and more upon its proper subject, and so he set himself to think through the whole of theological knowledge in such a way that it might be consistently faithful to the concrete act of God in Jesus Christ from which it actually takes its rise in the Church, and, further, in the course of that inquiry to ask about the presuppositions and conditions on the basis of which it comes about that God is known, in order to develop from within the actual content of theology its own interior logic and its own inner criticism which will help to set theology free from every form of ideological corruption.[95]

Torrance's consistent and uncompromising representation of Barth's thought as the concretisation of the inner logic of revelation itself realised through a conception of absolute, self-positing truth is an intellectual strategy fraught with unacceptable dangers. It appears to offer to the putative believer a form of theological re-armament with absolutist overtones all too reminiscent of other twentieth-century descendants of German idealism and its inversion. Torrance's mode of Barthian epistemological positivism would seem largely alien to the Anglo-Saxon mind. The reality of God, so conceived, puts the intellectual proclaimer of the Word in a dangerously ambiguous and less than wholly disciplined position with regard to the Subject about which he speaks. Torrance has, nevertheless, been responsible for the dominant interpretation of the mature work of Barth in Britain, and accompanying this have appeared the

[94] A forerunner of Torrance's approach may be detected in G. Howe, 'Parallelen zwischen der Theologie Karl Barths und der heutigen Physik', in *Antwort Karl Barth zum siebzigsten Geburtstag am 10 Mai 1956* (Zollikon-Zurich, 1956), pp. 409–22.

[95] *Theological Science* (London, 1969), p. 7; see also pp. 131–2 and T. A. Longford's 'T. F. Torrance's *Theological Science*: a reaction', *Scottish Journal of Theology*, vol. 25 (1972), pp. 155–70.

repeated affirmations of the latter's stature as the full equal of the greatest doctors of the Church.[96]

(vi)   *Barth and the 'death of God': secularising assimilation*
Some indication of the stunning diversity within the reception of Barth in the post-war, post-dialectical 'ordinary' period of his work is apparent when we appreciate the apparent contrast between T. F. Torrance's hyperbolic assessment of Barth, as compared with the attribution to Barth of the radical 'death of God' movement in the 1960's, a development associated with the collapse of Neo-Orthodoxy itself.[97] Some indication of the incipient tensions that underlaid the fairly sudden transition from revelational 'positivism' and biblical 'realism' into 'secular theology' is given by the Scottish theologian Ronald Gregor Smith, who, as a seminal thinker in the tradition of Bonhoeffer, put Barth in context:

> In Barth we have the last, and possibly the greatest, certainly an awe-inspiring, effort on the part of traditional metaphysical theology to overcome the difficulty of relating 'God in his being for himself' with 'God for the World in Christ'. But if you begin with 'being', is there any way to the world of time and movement, the historical world where Faith takes its rise?[98]

[96] The most recent of these is 'The Legacy of Karl Barth (1886–1986) in *Scottish Journal of Theology*, vol. 39, pp. 289–308. Earlier Torrance wrote 'Karl Barth is incontestably the greatest figure in modern theology since Schleiermacher, occupying an honoured position among the great elite of the Church – Augustine, Anselm, Aquinas, Luther and Calvin', *Union Seminary Quarterly Review*, vol. 12 (1956), p. 21. The ferocious attacks upon Barth by American-Dutch Calvinists, led by C. van Til were of course the strongest repudiation of any endorsement of Barth's orthodoxy. See *The New Modernism An Appraisal of Barth and Brunner* (London, 1946), and *Christianity and Barthianism* (Philadelphia, 1965).

[97] See James M. Robinson, 'Die ersten heterodoxen Barthianen' and Paul Hesser, 'Barthianische Wurzeln der "Radical-Theology"', both in W. Dantine, K. Luthi (eds.), *Theologie Zwischen Gestern und Morgen Interpretationen und Anfragen zum Werk Karl Barths* (Munich, 1968), pp. 13–37; 235–246. In addition, G. Vahanian, *The Death of God* (New York, 1961), provides important evidence for this 'radicalization' of Barth upon which P. Lehmann comments (1970), op.cit., pp. 116–117.

[98] *The Doctrine of God* (London, 1970), p. 91. In addition, Paul van Buren's personal history (as one of Barth's doctoral students) and his role in the 'death of God' theology represent par excellence this problematic dimension of Barth's reception.

The simultaneous heightening of the profile of quasi-metaphysical transcendence (formalised as we saw by Torrance in epistemological terms) took place in a socio-cultural historical context marked by an unprecedented turn towards individualism and consumer materialism, combined with a concern, above all, for 'human potential' during the relative optimism of the decade 1955–65. This led at the very least to a scarcely sustainable tension between the nature and content of theological assertions and the context of their social realisation. A post-war phrase coined by Daniel Bell, 'the end of ideology' was symptomatic, for comprehensive systems of thought imposed in the inter-war totalitarianism of Hitler and Stalin had lost their lustre and attraction. Likewise social moves towards individual self-realisation, demands for effective praxis and the emergence of the theological equivalent of 'pressure-group' politics had their effect. The troika of Barth, Bultmann and Tillich were to be among the last great monolithic ideological exports; an era of theological pluralism had truly begun. The orthodox Barthian either/or: *either* enter into the 'safe stronghold of transcendence' (to use Ernst Bloch's resonant phrase: '*eine feste Burg der Transzendenz*') or depart into the chaotic realm of 'unhinged thought' (reflecting T. F. Torrance's equally potent imagery) was a dilemma perhaps unsustainable in a new, and perhaps unprecedented, era.

(vii) *Barth and the sociology of religion*
The massive post-war expansion of higher education in both Britain and North America was attended by a corresponding increase in the teaching of sociology and of the sociology of religion. The latter provided (especially when presented within the ambit of 'religious studies') an acceptable way of introducing the study of religion into undergraduate teaching without the apparent stigma of dogmatic or denominational prejudice. In this post-war context the sharp distinction in the Barthian position between 'faith' and 'religion' allowed for the intellectual strategy, exploited by Peter Berger, of participating in and promoting the strictly objective discussion of the latter, whilst simultaneously by sleight of hand retaining a sharply differentiated implicit commitment in the former. The retention of a faith commitment as a means of escaping thorough-going sociological reduction was

a tactical ploy from which Berger later distanced himself.[99] The dominance of the positivist revelational image of Barth embodied in Neo-Orthodoxy, encouraged through the formulation of analogies between Christian dogmatics and ideas drawn from pure science as in Torrance's work, has been pursued at the expense of adequate understanding of the constitutive role of sociological factors in the evolution of religion, theological and, indeed, all intellectual constructs. Needless to say, the sociology of theology (including that of Barth) now opens up areas of great interest and importance.[100]

(viii)   *Barth and the philosophy of religion*
Again seen in the context of the post-war expansion of the liberal arts and social science in higher education, the apparent 'fideism' within Neo-Orthodoxy became the stock-in-trade object of philosophical critique. R. W. Hepburn in Britain[101] and W. W. Bartley III[102] in the United States, amongst others, attacked the status of a belief-system which had apparently lost effective touch with other spheres of discourse. The Neo-Wittgensteinian riposte, the assertion of the autonomy of spheres of discourse using the images of the 'language game' and 'form of life', and the formalisation of this 'conceptual relativism' in such popular works as Peter Winch's *The Idea of a Social Science*[103] provided at the very least an epistemological and structural support to the type of response identified below with 'narrative theology' and, moreover, with the contemporary academicism to which we also refer.

(ix)   *Barth and politics*
Examination of contemporary journals reveals regular if not extensive pre-war accounts of Barth's political interventions at Barmen, on the occasion of the invasion of Czechoslovakia in 1938

[99] See P. L. Berger's critical self-assessment in *The Social Reality of Religion* (Harmondsworth, 1969), pp. 186ff.

[100] As in the pioneering work of the prolific West German sociologist Niklas Luhmann. See Garrett Green, 'The Sociology of Dogmatics: Niklas Luhmann's Challenge to Theology', *Journal of the American Academy of Religion*, vol. 50/1 (1982), pp. 19–34.

[101] *Christianity and Paradox   Critical Studies in Twentieth Century Theology* (London, 1958), esp. ch. 5, 'Meaning and Mediator', p. 201.

[102] *The Retreat from Commitment* (London, 1984²).

[103] P. Winch (London, 1958).

and, most notably, in his exchanges with Reinhold Niebuhr at the Amsterdam meeting of the World Council of Churches in 1947. Whilst for the most part Barth's political intervention from his Safenwil period onwards have been the object of keen discussion in West Germany, and despite G. Hunsinger's[104] efforts at mediation of the highly contentious Marquardt thesis[105] concerning the political character of Barth's *theology*, the Anglo-Saxon evaluation of the significance of this element has been generally sceptical.[106] The political events upon which Barth commented and in terms of which his theology might be understood are vital to contemporary German identity in a way not shared, for better or worse, by Britons and North Americans. Most significant here is the Anglo-Saxon theologian's relative ignorance of, and ideological exclusion from, the issues raised by Marxism during the period in question. In this context Charles West's unsurpassed study was the notable exception.[107] Recent interest in the reappearance of Marxist ideas in liberation theology coincides, broadly-speaking, with a decline in commitment to the theological 'grand theory' approach characteristic of Barth, despite his own and his followers' disclaimers.

(x) *Narrative theology*

The decline of Neo-Orthodoxy and the secular theology of the sixties and its attendant social phenomena have, in recent years, been succeeded by a re-assertion of interpretation of the biblical texts on a literary, rather than a historical-critical basis. Central to this has been the exploitation of 'story' and 'narrative' as the starting-point for theological use of biblical texts. It would appear that the close contiguity of the growth of 'narrative theology' with the assimilation of the later volumes of the *Church*

---

[104] See *Karl Barth and Radical Politics* (Philadelphia, 1976), and 'Karl Barth and radical politics: some further considerations', *Studies in Religion/Sciences Religeuses* (1978), pp. 167–91.

[105] Fr. Wilhelm Marquardt, *Theologie und Sozialismus – Das Beispiel Karl Barths* (Munich, 1972).

[106] One hostile example will suffice: W. R. Ward, the Durham modern Church historian, has likewise attacked the integrity of the 'cult-figure' of the 'unpolitical Barth' prior to 1935 in 'The Socialist Commitment in Karl Barth', *Studies in Church History*, vol. 17 (1978), pp. 254–65. There is prolific further biography.

[107] C. West, *Communism and the Theologians* (London, 1938).

Dogmatics, notably volume IV, was not merely coincidental, indeed G. W. Stroup's programmatic *The Promise of Narrative Theology*[108] can be understood as an extended commentary upon theological possibilities inherited from Barth and first opened up by Hans W. Frei in two linked, but dissimilar works.[109] The location by Frei of the focal point of theological reflection in 'history-like', 'realistic' narratives on the basis of a methodological appropriation of elements culled from Eric Auerback's *Mimesis*[110] would appear to free the theologian from the restrictions of historicism. Whether in fact Barth's theology would legitimate this strategy of evading historical-critical reductionism through exploitation of the literary mode of novel-like realistic narrative is open to question. Indeed, moreover, the use made in this context of Auerbach's contrast between the intense known particularity of the ultimately closed Homeric narrative and the witnessing transparency of the Old Testament narrative is also doubtful. It is only by prising apart the early and later volumes of the *Church Dogmatics* that ontological claims and narrative meaning can be divorced in order to exploit the latter.

(xi) *Mythopoesis and Post-Modernism*
The sanction given to the relatively unfettered employment of the theological imagination apparently afforded by the later volumes of the *Church Dogmatics* was noted by the American feminist theologian R. R. Ruether in a perceptive, but neglected article published in 1968.[111] Looking for the freedom to re-form tradition herself, Ruether openly proceeded along the lines hinted at above, taking volume IV of the *Church Dogmatics* as her starting point

[108] C. W. Stroup (London, 1981/4), see pp. 139ff. where Frei's dependence upon Barth is made clear.

[109] H. W. Frei, *The Identity of Jesus Christ: An Inquiry into the Hermeneutical Bases of Dogmatic Theology* (Philadelphia, 1976); *The Eclipse of Biblical Narrative A Study in Eighteenth and Nineteenth Century Hermeneutics* (New Haven and London, 1974). D. F. Ford renders explicit the link between Barth and the narrative mode in *Biblical Narrative and the Theological Method of Karl Barth in the Church Dogmatics* (Bern, 1981). The early work of Dietrich Ritschl is also important.

[110] E. Auerbach, *Mimesis The Representation of Reality in Western Literature* (Princeton, 1953), see especially ch. 1.

[111] R. R. Reuther, 'The Left Hand of God in the Theology of Karl Barth. Karl Barth as Mythopoeic Theologian', *Journal of Religious Thought*, vol. 25 (1968/9), pp. 3–26.

for a presentation of Barth as a theologian of the unfettered imagination caught up in sublime *mythopoesis*, having effectively abandoned all metaphysical questions of truth and indeed narrative criteria other than the aesthetic. Whilst such a loosening of restraints might be justified in the context of an attack upon Barth's 'patriarchal' theology, it opened up a possibility within Anglo-Saxon theology not hitherto regarded as legitimate within main lines of the tradition. The theologian could, following Ruether, act with a sovereign freedom not merely to restate, but effectively to re-create a tradition using the narrative basis as a mineable seam containing images and motifs exploitable within belief-systems tailor-made for the ideological needs of sub-groups (however aberrant) within the pluralistic *corpus Christianum*.

A perhaps less irresponsible approach to the new imaginative possibilities detected in Barth's late work can be found within the 'post-liberal' or 'post-modern' movement in which the demand of both context and tradition are, so its proponents argue, contained. Thus G. A. Lindbeck in his important work *The Nature of Doctrine* asserts that: 'Karl Barth's exegetical emphasis on narrative has been at second hand a chief source of my notion of intratextuality as an appropriate way of doing theology in a fashion consistent with a cultural-linguistic understanding of religion and a regulative view of doctrine.'[112] Thus the more positive aspects of the fideist interpretation of Barth are re-earthed in the context of the religious life of a tradition and its socio-cultural matrix. Even here the failure to distinguish between and to relate together satisfactorily questions of truth and the exploration of meaning is not without its problematic aspect.

(xii)   *Literary assimilation: 'fallen' Barthians*
There is undoubtedly a sense in which Barth's theology has served as a transitional intoxication in the lives of some distinguished twentieth century thinkers who have passed through a Barthian adolescence as a prelude to the adoption of other positions. The transition from faith to scepticism may be sudden and complete. Such 'fallen' theologians sometimes retain a persistent Barthian

[112] G. A. Lindbeck, *The Nature of Doctrine Religion and Theology in a Postliberal Age* (London, 1984), p. 135.

core, almost as it were a gnostic 'spark', overlaid with consistent practical atheism: these have now through the good offices of the distinguished Episcopalian novelist John Updike, a dauntless explorer of the Alpha and Omega of sexuality, entered the pantheon of literary types. The central character of Updike's recent *Roger's Version*,[113] Professor Roger Lambert, brilliantly exemplifies this, and his exploits belong entirely to the (pre-Aids) era of the pursuit of unrestrained, but ultimately tragic sexual fulfilment. This is, to use MacKinnon's phrase, another 'dark theme' in the history of twentieth century Christian theology.

(xiii)   *New Fundamentalism and Academicism*
There is evidence, finally, of increased interest in Barth on the part of main-line Evangelical theological thought as it struggles between the resurgent and uncompromising demands of modernity over against Fundamentalist versions of Moral Majority and the 'New Age'. Whether such belated attempts to retain contact with modernity in the face of the ultra-conservative threat are more than the mis-employment of Barth's thought as an ideological convenience remains to be seen. Over against the conflicts within Protestant conservatism, North American university theology has moved decisively in the direction of an academicist liberalism exemplified in the widely-used textbook, *Christian Theology*[114], edited by P. C. Hodgson and R. H. King. This work in its original form, without the later addition of S. W. Sykes' paper on church, ministry and sacraments, is a classic example of the virtual elimination of any vestige of Barth's healthy insistence upon the church- and witness-related character of Christian theology. The ideological consequences of such well-funded Olympian detachment within universities for theological work effectively divorced from the painful contingency of reflection upon the proclaimed Word is all too evident. It would appear to reinforce the tendency within certain forms of 'post-modernism' and 'post-liberalism' to subsume theological reflection into the mere clarification of meaning within the

---

[113] J. Updike (London, 1986).
[114] *Christian Theology An Introduction to the Tradition and Tasks* (Philadelphia, 1982).

ideological superstructure of belief-systems, a process which in its turn resolves the rhetoric of 'praxis' into the practice of 'theory'.

IV   *Prospect: the Past and the Future of the Theology of Karl Barth*
Without doubt, it may be said that the thought of Karl Barth has had a constitutive influence upon the development of German Protestant theology in the twentieth century. It is also evident that Barth has earned a prominent place in modern German Church history. As regards the Anglo-Saxon world, he has made a major, but less decisive contribution; indeed it might generally be said that Barth is often seen as one in a series of major continental thinkers along with Bultmann, Tillich, Berdyaev, and so on, who have influenced English-speaking theology and religious thought in the mid twentieth century; and his status in this process of intellectual transmission is a contested question. It is a relatively select minority who have, like Torrance, accorded Barth the status of master theologian and drawn prescriptive recommendations from his connection. As we have shown above, the reception and influence of the theology of Karl Barth has not been uniform but diversified in accordance with the time and the mode of its cultural insertion. Barth's most fruitful and indefatigable champion in the Anglo-Saxon world, T. F. Torrance, saw in his work a radical clarification of the ground and grammar of theology, a gift to the Church that could only be ignored at the risk of grave loss. Such claims are difficult to assess but the extraordinary range and quality of the secondary literature does bear witness to the rich, ripe depths of Barth's achievement.

Contrary to Torrance's hopes, something other than the exploration of the inner logic of revelation has emerged, and this is a function not merely of the structure of an extensive organised body of thought but also of obscurely felt and imperfectly understood social forces which put in radical question the total status of such a complex system. What we find when we confront and penetrate the epistemological and ontological either/ors implicit in Barth is a series of profound questions, which although applicable to the whole conspectus of the theological task, take on in the case of Barth a coherent, distinctive and pressing particularity. Karl Barth was a very great theologian: great in terms of a highly original recapitulation of the tradition, which, at the same time, is a masterful representation of the wider difficulties of that tradition in the face of a hostile modernity. These difficulties are evident when we juxtapose Barth's recovery of the tradition with Eric Auerbach's poignant account of the penalties of the historical distance of Biblical narrative from its original context:

> If the text of the Biblical narrative, then, is so greatly in need of interpretation on the basis of its own content, its claims to absolute authority force us still further in the same direction. Far from seeking, like Homer, merely to make us forget our own reality for a few hours, it seeks to overcome our reality: we are to fit our own life into its world, feel ourselves to be elements in its structure of universal history. This becomes increasingly difficult the further our historical environment is removed from that of the Biblical books; and if these nevertheless maintain their claim to absolute authority, it is inevitable that they themselves be adapted through interpretative transformation. This was for a long time comparatively easy; as late as the European Middle Ages it was possible to represent Biblical events as ordinary phenomena of contemporary life, the methods of interpretation themselves forming the basis for such a treatment. But when, through too great a change in environment, and through the awakening of a critical consciousness, this becomes impossible, the Biblical claim to absolute authority is jeopardized; the method of interpretation is scorned and rejected, the Biblical stories become ancient legends, and the doctrine they had contained, now dissevered from them, becomes a disembodied image.[115]

Barth's work, like the Biblical narrative, bears the marks of something all too close to the claim of an absolute authority manifesting itself in a disembodied image; that is, as a 'strange new world', that first appears as a Kierkegaardian 'Moment' and is then extended in the linearity of the temporal order.[116] Barth's work progresses from dialectic and paradox to the sublime majesty and ontological solidity of a regular dogmatics; but this was perceived merely as a reinstated 'ordinary' theology. The risks are revealed when we push further the affinity between Barth's progress and that of other earlier major thinkers of the

---

[115] Auerbach, op.cit., pp. 15–16.
[116] I have outlined the temporal structures informing this danger in my contribution to S. W. Sykes (ed.) (1979), see note 2 above. See ch. 1 above.

Germanophone idealist tradition, of which Hegel and Marx are the obvious examples. Each moves from early, essentially dialectical insecurity towards regenerated ontological certainty: thus Hegel's *Phenomenology of Mind* precedes the *Logic* and then moves to narrative application in the massive series of historically based lectures including the posthumous *Lectures on the Philosophy of Religion*. Marx's *Paris Manuscripts* are followed by the *Grundrisse, Capital* volume I and then the historical justifications of the later volumes of *Capital* and *Theories of Surplus Value*. So Barth effectively begins with the dialectical *Römerbrief*, crystallises an ontology in the *Prolegomena* to the *Church Dogmatics* and then progresses into the 'history-like' narrative textuality of the latter volumes. Yet the ease of making such an analogy may suggest that the imposition of the disembodied image, the *stasis* and immobilism of a strange new world, is far too simplistic a response to what is not merely in its internal relations a complex phenomenon (as a synthetic re-interpretation of the tradition) but is also as regards its external relations equally difficult to comprehend and represent. Rather closer to the truth than Auerbach's insight may be the clue to be found in T. W. Adorno, where he referred to Beethoven's *Missa Solemnis* as an 'alienated masterpiece',[117] by which he intended to indicate that it was *both* great *and* problematic. Likewise with Barth's contribution we are in no position to confront it with a false and misleading dilemma, another either/or: either enter the world of alienated majesty *or* depart into secular aridity. This is the choice, a parting of the ways imposed by the consistent 'orthodox' Barthian; but does it represent the real nature of the situation? Far from being confronted with a simple choice between ideologies or with a disjunction between fantasy and reality, we have here to articulate what it would mean to go *through* rather than merely *around* Barth in a passage not as yet accomplished in the fullest sense by Anglo-Saxon theology.

In this essay it has been our purpose to indicate how, through initial, comparative historical surveys the initial stages of the reception of the theology of Karl Barth were delayed and distorted by contextual factors both social and cultural. Once Barth's

---

[117] This parallel is taken from 'Alienated Masterpiece; the *Missa Solemnis*', *Telos*, vol. 28 (1976).

thought, albeit imperfectly and incompletely mediated, had taken root in the consciousness of the English-speaking theological world then its secondary assimilation was to give rise to a series of responses which we have presented in terms of a typology. The alternative to such categorisation would have to be a complete history of the theology of the mid-and later twentieth century. Our typology indicates the modes of response related to the often delayed transmission of vital elements in Barth's *oeuvre*. Serious efforts at presentation tend to fall victim either to the kind of superficiality that stems from dogmatic and partisan over-commitment, or to an equally misleading instrumental use of Barth to justify individual intellectual strategies. There has been no definitive Anglo-Saxon interpretation of the theology of Karl Barth which respects its context, content and consequences.[118] An adequate passage through this body of thought and its total *Sitz im Leben* would present considerable, some might think insuperable difficulties. At the very least such an Anglo-Saxon reception ought to bring to bear virtues of restraint, analytical skill and clarity; but beyond this it would demand the full deployment of intellectual insights – historical, philosophical, sociological, linguistic and theological, besides those of literary theory – in what would amount to a 'genealogy' of Barth's thought conceived in the field of force of its historical emergence.[119] In this way it might prove possible to displace the dominant Anglo-Saxon interpretation of the theology of Karl Barth with its misleading totalitarian demands.

Barth's theology is in Adorno's phrase an 'alienated masterpiece' that represents to us in an extremely powerful way

[118] A quarter of a century ago John Baillie wrote of Barth in his posthumously published Gifford Lectures of 1961–2: 'there can be no hopeful forward advance beyond his teaching . . ., if we attempt to go *round* it instead of *through* it', *The Sense of the Presence of God* (London, 1962), p. 254. My argument is, in effect, that the failure to confront Barth's work (however it might appear dated) is part of the 'unconquered past' of English theology.

[119] 'Genealogy' and the associated 'archaeology of knowledge' are procedures drawn from Michel Foucault's methodological insights. See Alan Sheridan's comments 'The Foucaldian genealogy is an unmasking of power for the use of those who suffer it. It is also directed against those who would seize power in their name', *Michel Foucault The Will to Truth* (London, 1980), p. 221; this admirably summarises the nature of the enterprise and the moral goals underlying my own approach.

simultaneously both the recreation and the distance of tradition from modernity; in grappling with this dilemma we engage with something affecting the torn soul of European culture. To dare to venture a healing here would be to probe a universal wound. The prospect of such a recovery would be no mere dismantling or salvage of the stricken hulk of the great Dreadnought of Barth's lifework, but a means to the recovery of a *theologia viatorum*, reintegrated with possibly unforeseeable consequences into the fabric of human commonality. It *is* the task and purpose of the Church to incarnate the 'impossible possibility' of the active Word; part of this task implies an Anglo-Saxon *mediation*,[120] as opposed to a merely passive *reception* of the theology of Karl Barth. This in its turn requires the unsparing *Einsatz* of intellectual energy and dynamic intellectual *praxis* on the part of a theological tradition that all too often relapses into a flabby complacency and into an indifference born of a premature resolution of antitheses into *via media*.

As Hegel has taught the world, the unreflective consciousness of dominance awaits the challenge of the oppressed, the Bondsmen, those who through confrontation with fear, experience that inferiority (likened to the state of thinghood) out of which they may possibly emerge through struggle and labour into the dynamism of fully reflective self-consciousness. Such is the burden and the possibility incumbent upon the Anglo-Saxon tradition in confrontation with Karl Barth, the Goliath of twentieth century German-speaking theology. Indeed, as regards English theology it must learn to live dialectically (and thus dangerously) or it will die, suffocated in the cocoon of its own myopic misapprehensions; a process all too apparent in its reception of the theology of Karl Barth.

---

[120] This term here carried the fullest dialectical implications of the struggle for, and towards, reality to be found in Hegel's *Phenomenology of Mind*; see pp. 229–240 of the translation by James Baillie (London, 1910).

5

Theological Rhetoric and Moral Passion in the Light of MacKinnon's 'Barth' *(1987)*

1 *Introduction*

Donald MacKinnon has been a central figure in the pursuit of theology in Britain for half a century. To state this platitude, is, however, but to uncover a seething mass of difficulties presented not only by the intrinsic characteristics of MacKinnon's work, which is often both brilliant *and* highly obscure, but also by his position as an 'outsider' subsisting at the *centre* of the network of personal relationships, which, for better or for worse, has constituted the established core of a tradition not notable for either consistency or dialectical penetration. The resistance to the codification of tradition, particularly in England and in English theology, and the context of that tradition understood in comprehensive historical terms, mean that for those of us who have grown up in the post-war context the personal environment of pre-war and wartime Oxford in which MacKinnon himself developed is becoming rapidly less well-known and increasingly distant.[1] Thus, even where serious work is in evidence (as in, for example, the dominant account of Anglican social teaching, by E. R. Norman) this tends to subvert and distort the seriousness of socially concerned groupings (such as the Christendom Group) by a ruthless stress upon their alleged naivety and short-

---

[1] An obvious *lacuna* in this respect is a comprehensive account of the influence of E. C. Hoskyns' mediation of Barth.

sightedness that devalues our understanding of the immediate context of MacKinnon's intellectual youth. It is because of this and other factors that the interpretation of MacKinnon and his work as an inside 'outsider', presents very considerable difficulties. In addition, for those of us who have undergone some degree of 'formation' under his direct influence, the task is even more taxing because of the process of psychological embodiment which means that criticism has at the same time to be self-criticism. Moreover, the often highly oblique and sometimes seemingly perversely allusive aspects of MacKinnon's style invite the possibility of disastrous imitation. Such a self-cancelling and nugatory step has at all costs to be avoided.

Thus far I have concentrated in my remarks upon a cluster of difficulties (and there are more than I have alluded to) which attend serious engagement with the thought of Donald MacKinnon. How, more positively, might we apply ourselves to it? Reading and re-reading of MacKinnon's *oeuvre* convinces me that his most obvious achievements lie in the ruthless exposure of intellectual flabbiness in theological writers who venture incautious judgements. The deflation of pretension is, of course, a necessary but scarcely a sufficient condition of a positive contribution to theological self-understanding. MacKinnon's participation in the latter is contained mainly in four works: the wartime expanded pamphlets ('tracts' would be a happier term), *God the Living and the True* and *The Church of God* of 1940, and the substantial post-war texts, *A Study in Ethical Theory* (1957) and *The Problem of Metaphysics* (1974). It is relatively easy to couple the first and second and the third and fourth and to see in each pair internal consistency and coherence. What are we to make, however, of the relation between the two groups of texts? It is not good enough, I believe, to disclaim the former or consign them to the category of fevered juvenilia. If we tackle MacKinnon's work on lines applied to other significant constructive theological and philosophical writers then it would be reasonable to assume a pattern of initial dialectical exploration of issues which later, in maturity, undergo attempted resolution. If, then, we may assume the possibility in principle of such a pattern of question and attempted answer, what may it be that relates the 'early' to the 'mature' MacKinnon? Is there continuity despite the discontinuity? How, beyond such an internal investigation, do MacKinnon's most fundamental concerns relate to the wider history of British theological reflection? In this essay I attempt to begin a substantial answer to the former question, but must, through pressure of space, merely allude to the latter, contextualizing question. I shall focus primarily upon one text, the first, *God the Living and the True*, and on this basis generate a series of supplementary questions that will show the continuing historical relevance (yet also the highly problematic character) of the 'early' MacKinnon to the present day.

II *Dialectical initiation: theological rhetoric and the crisis of 1940*
I have chosen to use the provocative term 'theological rhetoric'[2] to characterize MacKinnon's early work because it best encapsulates the difficulties in interpreting the curious extremity and stridency of tone in both *God the Living and the True (GLT)* and *The Church of God (CG)*. I, and I suspect most of my readers, are not in a position to speculate upon the personal genesis of these texts. It is largely as self-subsistent entities that we must take them and in these terms we must try to understand why they failed, certainly so far as I can judge, to have any significant *Wirkungsgeschichte* upon contemporary or subsequent discussion. Why should this be? It is my interpretative contention that these texts have a 'surface grammar', a brutal style, which, as we shall see, functions as a near-totalitarian rhetorical diatribe, imposing impossibilist demands upon Christians and the Church (and here by 'Church' we must certainly mean the Church of England as by law established in the first instance) that were not eventually met. This sophisticated fundamentalism, the 'surface grammar', conceals to a large degree the 'depth grammar' of a growing, pervasive concern with the transcendental capacity of the human,

---

[2] I mean 'rhetoric' here primarily in the sense of an 'art of using language so as to persuade or influence others', but also in the potentially deprecatory sense of 'language characterised by artificial or ostentatious expression' (*COD*, p. 2535). Macaulay's judgement upon Milton that he had 'the sublime wisdom of the Aeropagitica and the nervous rhetoric of the Iconoclast', *Essays* on Milton, 1825, indicates something of the sense of rhetoric as the language of emergency that I seek to convey here.

what I have called the 'moral passion'. This is the term which I intend to convey the fullest range of meanings, for at this deeper level we certainly have to do with a Christ- and a Cross-centred, as well as a moral 'passion'. It is the latter which, I believe, compels the allegiance, even the devotion, of many of those who have come under MacKinnon's influence. Here Karl Barth's truest words, that there can be no real theology without distress, yet none without courage in distress, have been realized in the individual: there is the authenticity that attracts despite the brutal rhetoric that repels.[3]

It is extremely difficult to summarize the early and certainly problematic texts of 1940. Running very close to the rocks of sheer perversity, MacKinnon could, while evincing a concern 'primarily with the character of God, Creator and Redeemer, as he is presented in the Christian Gospel' (*GLT*, 9), see this in the light of Fr Victor White's gloss upon *Quem Deus vult salvare, prius dementat*, that is, 'Whom God wills to save he first drives mad' (*GLT*, 14).[4] Thus, in terms surely inseparable from Hoskyns' brilliant mediation of Barth's second *Römerbrief*, grace appears under the form of contradiction, even to the point of 'dementia'. This form of linguistic shock treatment is surely both rhetorical, a tactical ploy intended to obtrude upon a cultural consciousness weary of religious commonplace, and yet, in a sense, frighteningly, even if tangentially, true. Whilst MacKinnon wrote, that process of the estrangement of religion from social normality gathered pace, and it has now, possibly, extended over the whole of a sick social system and its degraded culture.

In *God the Living and the True* the ambiguous dalliance with divinely-induced madness is not pursued at length. We note, however, on the one hand the emergence of a persisting theme – the equal inevitability of the historical form of the

[3] The analysis of rhetoric in theology offers important possibilities which are explored more fully in R. H. Roberts, J. M. M. Good (eds.) *The Recovery of Rhetoric* (forthcoming).

[4] This is a deliberate reformulation of '*Quem Deus vult perdere, prius dementat*'. A Latin phrase originating in a scholastic's quotation of an unknown poet commenting on Sophocles' *Antigone*. I am indebted to Dr E. D. Hunt of the Department of Classics, University of Durham, for tracing the origin of this reference.

Gospel narrative and of the wider implications of its
language, which is 'of necessity metaphysical in character'
(*GLT,* 15). On the other hand, we also note the description of this
narrative scheme through the use of such conceptions as a 'meta-
history' that 'invades the historical series' (*GLT,* 16) and of time
broken in upon and 'invalidated' (*GLT,* 15) by God's eternity,
besides the use of the adjective terrible' to describe the 'tale of
Christ's coming and rejection' (*GLT,* 16), conceptions which
once more owed much to MacKinnon's 'Barth', despite the
disclaimer that he had not 'surrendered himself to the
contemporary mood of anti-rationalism' (*GLT,* 16).
MacKinnon's further defence against the charge of 'Barthianism'
consists of an appeal, again later consistently pursued, to the
combination of rationalism in method with a recognition of the
incapacity of reason exemplified in the scholastic theologies of
Gardeil and Penido. MacKinnon's recognition, with Barth, that
'There can be no way from man to God unless there has been first
set in the wilderness a way from God to man' (*GLT,* 21), is
complemented by the equally mutual (although differently
executed) appeal to analogy. The rhetorical use of a conceptual
vocabulary drawn from dialectical theology (in the first instance,
as regards its extremity, Barthian, but later, with the increasing
stress upon rationality, Brunnerian), coexists with scholastic
conceptions flowing from the neo-Thomist revival.
Overshadowing all is a massive commitment and adherence to the
paradoxes of Crucifixion and Resurrection into which the
dialectic of nature and grace is assumed (*GLT,* 20). In a passage
specifically prefiguring the staurological revival in recent German
Lutheran theology, MacKinnon focused upon the Crucifixion in
the Biblical narrative:[5]

> Any exposition of the Christian doctrine of God must first posit
> the Cross. For Christians, theology is, and must be, a *theologia
> crucis,* a theology of the Cross. (*GLT,* 22)

There are other features (including the polemic conducted
against 'idealism') which strengthen the parallel between the 'early
MacKinnon' with the 'early Barth', Barth, above all, shares a

[5] The 'prophetic' prefiguring of the fully developed theologies of Jürgen
Moltmann and Eberhard Jüngel is unmistakable.

rhetorical stridency, a tendency towards excess which is, it is to be feared, a function of weakness rather than strength. Is it not possible, moreover plausible, that the very extremity of the presentation of the disruption of the created order by the onset, as MacKinnon puts it later, of God's 'attack' upon man in the incarnation, should be understood as varying *inversely* with the *actual* categorical purchase of the 'mighty acts of God' upon reality? The context of this poignant dilemma is recognizably social: we can deny revelation because 'around us, furnishing the centre of our national life, is an elaborate social structure that is the fruit of human apostasy' and 'we are its prisoners more intimately than we know' (*GLT*, 25). Here MacKinnon displays a refracted response to the concerns of the Christendom group to which he owed a critical allegiance, even to the extent of acknowledging the social fact that in 'liberal culture, which we all inherit to a greater or lesser degree, religion is an adventure of the privileged few' (*GLT*, 26).

I have already presented sufficient material to indicate that there is, in however problematic a form, a systematic theology *in nuce* in *God the Living and the True*. This theology was never expanded and developed: it remains a strident and rhetorical combination of insights drawn from the dialectical and neo-scholastic traditions, set over against the pervasive corruption of liberal theology. It has, to use an offensive image, the potential and the pathos of a stillborn foetus. Why was it that MacKinnon turned from this area of intellectual operation into the 'borderland' that is the dominant feature of his mature work. The answer to this question may lie at least in part in the extreme rhetorical character of the early work, which carried MacKinnon into a form of untenable theological and moral absolutism, the presuppositions and conditions of which remained both problematic and obscure. What were the transcendental conditions of the juxtaposed categories of philosophy and theology? Unlike many more famous but perhaps less courageous thinkers, but again like Barth, MacKinnon did not pursue a programme of simple question and subsequent answer, but had to reformulate and redirect the questions themselves. Thus, on an immediate level MacKinnon presumed to exploit the theological analogue of philosophical positivism:

> It is not for philosophy, whatever philosophy may be, to tell us whether or not God has intervened in the way in which he must have intervened for that intervention to merit the name of a revelation. That he has or has not is a matter of fact. We can only look and see. (GLT, 33)

Both at a deeper level of transcendental presupposition *and* in terms of global plausibility, tensions mounted which would lead to a philosophical redirection of effort accompanied by what must have surely been a pain-bound personal advocacy of the *disciplina arcani* and ascesis with regard to the sphere of theology itself. It is not then surprising that the divine self-communication is understood as tragedy informed by kenosis:

> The tragedy of our situation is that God can speak no other language to us, and that is the language we find it hardest to understand. For that sets over against human achievement divine failure. It is not a transvaluation, but an inversion of human failure. (GLT, 40)

The Nietzschian overtones indicate how close to the wind MacKinnon attempted to sail in the exploration of paradox. It is not, I believe, implausible to conceive of MacKinnon's professional commitment to the philosophical mode of discourse as a means of expressing what must ultimately be judged as a profound and yet risk-fraught engagement with the contemporary theological expression of the Christian tradition. This has as its leitmotif that acceptance of self-denigration, even self-destruction, which has constantly haunted MacKinnon's grasp of the Christian Gospel and twentieth-century reality. To this we shall return.

I am trying to indicate in this substantial passage devoted to MacKinnon's first book that a variety of currents of thought coalesce, but that their strident, forced synthesis is, once seen with historical hindsight, a staying operation. In contemporary terms it was otherwise, because whilst the demand for transcendental justification existed in the 'surface grammar' and its potent, violent rhetoric, it then found expression in an extension of that rhetoric into a form of transcendental ecclesiology in *The Church of God*,[6] the first signs of which we find in the later chapters of *God the Living and the True*. It was upon the rock of the Church that MacKinnon's desperate and paradoxical optimism was to founder; this ecclesiological betrayal still confronts us, as it was to confront MacKinnon in the aftermath of war. What are we to do with a Church that has effectively entered into a state of contradiction with its original nature?

Despite MacKinnon's recognition within Christianity of an analogue to the classical Greek virtue of *sophrosune*[7] in the 'continual tragedy of frustrated achievement' (*GLT*, 46) and his juxtaposition of the ultimacy of the Cross with the penultimacy of all human achievement, he nevertheless invests very heavily, too heavily, in the Church. In a passage that combines intense ecclesiological optimism with the Barthian dialectic of 'dissolution' MacKinnon tries to generate a conception of the Church that fuses social critique, theological objectivity and the renewal of the human:

> To some extent the Christian baptised into the death of Christ must always, if he is loyal to his Master, be a disruptive force in society. For in and through his baptism he accepts the verdict of rejection pronounced from the Cross upon man's cultural achievement and is thereby irrevocably committed to the task of pointing the whole social frame to its origin beyond itself. The Church in its members is both involved in, and independent of, the historical cultural moment. It is involved in it, for it is [a] compact of individual historical men and women who are here to-day and gone to-morrow, but it is independent of it, for it is at the same time the Body of him who is the dissolver of all cultural forms that destroy and impede the attainment by the creature of his true status. The instrument, whereby the sub-human processes that ever threaten to absorb the individual persons are themselves revealed as demonic, is the revelation of the Cross of Christ. (*GLT*, 47)

[6] For example, MacKinnon asserted that changed (and more sympathetic) attitudes towards Rome in England indicated that 'the Church of God suddenly again stands for something. And that something we may describe as the final and absolute revelation of Almighty God, given in the Word made flesh' (*CG*, 13). The difficulty of reconciling 'absoluteness' with the 'scandal of particularity' on the Cross remains with us.

[7] A word defined as 'soundness of mind, providence, discretion, moderation in desire'. See H. G. Little and R. Scott *A Greek-English Lexicon*, revised edn. (Oxford, 1958), p. 1751.

It is perhaps understandable that in the heat and dust of 1940 the pacifist MacKinnon should lay considerable reliance upon the invasive metaphor (as indeed the Swiss neutral Barth had done in the context of the First World War), but to this is added what we may describe analogously as *Gleichschaltung*. Thus whilst the Church originates in

> an event in time that is the fruit of the interaction of time by eternity. It is the mission of the Church, the mystical body of Christ, to be his instrument for the extension of that irruptive and disruptive activity that was his coming. In a memorable phrase, Kierkegaard described the Incarnation as God's attack upon man. (*GLT*, 53–4)

Are we wholly unfair if we see in this conception of the Church something of a triumphalist *Gleichschaltung* in the practical enactment, the ecclesial praxis, that is to follow *immediately* upon the incarnational 'fact'? This is a twentieth-century repristination of the Christian *Mythos* with, on the face of it, distinct totalitarian implications.

> Our scheme has been to lay bare the whole character of the impact of the saving work of Christ upon our particular cultural situation. The Church exists for no other purpose than that through her ministry and her life she may continually refer human conflicts to the point in history at which they find their resolution. Apologetics properly conceived is the allotting to successive human aspirations and human tragedies of their place within the whole context of the Christ-drama. (*GLT*, 55)

Again the Germanic undertones are further emphasized by MacKinnon's assertion of Brunner's conception of 'verbi-competence' in the setting of Maritain and Demant's neo-Thomism; for in 'the sphere of decisions rather than that of intelligence is to be found that potentiality which Christ in his coming actualises' (*GLT*, 58). That supremacy of *Tat* (act) over *Wort* (word), traceable to Goethe's self-conscious revision of German cultural expectations and values in the opening passage of *Faust*,[8] has its darker side, not least apparent when a theologian struggles with the internalization and privatization of Christian practice in contemporary industrialized culture and society. The

---

[8] Notoriously 'Am Anfang war die Tat'.

question is still with us: how do we renew Christian obedience
without, putting it as directly (and crudely) as possible, relapsing
into forms of authoritarian 'Christian fascism', or, as is all too
apparent in the sociological literature, the analogous
heteronomous and infantilized patterns of behaviour to be found
in some new religious movements? In this further sense
MacKinnon's early work remains topical.

From under this potentially questionable 'surface grammar'
emerges MacKinnon's positive engagement with the interconnection of intelligence and will that preludes any encounter
with revelation. This is beautifully expressed in a passage which
itself prefigures his later concerns with the foundations of moral
discourse as the presupposition of divine knowledge:

> We can and must so scrutinise the human intelligence as to
> understand how it is that man can even in a measure comprehend
> the possibility of an intersection of the historical by the meta-
> historical. It is impossible to maintain the primacy of the practical
> reason in the face of the necessity that man should, at least in a
> measure comprehend the character of that which has shattered his
> conceit . . . the character of that act of decision is itself open to a
> distinctively intellectual scrutiny. His character as decision is
> discerned by an act of definitely intellectual recognition.
> (*GLT*, 60)

This intricate and sophisticated discourse, the 'depth grammar' of
God the Living and the True, cohabits uneasily with the
totalitarian demand encapsulated in the rhetoric of staurological
obedience:[9]

> Christian theology is a *theologia crucis* simply in so far as it is the
> operation whereby the human intelligence adjusts its own
> appreciation of the human situation in the light of the impact
> upon it of the divine Word. (*GLT*, 63)

If we were to scrutinize these levels of assertion in terms of the
'post-modern' debate how would we categorize MacKinnon's
assertions? There are, I believe, all the three elements, pre-critical,
modern and post-modern, at work. Indeed, part of MacKinnon's
great strength has been a refusal to accept any premature

[9] The affinity between the view expressed in the following citation and that
developed at length in T. F. Torrance's *Theological Science* (London, 1969)
scarcely needs to be stressed.

resolution of this restless tri-polarity, not least because of his constant interest in, and appreciation of, the particularities of pastoral life in which the struggle in and for faith is so informed. In the rhetoric of 'catastrophe', contradiction and saving act jostle upon the surface of MacKinnon's discourse, and this occasionally reaches a point near to *reductio ad absurdum*: the incarnational narrative of the Fourth Gospel is seen as 'the description of a divine attack upon man in mercy and a corresponding counter attack of man upon God in hate' (*GLT*, 72). At the same time the nascent 'depth grammar' intones themes that are to be pursued with both passion and agnostic caution in the mature work:

> We have seen how tenuously man retains hold upon that sense of the transcendent character of the ground of his existence. We have seen again and again in human history how that intuition of finitude which is the most profound natural human intuition is debased, and how the infinite by reference to whom alone man discerns his individual finitude is located within and not without the initial process. None the less, the possibility of that intuition remains itself a guarantee of the at least partial validity of human ratiocination and of the possibility of man's being not unable to represent to himself the content of that which in Christ is revealed to him. (*GLT*, 66)

I am acutely conscious that in trying to juxtapose the 'surface grammar' of extravagant and violent theological rhetoric with the 'depth grammar' and the birth of a subtle and agnostic moral passion I have not done justice to the emergent intellectual personality which finds fuller expression in the mature works, *A Study in Ethical Theory* and *The Problem of Metaphysics*. This deliberate exploitation of the unresolved ambiguities of the 'early' MacKinnon has, however, a further motive. Recent doctrinal controversy in the Church of England indicates, in my judgement, that an analogous irresolution persists in the wider context which allows public discussion to proceed with no real meeting of minds. Thus it would be possible for a conservative of High or Low Church persuasion to appeal to MacKinnon's consistent insistence upon the historical particularity of the Crucifixion and Resurrection narratives, or, alternatively, for a liberal to draw upon MacKinnon's cautious, even agnostic, explorations of epistemology and ontology such as we find them in the mature work.

MacKinnon concludes *God the Living and the True* with an emphatic flourish: 'It is through man's cruelty that the glory of God is revealed' (*GLT*, 88). This little book culminates in a brutal attack upon the domestication of the doctrine of the Incarnation in English Anglican theology, and if intellectual convulsion therapy could bring back critical life to a tradition then this perhaps ought to; but signally it did not. But are we not now in a position to see, with hindsight, that the malaise in Western European Christianity is certainly more complex, if not more profound, than MacKinnon then understood it? MacKinnon then stated the Christian vocation in perennial terms:

> We can only come to ourselves through the death of ourselves,
> and the place of our burial we share with him whom we crucified.
> To know our worth we must admit we are worthless. Rather . . .
> to say that we are, we must first say that we are not. (*GLT*, 88).

This indicates more precisely that pattern of 'intellectual apostleship' to which we have already alluded. Whilst he was professionally to be a philosopher, MacKinnon's vocation was undertaken, may one suggest, as an incognito, a deliberate or perhaps not fully conscious assumption of a contrary nature behind which there still burns a theological furnace ignited under the original influence of Hoskyns. Purged of sentimentality and flaccid incarnationalism, MacKinnon glimpses the Cross through the mysterious mutual involution of knowledge of God and of self-knowledge, and in that instant we know that of ourselves; we, the perpetrators of cruelty, *hate* what we see there displayed. Now we know why, in Hoskyns' words, the incarnation is 'a dagger thrust in the heart of the world':

> As he is . . . we need to see him as he is. When we see him, we are
> at first shocked that his face is marred above the sons of men. But
> as he confronts us, we are enabled to see of what stuff we ourselves
> are. Then no longer does it surprise us that there is no beauty that
> *we* should *desire in him*.[10]

---

[10] Further to this, 'It is the recognition that his being is contingent upon the necessary Being that is ever against him which constitutes the deepest intellectual appreciation of which he is capable. And the corollary of this discernment is the recognition that we do not know what God is; we know only what he is not and what relation everything else has with him. We cannot deny that this particular metaphysical assertion is vested with the ethical character of genuine humility

Here, at what is inevitably the attainment of the first summit of a long mountain-range to be traversed in the years that were to come, MacKinnon's uncompromising renewed refraction of theological language owes much to Barth, certainly, but beyond that acknowledged influence there lies something even deeper and more tremendous. I suspect that it is perhaps Calvin, and his sense of the awful nature of God rejected by a perverse and depraved humanity, mediated through the Scottish Reformed tradition, that has likewise so impressed itself upon both MacKinnon and his great Scots compatriot Thomas Forsyth Torrance. Whatever else this consciousness may be, it succeeds in making unconditional grace in respect of both human particularity and structural sin the incontrovertible departure point of the Christian life and its conception of human growth. The apparent contradiction between this conviction and the lived doctrine and behavioural pattern of the Church (not least the Church of England) and, in particular, its senior ecclesiastics, has, I believe, led a considerable number of MacKinnon's disciples either consciously or unconsciously to follow his example and resist the temptation of ordination.

III   *Conclusion: moral passion and the failure of the Church*
In *The Church of God*, MacKinnon further outlines, again in language at times of considerable brutality, the role of the Church, using the 'Messianic' motifs then current in Anglican theology (one has only to recall A. M. Ramsey's *The Gospel and the Catholic Church* for confirmation of this). Where the former misperceived the nature of the Church was in the presentation of a *contrasting* rather than a *similar* parallel between Israel and the Church. Whilst in the liturgy the Church 'stands most assuredly as witness to a tortured world that, where its self-contradiction was most hideously manifest, in the apostasy of the very chosen

---

(here the obliqueness of double negation almost subverts the statement of this, one of MacKinnon's most fundamental and continuing postulates – R. H. R.). In the individual the appreciation of his own contingency is a psychological event which is fraught with a consciousness of his own insignificance. It is surely plain that such a recognition is distinguishable both in content and quality from the suggestion that man's significance is discernible in his own spiritual and material achievement.' (*GLT*, 73)

people of God, there was Christ attested as victor in his resurrection from the dead' (*CG*, 30) this contrast can no longer be sustained: it is the Church of God as a 'chosen people' that stands apostate, completing a deep irony in that the Church has *become* what it was called into existence to *deny*. The emblematic measure of this apostasy, seen by MacKinnon in his repeated later allusions to Bishop G. K. A. Bell and to the actions of senior ecclesiastics, is a recurrent theme that stems from an ecclesiological impossibilism grounded at least in part in an appropriation of dialectical theology, a MacKinnon's "Barth'" that stalks the pages of *God the Living and the True* and *The Church of God*. There is a legitimate sense in which it could be asserted that the history of twentieth-century Western theology ought to be written around the attempted responses to Barth's impossibilism, his dialectical reduction. In *A Study in Ethical Theory* and *The Problem of Metaphysics* MacKinnon was, however, to promote a highly Anglo-Saxon version of a 'back to Kant' move, effectively abandoning the explicit use of the dialectical mode.

If, as I believe is the case, dialectical theology continues to be the key to understanding the fate of Christian theology in this century, and if, as I also believe, it contains the only *theological* tools capable of cutting through the entangled misconceptions that obscure the enactment of the tradition in contemporary reality, then MacKinnon's early work as the supreme British assimilation of that theology as mediated by Hoskyns deserves a partial and qualified rehabilitation. Such a rehabilitation has to be an *interpretation*, a hermeneutical mediation that recognizes the different, even incommensurable levels of argument and conflicting centres of intellectual consciousness which have, as I indicated at the outset, to be understood *both* in relation to MacKinnon's development *and* in the historical social and cultural context of that development. Last but not least, a serious appropriation of the 'early' MacKinnon might help that lame, often lazy and financially undernourished English tradition to crystallize the Church of England's historical sense of time and place and wean it from the vaporous confusion of recent, often ineffectual theological controversy into serious theological engagement in the late twentieth century.

6

Barth and the Eschatology of Weimar: A Theology on its Way? (1988/91)

It is, perhaps, a truism to assert of contemporary culture and society that it is fragmented, and, furthermore, to repeat that the sustained and relatively stable grand narratives of Western and indeed world cultures have given way to the iridescent play of fluid identities competing with each other for our allegiance in a global market place. In this concluding paper we proceed on the assumption that the chaotic, unhinged state of German society[1] that followed the First World War may in certain relevant respects be understood to presage the 'postmodern condition'[2] as it is at present

[1] I am grateful to my Lancaster colleague Professor John Clayton for comments upon the earliest and the final drafts of this paper.

[2] The following provides a useful entry point into the discussion: J. F. Lyotard, *The Postmodern Condition* (Manchester: Manchester University Press, 1984). More recently David Harvey surveys the all-pervasive cultural import of postmodernity in *The Condition of Postmodernity An Enquiry into the Origin of Cultural Change* (Oxford: Blackwell, 1989). See also the clear, comprehensive and bibliographically well-supported essay by Roy Boyne and Ali Rattansi, 'The Theory and Politics of Postmodernism: By Way of an Introduction' in Boyne and Rattansi (eds.), *Postmodernism and Society* (London: Macmillan, 1990). For comparison on the level of spatio-temporal conceptualisation (a central issue in post-structuralism and postmodernity) see Paul Forman, 'Weimar Culture, Causality, and Quantum Theory, 1918–27: Adaptation by German Physicists and Mathematicians to a Hostile Intellectual Environment', in C. Chant and John Fauvel (eds.) *Darwin to Einstein Historical Studies on Science and Belief* (London: Longman/Open U.P., 1980), and D. Harvey, op. cit., chs. 16 and 17, 'Time-space compression and the rise of modernism as a cultural force' and 'Time-space compression and the postmodern condition'. See also J. Habermas, 'Modernity's Consciousness of Time and Its Need

experienced in the Anglo-Saxon world. Then, as now, the general sense of structure and stability, a complex of presumptions conveyed in and through ancestral identities, was called into doubt. Yet more alarming was and is the apparent loss of the subject, the victim of progressive attrition in the *Neuzeit* that has culminated in its nihilistic dispersal. This is a situation presupposed by the creative construction of identities through dynamic assertion rather than either pre-modern passivity and reception of the symbolic capital[3] of a monolithic tradition or the modernist imposition of identity through function in a social system determined by a Fordist division and organisation of labour. The characteristics of the first postmodernity of the period of the Weimar Republic (1919–33) were both fear-inducing, and potentially liberative: responsibility for the self and its identity devolved upon the individual. This insecurity can well be represented in the culture of Weimar by a pervasive crisis of the 'Word'.[4] Now, in the poststructuralist era of deconstruction, both self and language are once more called into question. Yet in the earlier era, through the creation and projection of dialectical theology, Karl Barth was able to confront and influence significant areas of a culture and society steeped in crisis. Given the parallel we have drawn, it is the understanding and positive interpretation of the function of Barth's theological agency, understood in its particular socio-cultural context, that remains a matter of continuing concern to us.[5]

---

for Self-Reassurance' in F. Lawrence (tr.), *The Philosophical Discourse of Modernity Twelve Lectures* (Cambridge: Polity Press, 1987), pp. 1–22. On the theological aspects see E. Wolfel, 'Theologische Hermeneutik in der Postmoderne', *Neue Zeitschrift für systematische Theologie und Religionsphilosophie*, vol. 29/2 (1987), pp. 210–27.

[3] A useful conception taken from Pierre Bourdieu, *Outline of a Theory of Practice*, R. Nice (tr.) (Cambridge U.P., 1977), pp. 171–83.

[4] Moeller van den Bruck's portentous utterance sums up an era: 'At bottom it is all very, very, very, simple: only by using concepts do we make everything complicated. What we seek is the Word.' This is a decadent parody of the German preoccupation with the nature and efficacy of language. This from the author of *Das Dritte Reich* (1922). See Fritz Stern's fascinating account of the wider background, *The Politics of Cultural Despair: A Study in the Rise of the Germanic Ideology* (Berkeley: California U.P. 1961).

[5] We thus disagree with those commentators upon Barth who try to divorce his theology from its context, declaring the latter a virtual irrelevance. We wish to capture a fuller understanding of the socio-rhetorical function of theological texts in context and we regard this as a necessary step in the generation of *theological* argument itself.

Karl Barth and his significant contemporaries lived the years of their early maturity in the aftermath of the First World War and thus witnessed the concomitant collapse of the imperial legacy of the nineteenth century.[6] We now in our turn observe the crisis of the Marxist-Leninist imperialism, the birth of which, Barth and many of his contemporaries initially regarded with near messianic enthusiasm.[7] Contrary to many predictions it is apparent that capitalism has survived albeit in continuing crisis.[8]

Central to the cultural context in which the theology of the young Barth was to make its mark was an intoxicating combination of nihilism and eschatological consciousness. This is an era under the sign of Nietzsche (*Im Zeichen Nietzsches* – H.U. von Balthasar). From bolder spirits it drew forth responses which owe much to Nietzsche's transvaluation of values (*Umwertung*

---

[6] Apart from the standard literature on Barth (beginning with E. Busch, *Karl Barth His life from letters and autobiographical texts* (London: SCM, 1976) see the following: C. Gestrich, *Neuzeitliches Denken und die Spaltung der dialektischen Theologie Zur Frage der naturlichen Theologie* (Tubingen: J. C. B. Mohr, 1977); the masterly essays of E. Przywara, *Ringen der Gegenwart Gesammelte Aufsätze* (Augsburg: Dr. Benno Filser Verlag, 1929); vol. I, in particular 'Um das Erbe Friedrich Nietzsches' pp. 169–79; and E. Troeltsch, *Der Historismus und seine Probleme* (Tübingen, 1922) vol. I, pp. 495–472; also Hans-Walter Krumweide's recent and excellent survey: *Evangelische Kirche und Theologie in der Weimarer Republik* (Neukirchen-Vluyn: Neukirchener Verlag, 1990); G. Rupp, *Culture Protestantism. German Liberal Theology at the Turn of the Twentieth Century* (Atlanta: Scholars Press, 1987[2]); and the earlier, K. Scholder, *Die Kirchen und das Dritte Reich*, vol. I, *Vorgeschichte und Zeit der Illusionen* (Frankfurt am Main, 1977). Useful collections are: K. D. Bracher, M. Funke, H.-A. Jacobsen (eds.), *Die Weimarer Republik 1918–1933. Politik, Wirtschaft, Gesellschaft* (Dusseldorf, 1987); and G. Schulz (ed.), *Ploetz: Weimarer Republik. Eine Nation in Umbruch* (Freiburg/Wurzburg, 1987). Further background is provided by P. Gay, *Weimar Culture: the insider as outsider* (London: Secker and Warburg, 1969); and H. S. Hughes' classic, *Consciousness and Society* (1958[1], repr. Brighton: Harvester, 1979).

[7] The publication of the political speeches of the young Barth are still awaited; the appearance of these might substantiate (or undermine) F. W. Marquardt's highly contentious representation of Barth's work as the theological concretion of Marxism-Leninism, see *Theologie und Sozialismus Das Beispiel Karl Barths* (Munich: Kaiser, 1972).

[8] The metaphorical extension of the 'rise', 'decline', 'persistance', and 'resurgence' of capitalism is commented upon in a series of works by R. H. Tawney, V. A. Demant and R. H. Preston. For a recent review of the career of these metaphors and an analysis of the tropes employed, see R. H. Roberts 'Rhetoric and the Resurgence of Capitalism' in R. H. Roberts and J. M. M. Good (eds.) *The Recovery of Rhetoric: Persuasive Discourse and Disciplinarity in the Human Sciences* (forthcoming).

aller Werte): thus Barth conceived of the eschatological crisis (*Krisis*), and Ernst Bloch of the anticipatory refunctioning (*Umfunktionierung*) of culture in the face of the nihilistic impulse.[9] Indeed, it would not be too extravagant to regard all these attempted transformations as attempts to enact supercession (or *Aufhebung*) in the realm of history (rather than on the Hegelian level of the idea).[10] Barth's *Römerbriefe* (in particular the second edition of 1922) presents the reader with a truly remarkable textuality in which a dialectical and eschatological supercession of the nihilistic condition is enacted, an act of realisation that implies a quasi-expressionistic creation *ex nihilo*.[11] This was undertaken in an era of which Gunther Wenz has written:

> The consciousness of total crisis and the necessity of a radical new beginning determined not only theology but the whole intellectual and spiritual climate of Germany in the early nineteen twenties. However varied the eventual outcome of the many alternative conceptions may have been, they were to a large degree at one in their diagnosis: the collapse of the old world was identified with the foundering of the individual self-determining will of the modern (*neuzeitlichen*) subject.[12]

[9] See Arno Munster, *Utopie, Messianismus und Apokalypse im Frühwerk von Ernst Bloch* (Frankfurt am Main: Suhrkamp, 1982).

[10] The word *Aufhebung* is notoriously difficult to render adequately in English, as Walter Kaufmann remarks 'Hegel's "*aufheben*" has been the despair of his translators', *Nietzsche Philosopher, Psychologist, Antichrist* (Princeton: Princeton U.P., 1950[1], 1974[4]), p. 236. *Aufhebung* denotes form of negation and dynamic positive transition into a higher sphere of existence; this may be a possibility wholly alien to the Anglo Saxon mind. For a profound commentary upon the ambiguities of this conception in Hegel's own thought (with particular reference to the *Phenomenology of Mind* and the *Lectures on the Philosophy of Religion*), see H. U. von Balthasar, 'Das Wesen der Aufhebung' in *Prometheus Studien zur Geschichte des deutschen Idealismus* (Heidelberg: F. H. Kerle Verlag, 1947[2]), pp. 589–611.

[11] The parallels between Barth's early post-war writings and those of the Expressionists are considerable; whilst this affinity has been noted this would merit fuller comparative study.

[12] 'Zwischen den Zeiten Einige Bemerkungen zum geschichtlichen Verständnis der theologischen Anfänge Karl Barths', *Neue Zeitschrift für systematische Theologie und Religionsphilosophie*, vol. 28/3 (1986), pp. 289ff. A useful introduction to the social and political background can be found (together with a wide-ranging bibliography) in Kurt Sontheimer, *Antidemokratisches Denken in der Weimarer Republik Die politischen Ideen des deutschen Nationalismus zwischen 1918 und 1933* (Munich: DTV, 1962[1], 1978).

The crisis of nihilism[13] was not as we have already implied, solely concerned with the dissolution of the subject as such. Moreover, as Michel Foucault has argued, in the modern period there is a loss of the original referent, the growing absence of the power of representation in language, a deficit sometimes referred to as the subversion of logocentricity; we all now mourn the loss of the 'word':[14]

> For now we no longer have that primary, that absolutely initial, word upon which the infinite movement of discourse was founded and by which it was limited; henceforth, language was to grow with no point of departure, no end, and no promise. It is the traversal of this futile yet fundamental space that the text of literature traces from day to day.[15]

[13] See K. Löwith, *Der europaische Nihilismus. Betrachtungen zur Vorgeschichte des europaischen Krieges* (1940), *Sämtliche Schriften*, vol. 2, pp. 473–540. Löwith's engagement with the origins of twentieth century nihilism is conducted through a series of essays on Nietzsche assembled in the *Sämtliche Schriften*, vol. 6. See also, D. Arendt (ed.), *Der Nihilismus als Phänomene der Geistesgeschichte in der wissenschaftlichen Diskussion unseres Jahrhunderts* (Darmstadt: WBG, 1974); Gottfried Hornig, 'Die Spaltung der dialektischen Theologie' in H. Andresen, op. cit., III, pp. 248ff.; H. Thielecke, *Nihilism* (London, 1962); and Hermann Rauschning, *Masken und Metamorphosen des Nihilismus Der Nihilismus des XX. Jahrhunderts* (Frankfurt am Main: Humboldt Verlag, 1954).

[14] Stephen Prickett reviews wider issues in *Words and the Word Language, poetics and biblical interpretation* (Cambridge: Cambridge U.P., 1986). The role of the discussion of the nature of language by the precursors of Barth is extremely important. Contributions by J. G. Herder, J. G. Hamann, Hegel, Wilhelm von Humboldt, and the devastating proto-Wittgensteinian riposte by F. Mauthner at the beginning of the present century are, together with the rise of modern linguistics with Saussure and subsequent developments, essential background to decipherment of the textual strategies of Barth and his contemporaries. Mark C. Taylor makes an interesting start in this direction in his *Deconstruction in Context: Literature and Philosophy* (Chicago: Chicago U.P., 1988). See also R. H. Roberts, 'Hegel and the "Synoptic Problem" – The New Translation of the *Lectures on the Philosophy of Religion*', *Journal of Theological Studies* (forthcoming).

[15] *The Order of Things An Archeology of the Human Sciences* (London: Tavistock, 1970), p. 44. The view of the nature of language here adopted is influenced by Foucault's discussion in chapter 2, 'The Prose of the World', where he records the decline of language as representation and the rise of literature as the locus of the 'being of language'; 'language', according to Foucault, 'gives the perpetual disruption of time the continuity of space, and it is the degree that it analyses, articulates, and patterns representation that it has the power to link our knowledge of things together across the dimension of time', p. 113. See also the methodological exposition in *The Archeology of Knowledge* (London: Tavistock, 1972). The implications of Foucault's thought for the study of religion are expounded by David Chichester, 'Michel Foucault and the Study of Religion', *Religious Studies Review*, vol. 12 (1986), pp. 1–9.

In Barth's early texts, and, indeed, in those of his contemporary Ernst Bloch, we find powerful individual strategies deployed in the context of this growing double crisis of the subject and of language itself. Looked at in broad historical perspective, this problematic is addressed in the course of Foucault's argument in *The Order of Things*, a text concerned with changes in the mode of representation and organisation of knowledge or the *episteme* by means of which the self-consciousness of each historical epoch and culture constitutes itself. In the modern period it is literature (having assumed the space vacated by theological discourse) that has been set the task 'of restoring absolutely primal discourse'.[16] Karl Barth, and equally Ernst Bloch, venture the reconstitution of such primal discourse, that is a recovery of the *Word* itself. Thus on the basis of such a contextualised parallel between the first and second postmodernities it is then as now feasible to pose the question as to whether, and in what sense Barth's theology, or a theology worked out in the spirit of Barth, may be said to be a theology on its way, a *theologia viatorum*.

With these issues in mind we proceed as follows. First, we set the broader scene with a presentation of the contrasting interpretations of the relation between secularisation and eschatology offered by Karl Löwith and Hans Blumenberg, respectively. Second, in the light of this contextualisation, we look more closely at the immediate intellectual setting of Barth's endeavours in which desperate measures were taken to ward off

[16] Foucault, op. cit., p. 41. Of course his argument is historical and directed in the first instance to the sixteenth century (and it is pertinent to recall Barth's comment in the Prefaces to the *Römerbrief* that he sought to bridge the gulf between the twentieth and the sixteenth centuries), yet, in the setting of postmodernism and its forerunner, what we have chosen to apostrophise as the 'eschatology of Weimar', the question as to whether this strategy is pre- or postmodern is unresolved. The ascription of a surrogate or even quasi-salvific role to literature is not of course unique, Terry Eagleton writes of F. R. Leavis' Cambridge journal *Scrutiny*, that whilst other subjects in the humanities 'had their place ; but it was a place to be assessed by the touchstone of literature, which was less like an academic subject than a spiritual exploration coterminous with the fate of civilization itself', *Literary Theory An Introduction* (Oxford: Basil Blackwell, 1983), p. 32. The theological overtones of the Jewish contemporary Walter Benjamin's posthumously published text of 1916, 'On Language as Such and on the Language of Man', E. Jephcott and K. Shorter (eds.), *One-Way Street and Other Writings* (London: NLB, 1979), pp. 107–23 are explicit and again provide an indication that the question of language and text as 'revelatory' artifacts had in effect passed from theology as such to literature.

and counter the complex threat of nihilism. These efforts were focused in the admission of the possibility of resolution in radical futurity, and this was then developed either in the self-consciously negative exploitation of an apparent window of opportunity presented in eschatological dialectics (Barth) or, more positively, in a quasi-apocalyptic categorial assertion (Bloch).[17] Third, through a limited but close textual study of parallel passages in the *Römerbriefe* of 1919 and 1922, it will become apparent in succeeding sections that in the second edition Barth abandoned the etiolated and threatened subject of 1919, and in place of this, dialectically combined the remaining possibilities of nihilism with the eschatological impulse and fused them together in a theology of *krisis* that skirts *katastrophe*. On this basis, we are able to draw out the implications of the strategy: Barth, having abandoned the subject, was obliged to create an eschatological discourse, a rhetoric of the dialectics of God and negation, which answered immediate contemporary needs with extraordinary efficacy. This discourse was, however, subject to the normal conditions of rhetorical success (that is the power to persuade and to establish an enduring commonplace), which depends upon the continuing congruence of the *ethos* of the originator of discourse and the *pathos* of the audience addressed. It becomes apparent that Barth fell victim of the overwhelming logocentric power of his own renewal of primal discourse. After the second *Römerbrief*, and supremely in the *Church Dogmatics* he became the entextualised, but no longer context-bound mouth of 'God', a god once tied to catastrophic circumstances of the Weimar era but then emancipated into its own temporality.

In conclusion, fourth, we shall argue that whilst the dialectical theology changed and progressively lost touch with all but its self-created audience (in the first place the collaborators in, and readers of, the journal *Zwischen den Zeiten*), this strategy nevertheless was, and *remains* of indispensable importance to contemporary and future theological endeavour. We shall in turn outline a *theologia viatorum* conceived in the spirit and tradition of the early work of Barth which takes as its point of departure the dialectical juxtaposition of three elements: first, an ongoing

[17] See R. H. Roberts, *Hope and Its Hieroglyph: A Critical Decipherment of Ernst Bloch's "Principle of Hope"* (Atlanta: Scholars Press, 1990), ch. 1.

historical 'archeology' of the displacement and migration of the
sacred as seen in the history of the emergence and differentiation
of the human sciences (*les sciences humaines*);[18] second, the active,
and initially dialectical juxtaposition of the thesis of wide-ranging
exploration of the inter-disciplinary manifold of the
contemporary human sciences with the antithesis of engagement
with the theological tradition; and, third, the generation out of
this confrontation of an *episteme* for refunctioned theological
discourse and the possibility of a post-Barth*ian* systematic
theology. This would be a theology true to Barth's dialectics of
concealment and disclosure yet informed by engagement with the
history of the human sciences, and generated in a discourse
projected beyond crude dialectical confrontation, yet fully
conscious of the implication of all discourse in the social context
of its own constitution.[19]

I   *History, eschatology and secularisation: Löwith and Blumenberg*
The gradual secularisation of European consciousness over the
last two hundred years is a complex phenomenon open to a
variety of interpretations[20] from which we draw two dominant

[18] The use of this term follows that of my Durham colleagues:
'human sciences', like the German *Geisteswissenschaft*, encompasses a
number of different disciplines, including sociology, psychology,
anthropology, and linguistics. Unlike 'social sciences' it suggests a critical
and historical approach which transcends these specialisms and links their
interests with those of philosophy, literary criticism, history, aesthetics,
law, and politics.
in the opening editorial of *History of the Human Sciences*, I/1 (1987) pp. 1–2.
[19] It would be possible to extend this analytical venture into a study of post
Second World War German literature, particular that of the 70s and 80s, see Paul
Konrad Kurz (ed.), *Apokalyptische Zeit Zur Literatur der mittleren 80er Jahre*
(Frankfurt am Main: Verlag Josef Knecht, 1987) where an awareness of an ending
of time is posed by the threat of nuclear war.
[20] Important but contrasting studies of this phenomenon indicate an engaging
lack of theoretical consensus: few doubt the facts of secularization, yet many
dispute the feasability of subsuming these into a single scheme of interpretation.
For contrasting viewpoints, see for example: Henry Chadwick, *The Secularization
of the European Mind in the 19th Century* (Cambridge: Cambridge U.P., 1975); W.
Jaeschke (in a response to Friedrich Gogarten), *Die Suche nach den
eschatologischen Wurzeln der Geschichtsphilosophie Eine historische Kritik der
Säkularisierungsthese* (Munich: Chr. Kaiser Verlag, 1976); David Martin, *The
Religious and the Secular. Studies in Secularization* (London: Routledge and Kegan
Paul, 1969) and *A General Theory of Secularization* (Oxford: Basil Blackwell,
1978); Bryan Wilson, *Religion in Secular Society. A Sociological Comment*

and contrasting examples, which admit rather than reduce theological discourse *a priori.* Both Karl Löwith in his book *Meaning in History*[21] and his critic, Hans Blumenberg, in *The Legitimacy of the Modern Age*,[22] venture global hypotheses that extend to the whole history of Western culture. Both operate in century marked, so far as religious thought is concerned, by the epochal work of Karl Barth; indeed, Löwith's response to the dialectical theology was lifelong. Both seek in different ways to come to terms with what we call the divine digression; they attempt to answer the question as to whether the history of the human encounter with God is the authentic destiny of humanity, or, alternatively, whether it should be understood as a persistent aberration that has been gradually corrected over centuries of philosophical reflection and scientific discovery.

(i)   *Löwith and reduced eschatological explanation*
In his book *Meaning in History* (published in 1949, a fateful year in German history) Karl Löwith propounded a form of common sense, doubtless born of recent experience, a 'detached position in which faith and scepticism coincide'. Löwith's reaction to a perverse modernity was true to eschatological inheritance of Augustine and to the spirit of dialectical theology, albeit in a somewhat reduced forms:

> More intelligent than the superior vision of philosophers and theologians is the common sense of the natural man and the uncommon sense of the Christian believer. Neither pretends to discern on the canvas of human history the purpose of God or of the historical process itself. They rather seek to set man free from the world's oppressive history by suggesting an attitude, either of scepticism or of faith, which is rooted in an experience certainly by

---

(Harmondsworth: Penguin, 1969) and *Contemporary Transformations of Religion* (Oxford: Oxford U.P., 1976). Useful bibliographical guidance is provided in Karel Dobbelaere, *Secularization: A Multi-Dimensional Concept* (London: Sage, 1981) and H.-H. Schrey (ed.), *Säkulisierung* (Darmstadt: WBG, 1981).

[21] (London,1949[1], 1967[2]). The German version, *Weltgeschichte und Heilsgeschehen Die theologischen Voraussetzungen der Geschichtsphilosophie*, appears in *Sämtliche Schriften* (Stuttgart J. B. Metzlersche Verlagsbuchhandlung, 1983) vol. I. The original was written in English during Löwith's American exile.

[22] R. M. Wallace (tr.), *The Legitimacy of the Modern Age* (Cambridge, Mass.: MIT, 1976).

history but detached from and surpassing it, and thus enabling
man to endure it with mature resignation or faithful expectation.
Religious faith is so little at variance with scepticism that both are
rather united by their common opposition to the prescription of
settled knowledge.[23]

Löwith resists the assertion of a dogmatic *Neuzeit* or modernity
and the concomitant existence of a hiatus dividing the present
from the pre-critical, non-historical past. Real history is not the
exclusive product of such modernity:

Against this common opinion that proper history begins only in
modern times, with the eighteenth century, the following outline
aims to show that the philosophy of history originates with the
Hebrew and Christian faith in a fulfilment and that it ends with
the secularisation of its eschatological pattern.[24]

Löwith substantiates his case through a detailed analysis of the
emergence of the philosophy of history in the work of Burckhardt,
Marx, Hegel, Proudhon, Condorcet, Turgot, Voltaire, Vico,
Bossuet, Joachim of Fiore, Augustine, and Orosius to the 'biblical
view of history'. We suggest that Löwith's ability to combine the
renunciation of hope (here Jacob Burckhardt is decisive in his
estimation) with a continuing loyalty to the biblical view (an
irreducible foundation) was paradoxically enabled by the role
dialectical theology played in the development of his thought.[25]
Indeed, according to Löwith, the interpretation of Western
history would be inconceivable without its biblical impulse which
makes a perennial search for theodicy the leitmotif of its
consciousness. Rejecting decisively any retreat into historically-
displaced reconstructions of consciousness and identity (like those
of Kierkegaard into early pre-Constantinian Christianity or
Nietzsche into pre-Classical Greek paganism), Löwith argues
that:

The outstanding element, however, out of which an interpretation
of history could arise at all, is the basic experience of evil and
suffering and of man's quest for happiness. The interpretation of

[23] Löwith, *Meaning*, op. cit., p. vi.
[24] Löwith, loc. cit.
[25] See 'Grundzüge der Entwicklung der Phänomenologie zur Philosophie und
ihr Verhältnis zur protestantichen Theologie' (1930) in *Sämtliche Schriften* vol. 3,
pp. 33–95 (esp. pp. 76ff.).

history is in the last analysis, an attempt to understand the meaning of suffering by historical action.[26]

History, that is Western historical consciousness, is resolved into two alternatives, even antitheses:

> In the Western world the problem of suffering has been faced in two different ways: by the myth of Prometheus and by faith in Christ – the one a rebel, the other a servant.[27]

Whilst the question as to the meaning of history 'takes one's breath away; it transports us into a vacuum which only hope and faith can fill',[28] this is, nevertheless, a vestigially Christian standpoint which is used as a basis for the repudiation of Nietzsche and his conception of the doctrine of eternal recurrence.[29] For Löwith, in the final analysis it is salvation history that provides the inner rationale of world history (hence the resonant German title of his book: *Weltgeschichte und Heilsgeschehen*). This viewpoint is sustained solely through eschatology:[30] The temporal

---

[26] Löwith, op. cit., p. 3.

[27] Op. cit., p. 3. Another approach in some ways parallel with these alternatives can be constructed through a hermeneutics of history suggested by Hegel's historical mythologisation of the parable of Lordship and Bondage in the *Phenomenology of Mind* (1807), a point well understood by Bloch in his depiction of the theology of Barth in 'Weiterung: Deutscher Quietismus und der Lutherherr', *Thomas Münzer als Theologe der Revolution* (1921), *Gesamtausgabe* (Frankfurt am Main: Suhrkamp, 1977), vol. 2, pp. 175–81. See also, R. H. Roberts, 'The Reception of Hegel's Parable of the "Lord and Bondsman"', *New Comparison A Journal of Comparative and General Literary Studies*, vol. 5 (1988), pp. 23–39.

[28] Löwith, op. cit., p. 4.

[29] Löwith has devoted a great deal of attention to this strange element in Nietzsche's thought, see, for example, the substantial essay: *Nietzsches Philosophie der ewigen Wiederkehr des Gleichen* (1935), *Sämtliche Schriften* vol. 6, pp. 101–384, and the brief note, 'Nietzsche's Doctrine of eternal recurrence' (1945), op. cit. pp. 415–426. Of the doctrine Löwith writes, 'It breaks asunder because the will to eternalize the chance fact of the modern ego does not fit into the assertion of the impersonal eternal cycle of the natural world', p. 426. Both Barth and Bloch resist the cyclic conception, despite their preoccupation with Nietzsche (transient with regard to the former, lifelong as regards the latter).

[30] Löwith's eschatological emphasis (like his Prometheus/Christ contrast) has remained a feature of undiminished importance in post-Second World War German theology. For example, J. Moltmann's collection of texts from the dialectical theology of the Weimar period in the *Anfänge der dialektischen Theologie* (Munich, 1966–7), 2 vols. and his *Theology of Hope: On the Ground and Implications of a Christian Eschatology* (London: SCM, 1967) are evidence of this. Indispensable sources for the background and persistence of eschatological motifs

horizon for a final goal is an eschatological future, and the future exists for us only by expectation and hope. The ultimate meaning of transcendent purpose is focused in an expected future. Löwith retains the possibility of the mythological conceptualisation of history (whilst resigning theology) and will not relinquish the eschatological horizon for:

> 'The future in the "true" form of history, provided that the truth abides in the foundation of the Christian occident, whose historical consciousness is, indeed, determined by an easchatological motivation, from Isaiah to Marx, from Augustine to Hegel, from Joachim to Schelling.'[31]

Löwith recognises the force of a post-Nietzschian modernity, yet he remains Augustinian,[32] and resists consistent secularity and relativism:

> We are neither ancient ancients nor ancient Christians, but Moderns, that is, a more or less inconsistent compound of both traditions. The Greek historians wrote pragmatic history centered around a great political event; the Church fathers developed from Hebrew prophecy and Christian eschatology a theology of history focused on the supra-historical events of creation, incarnation and consummation; the moderns elaborate a philosophy of history by secularizing theological principles and applying them to an ever increasing number of empirical facts.'[33]

Löwith therefore retains his allegiance to the Western Latin tradition, reinforced indirectly by the dialectical theology and in a form purged by the events of the twentieth century.

---

in twentieth century theology and philosophy are, for the early period: Elmar Fastenrath, 'IN VITAM AETERNAM' *Grundzüge christlicher Eschatologie in der ersten Hälfte des 20. Jahrhunderts* (Sankt Ottilien: Eos Verlag, 1982) (this work contains over one hundred and forty pages of bibliography), and for the later: G. Sauter, *Zukunft und Verheissung Das Problem der Zukunft in der gegenwärtigen theologischen und philosophischen Diskussion* (Zurich: Theologischer Verlag, 1965).
[31] Löwith, op. cit., p. 18.
[32] There are affinities between Löwith's qualified Augustinianism and A. J. Milbank's lengthy and complex rehabilitation of Christian social theory and critique of the Enlightenment project (and the contemporary sociology of religion) in *Theology and Social Theory Beyond Secular Reason* (Oxford: Basil Blackwell, 1990). Both are engaged with the repristination of forms of Augustianism.
[33] Löwith, op. cit., p. 19.

(ii)   *Blumenberg's "detour" and the legitimation of modernity*

In his magisterial work *Die Legitimität der Neuzeit* (1966) Hans Blumenberg attacked Löwith's conception of secularisation and hypothesised an alternative, negatively Nietzschian and anti-theological interpretation of the history of the West. The core of Blumenberg's book consists in an analysis of the history of dogma, of philosophy as it has existed in synthesis with Christianity, the rise of natural science, and the final retreat of the eschatological horizon which is conducted in terms dictated by Nietzsche. The theory is advanced that the Western tradition may be understood as a whole through an account of the interaction between the ancestral Augustinian model of knowing as *memoria* (and the consequent denigration of *curiositas*) on the one hand, and, on the other, the progressive exaltation of the spirit of inquiry and the displacement of theological explanation. Thus far from the Enlightenment appearing as a diversionary interlude, Blumenberg conceives it as the recovery of a quest that began long ago in certain strands of Classical, pre-Christian philosophy, but which was later stifled by Christianity. The recovery of a pre-Christian humanity from its false detour into the sustained false mediation of the doctrine of God in the Christian West is the exultant task of the enlightened philosopher. The modern age, *Neuzeit*, is for Blumenberg 'legitimate' and normative: the nineteenth and twentieth century crisis of the formation of humanity and the human awaits consistent completion. Marx, Nietzsche, Dilthey, Weber, Cassirer, Heidegger, Husserl, Adorno and Horkheimer all remain to some degree bewitched by an unconquered past. Blumenberg ambitiously proposes the historical hermeneutics of final conquest, an undercutting of the basis upon which the very discourse of 'secularisation' has drawn for its continuing social and cultural leverage:

> We are describing something that would not even exist for us if we were not still in position to understand what had to precede it, what the hope of salvation, what the next world, transcendence, divine judgement, refraining from involvement in the world and falling under the influence of the world once meant – that is to understand the elements of that 'unworldliness' that must after all be implied as a point of departure if we are to be able to speak of "secularisation".[34]

[34] Blumenberg, op. cit., p. 3.

Paradoxically, it was both the original form of dialectical theology (and by direct implication the work of Karl Barth) and its renewal in the 'radical theology' of the nineteen sixties which, according to Blumenberg, went far to expose the convolutions of 'secularisation':

> The very people who were attempting to restore the radicalness of the original religious distance from the world and to renew theology's declaration of transcendence 'dialectically' could see in the massive evidence of the world as 'worldliness' the advantage of its unmistakeable character of immanence ... A theology of 'division', of crisis, had to be interested in making clear the worldliness of the world rather than in overlaying it with the sacred. That is what gave the use of the term 'secularisation' its specific theological pathos.[35]

Blumenberg then baldly poses the question which cuts through the entanglement and disposes summarily of the cultural aggregation of reason and faith in sceptical hope that had been proposed by Löwith. Would it not be more plausible to argue that the theological 'detour' had been 'illegitimate' in principle?

> The problem in such a case, quite logically, is not secularization but the detour that made it necessary in the first place. For detours, of course, we do have the trusty schema of the consciousness that finds its way to itself, that achieves consciousness of its own identity. What is in order after this detour is no longer the division of sheep from goats, the clarification of fronts, but rather the unveiling of the identity of the one interest for the realization of which a God had to exist at most as an assistant in the process of its accomplishment. But would it not have been better if He had not existed at all?[36]

Blumenberg locates the watershed in western history at the transition represented by Nicholas of Cusa and Giordano Bruno, the point at which theoretical curiosity (*curiositas*) ceased to be regarded as perverse and took up the direction which led to its becoming the normative scientific outlook of full-blown modernity. Löwith and Blumenberg stand, however, in opposition, on the one side the former defends the indispensable

[35] Blumenberg, op. cit., p. 5.
[36] Blumenberg, op. cit., p. 6.

role of an eschatologically-conditioned philosophy of history in the search for the generation of meaning in a reduced but inevitable theodicy; on the other, the latter regards the nostalgic interpretation of Western history as the record of the decline of eschatological consciousness into its secularised residuum as compounding a mistaken adherence to a false detour. This is the defence of a diversion away from an original pagan *homo curiositas* who was corrupted by the incursion of Jewish and Christian biblical consciousness of the divine in history and over against humankind. Both Löwith and Blumenberg respond to Barth and to the dialectical theology; both indeed sense a certain pathos in the continuing de-eschatologisation of Western culture. Yet, in the final account, they come down on opposite sides of the great divide which was re-energised and reformulated in an extreme and concentrated way by Karl Barth at a time of perhaps unparalleled social and cultural crisis, a turning point in religious history towards which we now turn our attention.

II   *Eschatology, Neokantianism, and the dialectics of extremity*
It has become apparent in our foregoing account of the reception of Barth's theology in the Anglo-Saxon world that the cultural transmission of 'dialectical theology' and the 'theology of crisis' was enabled or inhibited in accordance with the actual capacity of any given social context to facilitate the necessary cultural resonance. We now isolate some of those features of germanophone culture which helped Barth's early theology towards its quite remarkable success. This will, in turn, permit us to tease out some of the intricacies of Barth's own eschatology and to explain its dialectical ingestion and transmutation of radical nihilism.[37]

We also earlier saw how German culture and society were catastrophically affected in the aftermath of the Armistice. The theology of history implicated in the spirit of 1914 had proved a costly deceit, the pact between Church and state collapsed, and the Bolshevism threatened a political order already in disorder. The cult of Nietzsche and calls for a prophet sounded out over the

---

[37] Another way of looking at the crisis of the real can be found in J.P. Stern's important article "'Reality' in early Twentieth-century German Literature" in A. Phillips Griffiths, *Philosophy and Literature* (Cambridge: Cambridge U.P., 1984), pp. 41–57.

cultural wasteland of nihilism. For Karl Barth, Ernst Bloch, and Georg Lukács, besides Martin Heidegger,[38] nihilism was the point at which confrontation with the consequences of absolute immanence took place. Each had to strike out dialectically from this point of immanent departure. Adorno's epigram (in defence of Nietzsche) is applicable here: 'Thought honours itself by defending what is damned as nihilism'.[39] Writing with hindsight in 1954, Herbert Rauschning characterised twentieth century nihilism as:

> paradoxical . . . A nothing which is simple negation proves in its activity to be a meaningful something. Nihilism is not a condition; it is a process. It is a devaluation, not the absence of values. It is a 'de-realisation', not *das Nichts*. Nihilism is neither a teaching nor a goal in itself. However it 'unmasks' every teaching as arbitrary and opposes every action to its goal. It has no essence or form of its own. It is an activity, but it has itself no *being*. (*Er ist Wirkung, aber er selbst ist kein Sein*)[40]

Nihilism presented the alternatives of either seeking out a way of being-in-becoming or embracing annihilation: the only ontological space left in the material order, historical, social, and biological,[41] lay in the postulation of a final horizon of time in the 'last days', or a 'between the times' somehow inserted in the interstices of the temporal order itself. It is out of the unmasking of the pretensions of being that the new modes of realisation, the sustained dialectical protests and the attempted sublations were to arise, and in terms of which they may be understood. The very titles of Karl Kraus' *Die letzen Tagen der Menschheit* (1921) and of the journal of the dialectical theology, *Zwischen den Zeiten*, indicate that on the level of public consciousness,

---

[38] Jurgen Habermas provides an admirably lucid account of the function of Heidegger's thought in the context of the crisis of twentieth century philosophy in "The Undermining of Western Rationalism through the Critique of Metaphysics", op. cit., pp. 131–60.

[39] *Negative Dialectics* (London: RKP, 1973), p. 381.

[40] Blumenberg, op. cit. p. 7.

[41] Here the names and doctrines of other architects of German modernity: Troeltsch and historicism; Weber and the 'iron cage'; Ernst Mach and Eugen Dühring's positivism and Ernst Haeckel's '*Welträtsel*' of evolutionary materialism spring to mind, respectively. The currents of thought were concisely mapped at the turn of the century by Ernst Bloch's Würzburg teacher, Oswald Külpe, in *Die Philosophie der Gegenwart in Deutschland Eine Charakteristik ihrer Hauptrichtungen nach Vorträgen* (Leipzig: B. G. Taubner, 1902).

eschatologically-nuanced cultural commonplaces informed the thought of the time.[42] This popularly felt sense of time's end had a corresponding philosophical context[43] which now provide us with a framework for comparative analysis in which the strategies of the *Römerbriefe* and *Geist der Utopie*, besides Lukác's *Geschichte und Klassenbewusstsein* and Heidegger's *Sein und Zeit* make sense. Of this period, the last stage of the breakdown of classical German philosophy, the Marxist Georgy Lukács wrote as follows:

> Classical philosophy is able to think the deepest and most fundamental problem of the development of bourgeois society to the very end – on the plane of philosophy. And – in thought – it is able to drive all the paradoxes of its position to the extreme point where the necessity of going beyond this historical stage in mankind's development . . . can at least be seen as a problem.[44]

The drive to go 'beyond' had long been a feature of the German (ultimately Carolingian and Neoplatonic) dialectical tradition that culminated in the Hegelian '*Aufhebung*'. This urge has undergone displacement and consequent transmutation in the course of the nineteenth and twentieth centuries.[45] Our approach to the phenomenon is influenced by our interest in the eschatological and religious dimensions of such displacements of

[42] Another example is the (ironically entitled) Expressionist collection, K. Pinthus (ed.), *Menschheitsdämmerung. Symphonie jüngster Dichtung* (Berlin: E. Rowohlt, 1920). The thematic range is illustrated in T. Anz and M. Stark (eds.), *Expressionismus Manifeste und Dokumente zur deutschen Literatur 1910–1920* (Stuttgart: J. B. Metzler, 1982). The words of the critic Margarete Susman are indicative:

> Our world must be made new, but this can only come about in agonised convulsions – there is no other way. The days of serenity, of gracefulness, of reticence, of modesty are over. God does not come to us ill-starred mortals on the wings of a gentle breeze. Expressionism has a mission in which beauty plays no part. When expression has become the sole will and principle of an age, and when the naked soul kneels down and cries out to God, beauty is like a robe that has been consumed by flames, while despair manifests itself in forms filled only with the sound of screams and prayers.

cited in translation by Ronald Taylor, *Literature and Society in German 1918–1945* (Brighton: Harvester, 1980), p. 34.

[43] See P. Forman, op. cit., n. 1 above.

[44] *History and Class Consciousness Studies in Marxist Dialectics* (London: Merlin Press, 1971), p. 121.

[45] The long history of the philosophical traditions that led into German 'bourgeois' idealism is presented by Leszek Kolakowski in his brilliant resume: 'The Origins of Dialectic', *Main Currents of Marxism* (Oxford: Clarendon Press, 1978) vol. I, pp. 9–80.

the drive towards *Aufhebung*. The underlying intellectual currents
of the time have been investigated on a magisterial scale by Elmar
Fastenrath, who begins his monumental study IN VITAM
AETERNAM[46] with a fascinating account of the philosophical
context of Protestant and Catholic eschatological thinking in the
first half of the present century. Fastenrath first recognises with
R. Guardini (1940) the apparent distance of those matters of
which eschatology speaks from the sensitivities of modern man.
The late nineteenth century expression of this distance was
dominated by evolutionism and materialist monism, embodied
above all in the figure of Ernst Haeckel (1834–1919) who
transformed Darwin's theory of human descent into a causal-
mechanical doctrine and reduced consciousness to a function of
matter and the *Monistenbund*, the Monist League, which
campaigned for the public acceptance of these ideas.[47] Some, like
the philosophers Eduard von Hartmann and Rudolf Hermann
Lotze, struggled with the naturalistic and mechanistic world-
outlook of scientific monism in order to formulate an inductive
metaphysics underpinned by research in natural science. As early
as 1874 von Hartmann understood the implications of what he
saw as the retreat of the world into *das Nichts* and the
decomposition of Christianity.[48] The pattern of philosophical
developments that took place during this period is highly
complex, as a variety of strategies were evolved through the extensive
recycling of ideas drawn in the main from the earlier stages of the
German tradition, above all this is apparent in Neokantianism.[49]

[46] See Fastenrath, op. cit. The first part of this book, 'Der philosophie- und
theologiegeschichtliche Hintergrund fur die neuern Entwürfe christliche
Eschatologie' is an indispensable source, pp. 1–124.

[47] As we have seen earlier in our study of the reception of the theology of Karl
Barth it was the proselytising success of such groups amongst the working classes
which caused the churches particular alarm.

[48] *Die Selbstzersetzung des Christentums und die Religion der Zukunft* (Berlin,
1874). Fastenrath remarks as follows, and thereby gives an indication of von
Hartmann's prescience, '*In der Erlösung vom Dasein, in der Rückkehr dieser
leidvollen Welt ins Nichts, sah er das Ziel der ganzen Menschheitsentwicklung. Da er
das ganze Christentum fast allenthalben als in einem Prozess der Selbstzersetzung
befindlich sah*,' op. cit., pp. 18–9.

[49] Lewis White Beck's article 'Neo-Kantianism' in P. Edwards (ed.) *The
Encyclopaedia of Philosophy* (New York: Macmillan, 1967) vol. 5, pp. 469–73
though now somewhat dated still provides an excellent overview of the South
German schools.

In this transitional period regarded as a whole, marked at its extremes by the foundation of the first psychological laboratory in Leipzig in 1879 by Wilhelm Wundt (1832–1920) and ending with Edmund Husserl's first outline of the *Crisis of the European Sciences* of 1934,[50] two major streams of thought may be discerned of considerable importance for the religious and theological dimensions with which we are primarily concerned. These are Neokantianism and varieties of '*Lebensphilosophie*', respectively, tendencies that asserted formal order and the vitalist impulse against the reductive tendencies of materialist positivism and the nihilistic cult of Nietzsche. Neokantianism represented the idealist (as opposed to the vitalist) reaction to scientism, and in its founder Friedrich Albert Lange (1928–1875) and chief Marburg proponents, Hermann Cohen (1843–1918) and Paul Natorp (1851–1924), struggled to reconcile the invasive (and experimental) scientific outlook with the German idealist tradition. The structures provided by Neokantianism (expressed in the refunctioning of forms of transcendental argument, critique and the articulation of schemata) and the life impulse in *Lebensphilosophie* did not in themselves provide the basis of an ontology that could confound the pervasive relativism quintessentially expressed in Nietzschian nihilism. Immediately after the First World War the Catholic philosopher-theologian Erich Przywara represented the factors underlying the philosophical repetitions of the idealist tradition in Neokantianism in remythologised theological terms as the rediscovery of:

> the primal Lutheran Moment of the dynamic God who is restlessly present to struggling man as the ungraspable will of fate.[51]

Fastenrath represents Neokantianism as an overextended rationalism which was ultimately incapable of resisting its own conflicting tendencies seen in the materialist reduction into monism and the vitalist relapse into irrationalist mysticism, the latter being a tendency which was later to have devastating historical implications.

[50] David Carr (tr. and ed.), *The Crisis of European Sciences and Transcendental Phenomenology An Introduction to Phenomenological Philosophy* (Evanston: Northwestern U.P., 1970).

[51] *Ringen der Gegenwart*, op. cit., vol. I, p. 321.

A figure of great and continuing importance was Wilhelm Dilthey (1833–1911), who attempted to re-open a broadly-based and differentiated analysis of the human condition in the face of positivistic natural science by exhibiting multiple life-phenomena latent within the contexts of their historical development. With realism Dilthey had argued in 1911, that world-views (*Weltanschauungen*) were not simply:

> the products of thought. They do not arise out of the bare will to know . . . It is out of the behaviour experience of life itself that the structure of our psychical totality arises. The raising of life to the conscious knowledge of reality, the dignifying of life and the exercise of the will is slow and burdensome labour, which humanity has undertaken in the course of the development of its views of life.[52]

In Dilthey's historicist vision the conflicts within his typology of metaphysical systems is a reflection of different responses to questions about knowledge of reality, the evaluation of life and the setting of human goals. This was a historical and cultural anthropology pursued without arbitrary or tyrannical commitment to any reductive scheme, be it idealist or materialist monism. Dilthey's pursuit of something approaching a universal '*Wirkungszusammenhang*', the comprehension of the totality within a given world-view or system, and the contextualisation of these constructions within the whole of the intellectual-historical life-process, provide the basis for his differentiated pluralism which was in its turn immensely influential. Nevertheless, according to Fastenrath, Dilthey's historical pluralism legitimated the diverse streams of irrational mysticism behind which loomed the 'hidden guardian spirit (*Schutzgeist*) of Nietzsche'.[53] Equally, Dilthey's thought was not capable of restraining the forces latent within the emergent differentiation that he justified on the basis of value-free historical comprehensiveness.

[52] 'Die Typen der Weltanschauung und ihre Ausbildung in den metaphysischen Systemen' in H. Nohl (ed.) *Die Philosophie des Lebens. Aus den Schriften W. Wilthey* (Stuttgart, 1961) p. 92. Dilthey's seminal text (1927) in R. J. Betonzos (tr.), *Introduction to the Human Sciences: an attempt to lay a foundation for the study of society and history* (London: Harvester Wheatsheaf, 1988) gives the full picture.

[53] Fastenrath, op. cit., p. 35, see n. 147 for initial excellent bibliographical guidance.

It is on this foundation, the conjunction of Neokantianism, Dilthey's analysis of the human sciences and the burgeoning *Lebensphilosophie* movement, that Fastenrath builds a critique of subsequent developments. His thesis is that the shrinking of metaphysical thought and the pursuit of absolute, ever-valid truth and the emancipation of life-powers freed from responsibility to civic virtues had evil consequences. Particularly sinister, as E. Sommerlath pointed out in 1929, was the marginalised position into which the Christian purchase upon the current intellectual conception of reality had been forced: the community life mediated through Christ could only come into being in so far as this 'vital life' was given over into death, itself the passage into 'real life'.[54] So it was that *Lebensphilosophie* drove the seeker after 'true' or 'real' life into the embrace of a mysticism of death. This morbid preoccupation must be borne in mind when approaching the contribution of protestant authors to the so-called 'philosophy of life'.

At this juncture Fastenrath makes a important connection which, curiously, he then fails to develop: it is significant that 'in the epoch of an extreme *Lebensphilosophie* that a radical eschatologism arose'.[55] The line of biblical interpretation known as 'consequent eschatology', developed in a tradition extending from Johannes Weiss and Albert Schweitzer to Martin Werner and Fritz Buri, is congruent with the mainly German philosophical trend in which the exaltation and intensification of 'life' implied a transition through death. Here once more a displaced and reduced residuum of Christian self understanding can be seen to be part of the 'after-life' of a religion. The rendition of the life-death dialectic of Christianity in terms of philosophical immanence and liminal marginality[56] (attained through progressive philosophical fragmentation, aggressive naturalism and the prolonged cultural crisis attending secularisation) became an alternative to the neo-idealism of later Neo-Kantianism. In the

---

[54] '*Aber dieses Sterben sei Durchgang, ja Mittel des echten Lebens*' in art. '*Lebensphilosophie*', *Religion in der Geschichte und Gegenwart*² (1929), vol. III, 1510–1511.

[55] Fastenrath, op. cit., p. 35.

[56] I use the phrase 'liminal marginality' after some thought; it denotes the edge or horizon of existence which is ostensibly not as it were a closure or end but a threshold and beginning.

light of this we may justly regard the work of Barth and others active in what we have called the 'eschatology of Weimar' as the inheritors of this divided tradition. Our account of the general philosophical climate of the time is confirmed by the evaluation of a philosopher and pioneer sociologist of the period immediately preceeding the First World War, Georg Simmel (1859–1918).[57] In 1911 Simmel summed up an epoch in terms congruent with those of Lukács. The nihilistic provocation to *become* in order to *be* is suffused with quasi-eschatological unease:

> Life itself is an unceasing relativity of contradictions, the determination of the one thing through the other and vice versa in a flood of movement in which every entity can only subsist as something determined. As if proceeding out of high mountain peaks a presentiment (*Ahnung*) and a symbol confront us, that life at its point of climactic intensification (*Steigerung*) is in a form that no longer perishes but is that which stands above and over against life itself.[58]

It is in such a social setting and intellectual climate subsequently thrown into chaos and crisis by the War that Karl Barth was to toss his intellectual bomb, the dialectical theology, where it had to compete with other conceptions in the febrile ideological and spiritual bazaar of the first postmodernity.

III   *Barth, the Römerbriefe and the textual refraction of social crisis*
Karl Barth, the Swiss-German theologian schooled in the Liberal Protestantism of Bern, Tübingen, Berlin and Marburg prior to the First World War, succeeded in refracting in virtual isolation and distant from the scene of actual conflict the 'crisis' of war and its consequences. In his voluminous correspondence with his life-long friend Eduard Thurneysen, in the sermons of the period 1911–1919 inflicted upon his long-suffering congregation in Safenmil, and in the two *Römerbriefe*, supremely the second, rewritten text of 1922, Barth forged a new theological dialectic which entextualised the crisis of his time. This dialectical

---

[57] There is currently a marked renewal of interest in Simmel, see James Beckford, *Religion and Advanced Industrial Society* (London: Unwin Hyman, 1989), passim.
[58] *Philosophische Kultur. Gesammelte Essays* (Leipzig, 1911¹, 1919²) p. 141.

synethesis, when read from the standpoint of the historian of theology, embodies as we have seen at least the following: first, the revitalisation of the radical doctrine of justification by faith alone propounded by Kohlbrugge and rediscovered in the early Luther by Karl Holl; second, the progressively more relentless and extreme application in biblical exegesis and in systematic theology of the Weiss-Schweitzer-Overbeck consistent eschatology thesis; and, third, the 'infinite qualitative distinction' of time and eternity, the 'system' appropriated from Kierkegaard.

If, however, we interpret these developments from the standpoint of the *Zeitgeist* we first visited in our study of the reception of the theology of Barth then something distinctive becomes apparent. We encounter a theological strategy enacted through a re-mythologised discourse grounded in the exalted and inspired exegesis of scripture[59] which can be seen to correspond in remarkable ways with the philosophical limitations and residual possibilities of Neokantianism and the *Lebensphilosophie*, movements that Lukács regarded as the extreme expression of the contradictions of bourgeois rationality entering terminal crisis and decline.

(i)   *"Römerbrief I": salvific certitude and eschatological hope*
The two *Römerbriefe* are texts of great power. The general characteristics[60] that relate and distinguish them are best exposed through close examination of representative passages used as the basis of comparison and contextualisation. The texts in question, Barth's two 'comments' upon Romans 8^{24-5} ('readings' in the constitutive sense suggested by reception theory might be more apposite) encapsulate a radical change from an inspired and affirmed self in *Römerbrief* I to an endangered subject threatened by eschatological annihilation in *Römerbrief* II. This involves the

[59] Note the historian Adolf von Harnack's methods and outlook as recorded in H. M. Rumscheidt, *Revelation and Theology An Analysis of the Barth – Harnack Correspondence of 1923* (Cambridge: Cambridge U.P., 1972), pp. 105–6.
[60] See for accounts of Barth's early work see: Ulrich Dannemann, *Theologie un Politik im Denken Karl Barth* (Munich: Kaiser, 1977); Simon Fisher, *Revelatory Positivism Barth's Earliest Theology and the Marburg School* (Oxford: Oxford U.P., 1986) (the most important recent account in English); Werner M. Ruschke, *Entstehung und Ausführung der Diastasentheologie in Karl Barths zweitem 'Römerbrief'* (Neukirchen-Vluyn: Neukirchen Verlag, 1987); Tjarko Stadtland, *Eschatologie und Geschichte in der Theologie des jungen Karl Barths* (Neukirchen-Vluyn: Neukirchener Verlag des Erziehungsvereins, 1966).

displacement of the relatively secure, contemplative subject in the first *Römerbrief* and its replacement by a striving negative space in the second; this is what may be justifiably regarded as a deconstruction *avant la lettre* of the ontology of the subject. The intertextual contrasts between Barth's two comments on Romans 8[24–5] are of particular interest in this regard. Paul writes:

> For in this hope we were saved. Now hope that is seen is not hope. For who hopes for what he sees? But if we hope for what we do not see, we wait for it with patience.[61]

The nature and consequences of this 'hope' are markedly different in each edition and it is possible to unfold a wider contrast out of a detailed comparison. In *Römerbrief I* Barth first comments undialectically on the passage in a way which clearly implies a stable undeconstructed subject, a self that grasps with pietistic ardour the divine gift, the certainty and assurance of salvation. The commentary on verses 24–5 concludes with the assertion that: '*Heilsgewissheit und Eschatologie* (author's italicisation) *unzertrennbar zusammen gehoren*',[62] which we may render: 'Certitude of salvation and eschatology belong inseparably together'. Bearing this in mind we may work briefly through Barth's presentation.

According to Barth the Holy Spirit is not merely *in* us but is our *being* itself;[63] but, despite the free use of the language of Pietism, fellowship with God is not confined to inwardness (*Innerlichkeit*)[64] but is a direct and subordinate consequence of the

---

[61] Revised Standard Version. Hoskyns uses the Authorised Version.

[62] H. Schmidt (ed.), *Karl Barth Der Römerbrief (Erste Fassung) 1919* (Zürich: Theologischer Verlag, 1985), p. 337.

[63] '*Der Geist will nicht nur in uns sein, sondern, gerade weil er unser Sein ist, wachsen und siegen*', *Römerbrief* I, p. 333.

[64] '*Es gibt keine in der Innerlichkeit stehenbleibende Gemeinschaft mit Gott . . . Die wirkliche Sohnschaft Gottes, die wir noch nicht haben, sondern die wir erwarten, ist die "Erlösung unseres Leibes", der Sieg Gottes in der Leiblichkeit der gesamt Schopfung, von der unsere eigene ja nur Partikel und Inbegriff ist.*' *Römerbrief* I, pp. 334–5. The word '*Innerlichkeit*' is crucial in the context of German discussions of the meaning of human existence in the *Neuzeit*. It recalls a struggle with the relation between the inner and outer dimensions of existence which goes back to Kant's renowned discussion of the Enlightenment, and beyond, to Luther's seminal text *Die Freiheit eines Christenmenschen* (1620). In this century, Bloch (in *Geist der Utopie* and his study of Thomas Münzer), Adorno (in his doctoral thesis on Kierkegaard), and Herbert Marcuse (in his *Studies in Critical Philosophy*) have all engaged with this problematic.

victory of the saving God. The theme of 'victory' follows the insights of the famous Schwabian pietist, Johann Christoph Blumhardt of Bad Boll, who had earlier after much soul-searching and prayer wrought a victory over the demonic possession of Gottliebin Dittus of Möttlingen.[65] The structure of deliverance is proleptic yet ontologically affirmative. In the first *Römerbrief* the subject contemplates the 'contemporary situation (*gegenwärtigen Lage*)' and our 'blessedness (*Seligkeit* – following Blumhardt)' and observes these conditions through an organic, biological metaphor, the 'life process of the Body of Christ (*Lebenprozess des Leibes des Christus*)'. The horizon of transcendence (here the theological correlate of the philosophical horizon we isolated earlier in our comments on Neo-Kantianism) is at a distance; it is, to use the critical conceptuality of Marx's celebrated *Theses on Feuerbach*, knowledge in the mode of contemplation.

(ii) *"Römerbrief II": eschatology and the logic of negation*
Whereas for Marx it is the subject that must engage in praxis and transform the world, for Barth in the second *Römerbrief* it is God in the Eschaton who sweeps down from the future horizon and overwhelms the subject. Indeed, inasmuch as the doctrine of justification by faith alone is radicalised and recast through an identification of its epistemological and ontological possibilities, the subject in annihilated and by a dialectically conceived divine agency. Commenting upon the same passage in *Römerbrief* II, Barth wrote the famous words: '*Christentum, das nicht ganz und gar und restlos Eschatologie ist, hat mit Christus ganz und gar und restlos nicht zu tun*'.[66] This Sir Edwyn Hoskyns translated in a rather tamely: 'If Christianity be not altogether thoroughgoing eschatology, there remains in it no relationship whatever with Christ.'[67]

Hoskyns remains within a tradition that mediates extremity and resists the inclusion of the contextual factors which would allow for a reading of the text in its full force. Once understood against the background in the Marburg Neo-Kantianism with which Barth was directly acquainted with and indeed influenced

[65] See E. Busch, op. cit., pp. 83–6; and Friedrich Zündel, *Johann Christoph Blumhardt, ein Lebensbild* (1880).
[66] *Römerbrief* II, p. 298.
[67] Hoskyn's, ER, p. 314.

by, we reach the level that permits the eschatological cycle to enact itself.

In *Römerbrief* II the 'truth (*Wahrheit*)', as opposed to certainty and inner certitude, is presented as a 'deliverance (*Erretung*)' identical with 'God himself (*Gott selbst*)', a God 'for us (*für uns*)'. This allusion to the analytic of the mergence of selfhood in Hegel's *Phenomenology of Mind (1807)*[68] as 'in itself (*an sich*)' and 'for itself (*für sich*)' indicates that the totality of *both* subject *and* object is comprised in the eschatologically realised 'wholly other (*das ganz und gar Andere*)'. This, 'the unknown' (*das Unbekannte*) and the 'unapproachable' (*das Unzugängliche*) displaces eschatologically the epistemological structure of the subject-object relationship by contrast with *Römerbrief* I where it is retained as the locus of the religious experience. Whereas in *Römerbrief* I Barth writes of an 'inmost essence' (*innerstes Wesen*) that is saved by Christ[69] in harmony with the yearning and sighing of the whole cosmos for deliverance, in *Römerbrief* II the realised eschatology and a dialectical 'dagger of the Incarnation' (to use E. C. Hoskyns' image) is thrust into the victim and twisted rather than, as it were, unsheathed and held at a healthy proleptic distance, as we saw in our earlier exploration of the Barthian elements in the thought of Donald MacKinnon.

Thus without reference either to an analytic of subjectivity (like that present in the first *Römerbrief*) or a theological or philosophical anthropology, Barth draws a panoply of philosophical allusions into passages replete with dialectical ironies, in which the 'not yet' of eschatological tension is sustained in the face of the annihilistic onset of grace. Ironically the destruction wrought by grace (a theological ingestion of nihilism) is countered not by an appeal to a residual natural order but to a coming restoration sustained through the classic Neo-Kantian device of the 'as if' (*als ob*). It is by means of the latter that the dimensions of consciousness placed beyond the limits of the knowable by the Kantian critique were restored by philosophers such as, most famously, Hans Vaihinger.[70]

[68] "Lordship and Bondage", in J. B. Baillie (tr.) (London: Allen and Unwin, rev. ed. 1931).
[69] *Römerbrief* I, p. 337.
[70] C. K. Ogden (tr.), The Philosophy of "As if" (New York: RKP, 1924).

In an extraordinarily resonant passage formulated in the present conditional *Irreale*, Barth articulates the tensions and uncertainties of the new 'waiting' that attends the storm and stress of the existential enactment of eschatological annihilation (which in turn reflects the culture of the dialectics of nihilism). The certainty is of annihilation; the hope expressed in the intentionality and pragmatics of 'as if' is for a God who is as it were 'not yet':

> *Beharren,* als ob *es ein Jenseits gäbe von Gut und Böse, Freud un Leid, Leben und Tod, beharren,* als ob *wir im Glück und Unglück, im Aufstieg und Niedergang, im Ja und Nein unsres Da-Seins und So-Seins auf etwas warteten, beharren,* als ob *ein Gott wäre dem wir unterliegend oder siegend, lebend oder sterbend in Liebe zugewandt zu dienen hätten. Als ob? Ja eben das ist das Merkwürdige dass wir, wenn wir es auf unserm Weg durch die Zeit aufs Höchste bringen, Beharrende sind,* als ob *wir sähen, was wir doch nicht sehen, schauten das Unanschauliche. Die Hoffnung ist die Aufhebung dieses Rätsels, die Aufhebung des 'als ob'. Wir sehen eben* wahrhaftig, *wir sehen* existentiell, *was sir doch nicht sehen.* Darum *beharren wir.*[71]

In this passage the unmistakeable allusions to the Nietzschian '*Jenseits von Gut und Böse*', 'beyond good and evil', the Neo-Kantian philosophy of '*als ob*', the Hegelian conception of '*Aufhebung*', that is 'supercession' or 'sublation', and the Kierkegaardian '*existentiell*' are all unmistakeable, yet they lose their force and resonance in Hoskyns' translation which was, as we have seen, the main means of mediating the insights of the early Barth:

> And we – we must wait, as though there were something lying beyond good and evil, joy and sorrow, life and death; as though in happiness and disappointment, in growth and decay, in the 'Yes' and the 'No' of our life in the world, we were expecting something. We must wait, as though there were a God whom, in victory and in defeat, in life and in death, we must serve with love and devotion. 'As though?' Yes, this is the strange element in the situation. In our journey through time, we are still men who wait, as though we saw what we do not see, as though we were gazing upon the unseen. Hope is the solution of the riddle of our 'As though'. We do see. Existentially we see what to us is invisible, and therefore we wait.[72]

[71] *Römerbrief* II, p. 298.
[72] Hoskyns, ER, p. 314.

A crucial weakness is Hoskyns' use of 'as though', a locution which would appear to be a transposition of the Authorised Version's reading of Paul's depiction of his spiritual vision in Second Corinthians; its presence in the translation ensures the English reception of text, yet there is a price to be paid. This is an understandable domestication of a German text shot through with historical and contextual allusions, all of which energise and deepen Barth's full-throated engagement with the then *Zeitgeist*. What, then, are the contemporary lessons we can learn from this extraordinary episode in an equally remarkable period of what we have designated the 'first postmodernity' of the Weimar culture in the context of which Barth set out to refunction and empower a seemingly moribund tradition?

IV   *Barth and the Postmodern Condition; A Theology on its Way?*
It is now apparent that this concluding paper is a Janus-faced construction that faces back over an prolonged engagement with the person and work of Karl Barth, and then forward over the territory I intend to explore in the immediate future. As such it is built around the comparison between the setting of Karl Barth's early theology and features of our own time, a parallel between a first and second postmodernity. We are now in a position to draw the main strands of our argument together and indicate how it is possible to conceive of Barth's work as a theology on its way, a true *theologia viatorum*.

The undoubted achievement of Barth lay in his ability to refunction a religious tradition; the high point of this endeavour is to be found in the two *Römerbriefe* which refract the rapidly changing and fluid circumstances of the First World War and the dangerous and fertile period of social reorientation that followed it. The later work of Barth, notably that of the *Church Dogmatics*, possesses a pathos which we have amply illustrated in the foregoing book: strength and power were bought at the price of progressive isolation. This is a tendency chartable not only biographically through Barth's successive rejections of those with whom he came to disagree, but also within the inner logic of a theological system that struggles to regain reality through a strident theological rhetoric of the 'real'.

By profound contrast the two *Römerbriefe* taken together as a single intertextual whole constitute the richest and most important theological work of the twentieth century, not least because, unlike the *Church Dogmatics* and the efforts of his contemporaries, the *Römerbriefe* are both *open* and in the most extreme way *provocative*. They remain latent texts; they await a full awakening in the Anglo-Saxon world. The openness of these texts is twofold: first, in them the cultural *Sitz im Leben* of the theologian is addressed so that this context may itself become the dialectically appropriated source of the analogical transmutations that permit any given contemporaneity to address us and be interpreted by the Word of God; second, the 'God' thus encountered is the God whom we cannot predefine: He is to us from the future; He stands in judgement upon the *theological* articulations that we inherit from the past. Thus, rightly understood, Barth's theology in the *Römerbriefe* is first and foremost an atheology that mounts in intensity, consistency and severity in the transition from the first to the second edition. The deconstruction that they propound is no mere criticism of religion as such, a polemic developed and propagated with excess and misunderstanding zeal by commentators on Barth's endorsement of Feuerbach,[73] but a deconstruction of both 'God' and subjectivity. It is only in the condition of the second postmodernity, where the extreme fluidity first explored in the aftermath of the First World War as a first postmodernity has now become part of our normativity, that we are once more in a position to begin to understand the dialectics of negation, the necessary atheology that preludes the refunctioning of the experience of grace.

The provocation implicit in Barth's early theology is again twofold: first, and positively, it succeeded in launching a longstanding theological and church movement in an unpromising environment and in providing the ideological backbone of the Confessing Church during the Third Reich; second, and less positively, its strange, alienated quality and self-

[73] See Barth's famous lecture of 1926 which first appeared in *Die Theologie und die Kirche* (Zollikon-Zurich: Evangelischer Verlag, 1928) and is reproduced in the standard modern edition of George Eliot translation of Ludwig Feuerbach's *The Essence of Christianity* (New York: Harper and Row, 1957), pp. x-xxxii. This essay was written at the point Barth was moving from the dialecticism of the two *Römerbriefe* back to the renewed subjectivism of the *Christliche Dogmatik* of 1927.

presentation and representation in terms of the commonplace of "crisis" brought about (so far as the English-speaking world is concerned) that long history of partial mediation and miscomprehension we have explored in our account of the reception of Barth's theology.

Where Barth was, I believe, wrong, and where many of those influenced by him both positively and negatively also err, is in the following. The pursuit of the polemic against religion was a diversion away from more fundamental aspects of Barth's theological argument which enjoyed a transient timeliness but which failed to take root and establish themselves as a stable and enduring creative commonplace. The polemic against religion compounded a growing dichotomy between the pursuit of theology as a progressively more isolated discipline and the study of religion along positivistic lines, the growth of phenomonology notwithstanding.

It is therefore necessary to adopt a dialectical approach to the work of Barth in full recognition of both the indispensability and the manifest limitations of his early work. The dialectical developments of the *Römerbriefe* contain a theology which enjoyed a measure of success in an era bearing significant similarities to our own: thus the first and second postmodernities converge around certain possibilities. The other side of Barth's approach, the attack on religion, was hypostatised and has been incorporated in a tradition which has in many of its manifestations disastrously divided off theological enquiry from the study of religion, and often enough, has separated *both* from the human sciences as a whole. It is this polemic, and its associated consequences that have to be submitted to thoroughgoing critical revision. In its place it is not sufficient merely to reinstate some form of 'religious studies', narrowly conceived, precisely because this has failed to articulate an *episteme* that can convince. Such an articulation cannot be imposed, it must be discovered as the accompaniment and consequence of a full-scale "archeology" of the changing roles and displacements of religion and the sacred in the history of the emergence and differentiation of the human sciences (and thus of society and culture). Out of this analysis of

[74] See Peter Dews, *Logics of Disintegration Post-structuralist Thought and the Claims of Critical Theory* (London: Verso, 1987).

the processes of fragmentation[74] and the construction of disciplinary rhetorics it may prove possible to bring into existence an *episteme* that might in turn enter the sphere of public discourse as a effective commonplace, the transcendental principle of the construction of a benign, yet extraordinary normality, a constructive and integrative *sensus communis.*

Such an investigative procedure in the human sciences would in its turn be the preliminary to a systematic theology that might with some justification claim to articulate an interface between tradition and modernity/postmodernity. This might also claim to be a theology that, inspired by the grandeur and chastened by the pathos of the epochal achievements of Karl Barth, was a theology on its way.

Index of Names

Adorno, T. W. 152, 153, 192
Ahlstrom, S. E. 118, 119, 134
Anselm, St. 4, 66
Aquinas, St. Thomas 65
Aristotle 8
Auerbach, Erich 147, 151
Augustine, St. 35, 36, 52, 73, 85, 92

Baillie, John 153
Baillie, John and Donald 98
Balthasar, H. U. von 37, 171
Barr, James 140
Barrett, C. K. 111, 112, 140
Barth, Karl *passim*
    Christliche Dogmatik 13, 15, 67,
      129–30
    Church Dogmatics, general
      comment 12, 14, 55, 61–2
    CD I/1 15–22, 30, 63, 66–8, 87–9,
      91
    CD I/2 34–41, 63, 75
    CD II/1 23–8, 30, 44, 64, 68–9,
      71–2
    CD II/2 30–34
    CD III/1 43–7
    CD III/2 48–55, 70, 76–7
    CD IV/1 41–2, 75
    Das Wort Gottes und die Theologie
      106, 129
    Fides Quaerens Intellectum 4–5,
      66

Barth, Karl *passim (continued)*
    Protestant Theology 3–4, 65
    Römerbriefe 9–12, 102, 106, 110,
      158, 172, 191, 193–6, 197
Bartley III, W. W. 145
Beckford, J. W. 97, 190
Bell, Daniel 144
Bell, G. K. A. 168
Berdyaev, Nikolai 150
Berger, Peter 144, 145
Bixler, J. S. 131
Bloch, Ernst 144, 174, 192
Bloom, Harold xvn.3
Blumenberg, Hans 174 ff.
Blumhardt, Johann Christoph 193
Boethius 73
Bouillard, Henry 35, 65, 84
Bourdieu, Pierre 170
Bromiley, G. W. 81, 141, 142
Bruck, Moeller van den 170
Brunner, Emil 98, 129, 131, 133
Bryden, W. W. 136
Bultmann 50, 137, 144, 150
Buren, Paul van 143

Camfield, F. W. 115, 137
Cant, R. 116
Carradine, David 101
Cave, Sidney 112
Chadwick, Owen 101
Chaning-Pearce, M. 109, 110, 115

Childs, Brevard 140
Clarke, W. K. Lowther 103, 104, 112
Cobham, J. O. 111
Cohen, Hermann 187
Cranfield, C. E. B. 141
Cross, F. L. 117

Darwin, Charles 186
Davey, Francis Noel 111, 116
Deissman, A. and G. K. A. Bell 103
Deusen, H. P. van 133
Diels, H. 73
Dilthey, Wilhelm 188
Dittus, Gottliebin 193
Dodd, C. H. 116
Dühring, Eugen 184

Eagleton, Terry 101, 174
Eliot, T. S. 101, 109, 110, 116
Eucken, Rudolf 123

Farrer, A. M. 117, 140
Ford, D. F. 2, 12, 147
Forsyth, P. T. 100, 107
Foucault, Michel 153, 173, 174
Fastenrath, Elmar 186ff
Frei, Hans W. 131, 147
Feuerbach 197

Gogarten, Friedrich 128
Gore, Charles 98, 104
Graves, Robert 101

Habermas, Jurgen 184
Haeckel, Ernst 121, 184, 186
Haitjema, Th. L. 111
Hamann, J. G. 173
Hamer, J. 16
Hammer, Karl 102
Handy, R. T. 136
Harnack, Adolf von 123, 127, 191,
    What is Christianity? 123
Hartmann, Eduard von 186
Hartwell, H. H. 141
Hegel, G. W. F. xv, 3, 5, 7, 73,
    89–90, 97, 151, 152, 173, 179
Heim, Karl 133
Henson, H. Hensley 100
Hepburn, R. W. 145

Herbert, A. G. 116
Herder, J. G. 173
Hermann, Rudolph 186
Hodgson, P. C. 149
Hölderlin 52
Holl, Karl 191
Horton, Douglas 106
Horton, W. M. 133
Hoskyns, Edwyn Clement 97, 106,
    110, 166, 168, 193
Hoyle, R. Birch 108
Humboldt, Wilhelm von 173
Husserl, Edmund 187

Jenkins, Daniel 116, 138
Jenson, R. W. 12, 138
Jünger, Ernst 102, 127

Kant, Immanuel 5, 62, 65
Keller, Adolf 106, 132
Kelsey, D. M. 140
Keynes, J. M. 124
Kierkegaard, Soren 3, 7, 8–9, 62, 65,
    74, 133, 178
Kittel, G. 140
Kohlbrugge, H. F. 191
Kolakowski, Leszek 185
Kraemer, Hendrik 138
Kraus, Karl 184
Krüger, G. 126
Külpe, Oswald 184

Lange, Friedrich Albert 187
Langford, T. A. 99
Leavis, F. R. and Q. D. 101
Lehmann, Paul 139
Lempp, Richard 119–24
Lindbeck, G. A. 148
Löwith, K. 173, 174, 177–80
Luhmann, Niklas 145
Lukács, Georgy 185, 190
Luther, Martin 37n.30
Lyotard, J. F. 169

MacConnachie, John 132
MacDonald, A. J. 107, 108
Mach, Ernst 184
MacKinnon, Donald M. ix, xiv, 112,
    117, 138, 139, 155ff, 161

Mackintosh, H. R. 105, 107, 108
Marcuse, Herbert 192
Maritain, Jacques 111
Marquardt, Fr. Wilhelm 146
Marx, Karl 37n.30, 151, 152, 193
Matthews, W. R. 98
McConnachie, John 107, 108, 112
McGrath, A. 112
McKim, Randolph H. 118
Millbank, A. J. 180
Morrison, J. H. 107
Mozley, J. K. 98, 112
Münzer, Thomas 192

Natorp, Paul 187
Newbigin, Lesslie 138
Niebuhr, Reinhold 133
Nietzsche, Friedrich 122, 171, 178, 181, 195
Norman, E. R. 155

Parker, T. H. L. 141
Pittenger, Norman 132
Porteus, N. 107
Przywara, Erich

Quick, O. C. 115

Ramsey, A. M. 116, 140, 167
Rauschning, Herbert 184
Raven, Charles, 100, 115
Richards, I. A. 101
Ritschl, Albrecht 123, 127
Robinson, James M. 143
Rouse, H. C. 115
Ruether, R. R. 147
Rumscheidt, H. M. 136

Sassoon, Siegfried 101
Schleiermacher, Friedrich, *The Christian Faith* 82
Saussure, F. 173
Schleiermacher, Friedrich D. E. 82
Scholder, Klaus 102
Segundo J. P.
Shaw, Bernard 100

Simmel, Georg 190
Smart, Ninian ix
Smith, Ronald Gregor 2, 143
Smyth, Charles, 116
Sommerlath, E. 189
Spengler, Oswald 128
Steiner, George xvi, 57
Steiner, Rudolph 125
Stern, Fritz 170
Stewart, R. W. 110
Strauss 121
Stroup, G. W. 147
Studdert-Kennedy, G. A. 100
Sykes, S. W. 2n.1, 96, 98, 149
Sykes, Stephen W. x

Tasker, R. V. G. 116
Taylor, Mark C. 173
Temple, William 98, 104
Thomson, G. T. 81
Thornton, Lionel 116
Thurneysen, Eduard 190
Til, C. van 143
Tillich, T. F. 133, 144, 150
Torrance, T. F. ix, 3, 13, 35, 59, 77, 81, 83, 93, 98, 114, 139, 141, 142, 144, 145, 150, 164, 167, 112
Trendelenberg, Adolf 7, 74
Troeltsch, Ernst 127, 184

Updike, John 149

Vahanian, G. 143
Vidler, A. 138

Weber, Max 184
Welch, Claude 97
West, Charles 146
White, Fr. Victor 158
Whitehouse, W. A. 139
Williams, N. P. 103
Winch, Peter 145
Winnington-Ingram, A. F. 100
Wright, G. E. 140
Wundt, Wilhelm 187

Index of Subjects

Absolute Spirit, doctrine of 24
actualism, Barth's 44
actus purus (divine act) 56, 67
  and ontology 33
  and grace 16
alienation xiv
analogy of faith (*analogia fidei*) 3, 4,
  7, 53, 56, 65, 66, 69
  and being in act 73
  principle of, and doctrine of God
    48, 78, 79
  rejection of 22
  Roman Catholic 4
anamnesis, or Neoplatonic
  recollection 16
anthropology, theological 30, 48
antinomies of space and time, Kant's
  criticism of 69
Aufhebung, Hegelian conception of
  185, 195
Augustinianism, in Barth's theology
  73, 85
authority, trust in 100

Barth, and politics 145ff
  Anglo-Saxon responses to 137
Barthianism, the charge of 159
becoming, stream of (*Strom des*
  Werdens) 17
being in act, God's 2
being, modes of in the Trinity 91

Bible, the revealing God of the 19
Biblical narrative, 159
Biblical theology movement 117, 133
Boston Declaration (1976) 139

Christendom Group 155
Christian Science 125
Christianity, Hegelian 60
Christology 45, 54, 63, 76, 90
  Barth's 37
  classical 59
  hypostasis 40, 75
  and paradox 10
  in Protestant scholasticism 40
  temporal structure of 30
  two natures, doctrine of the 31
  unio hypostatica 63
Christomonist tendency, Barth's 86
Church of England 168
  theology of in 1946 116
churches, German, organised parties
  in 120
circle, theological (*circulus veritatis*
  Dei) 51, 54, 55, 61, 69, 87
contemporaneousness, contingent
  (*kontigente Gleichzeitigkeit*) 67
  of God's act and word 1, 17
covenant 44
creation, Barth's conception of 42
  and covenant 31
  and dialectics of temporality 43ff

creation *(continued)*
  ex nihilo, quasi-expressionistic 172
  and history 45
  true and genuine basis of 44
Creator and Creation, duality of 54
creed, Niceano-Constantinoplitan,
    and the Trinity 90
crisis of culture, religion as 128
crisis, eschatological 9
curiositas, denigration of 181

death of God 143
deconstruction 97
dialectic of grace 7
dialectic, Hegelian 24
dialectical theology, cultural
    transmission of 128ff., 183
disjunction, radical (*diastasis*), of the
    temporal and the eternal 8
divine grace, Reformation emphasis
    upon 33
divine perfections, and active
    freedom 24
divine simultaneity, Boethian notion
    of 29
divine will, and the doctrine of
    nothingness 32
Docetism, and the doctrine of time
    39, 76

ecclesiology 162
election of grace 30
Enlightenment 181
episteme 174, 176
Erfurt Programme of 1891 124
eschatology, annihilation 195
  consequent 189
  discourse of, 175
  realised 11
  'rediscovery' of by Schweitzer and
    Weiss 10
essence of the Church (*Wesen der
    Kirche*) 67
eternal Moment – the Now 16
eternity 27, 28, 53
  and divine freedom 25
  Nicaeno-Constantinopolitan
    Creed 21
  Barth's doctrine of 26–8

eternity *(continued)*
  Boethian conception of 71–3
  eternity and time 25–6, 34, 43, 45–7,
    52, 63, 82
existentiell, Kierkegaardian 195
Expressionism 185

Faust 163
finite and infinite 5, 71
First World War 7
  aftermath of 128
  and American theology 117, 118,
    119
  theological response to 96, 99, 100
freedom, God's sovereign 85
fulfilled time (die erfüllte Zeit) 16

God's act in Jesus Christ
    infinity 26
God, being-in-act of 23
  doctrine of 63
  Fatherhood of 20, 88–9
God, non-spatiality of 26
  as infinite Wholly Other 9
  and the *Now* moment 22
  prototype and foreordination 27
  super-infinity of 70
Gospel, message of 55
grace, and natural theology 54

Hartford Declaration (1975) 139
Hegelian dialectic 6
history, philosophy of 178
Holy Scripture, and the Trinity 91
horizon, eschatological 181
human existence, ontology of 20
human perception, *krisis* of 10
human sciences, emergence and
    differentiation of 176
  investigative procedures in 199

idealism, in *Church Dogmatics* 73
Incarnation 30, 40, 41
  Barth's doctrine of the 35–7
  determinants of doctrine of 34
  Hoskyns 166
  ontological dogma of 57
Israel, history of 30

Jesus Christ, the divine act 24
  being of 52
  error of docetic attitude to 50, 51

kenosis 161
kinesis 8
Kirchliche Dogmatik 15, 114, 130

Man, Barth's doctrine of 43
Marxist-Leninist imperialism, crisis
  of 171
memoria, and the Augustinian model
  of knowing 181
Moment, in Kierkegaard 74, 151
  dynamic God, Lutheran moment
    of 187
  in the eternal 12, 21
Monist League (*Monistenbund*) 186
Moral Majority 149
mythopoesis 148

narrative theology, growth of
    nature 36
Neokantianism 183–6, 187, 191
  Neo-Orthodoxy 141–3
    collapse of 143–6
  Protestant theology 133–4, 137
Neo-Thomism, 60
Neuzeit 170
New Age 149
nihilism, crisis of 173
  and immanence 184
nothingness (Nichtigkeit), Barth's
    doctrine of 32
Novum, epistomological 67
Now moment 1, 15
  Divine 18
nunc stans 29

overcoming (*aufhebung*) of
    contradiction 8

parousia 52
perfections, God's 21, 72
  attribution 69
Philosophy of Nature 7
philosophy, breakdown of classical
    German 185

post-liberalism 149
postmodern condition, presaged by
    inter-war social conditions 169,
    196ff.
post-modernism 130, 147–9, 199
postmodernity/modernity 199
predestination 30–1
  Christology 31
primal history 30–1
Protestant theology 6, 66
Protestantism, liberal 62, 190
providence, residual belief in 100

rationality 5
real time (*wirkliche Zeit*), and God's
    time 28, 29
reconciliation (*Versöhnung*), doctrine
    of 41
refunctioning, anticipatory, in Ernst
    Bloch 172
*Religion Within the Limits of Reason
    Alone* 5
religion xv
  after-life of xvi
  analysis of ix
  Marxist critique of 57
religious studies 198
  and sociology of religion 144
resurrection 1, 30, 34, 52, 91
revelation 44, 54, 91
  fundamental nature of 86
  the *Novum* of 68
  real-time of 69
  as self-authenticating 85
  and *transcendence,* renewal of 105
  and the Trinity 81
rhetoric, specific definition of 157
  theological 42, 135, 196

salvation, secularised substitutes for
    135
secularisation, in Löwith and
    Blumenberg 176ff
sin, and the election and rejection of
    Jesus Christ 32
substance 63, 67, 78
synthesis, nature of the 'proper object
    of' 6
System, Barth's 10

temporality 53
  and humanity 36
  and humanity in Christ 23
  man's need of 48
theologians, Neo-Orthodox 134
theology of crisis 1, 96, 126
  cultural transmission of 183
  in Germany 119
  ways of escape from 12
theology, Anglo-Saxon 152
  biblical 140
  Cambridge, in the inter-war
    period 111
  dialectical movement in 106
  natural 22, 56, 79
  post-war British 117
  radical 117
  realistic, in America 133
  traditional, reinterpretation of
    distinct categories of 32
Third Reich, Confessing Church
  during 197
time 56, 73
  Christ's life in 49
  doctrine of 75
  and eternity 1, 11, 29, 46, 54, 63
  God's time 34, 54, 71, 78
  God's time and human time 40
  God's time and the negation of
    the negation 43
  and the Incarnation 39
  midpoint of 34
  problem of 45

time *(continued)*
  real 43
  and resurrection 48ff
  and simultaneity 46
  source of 47
  and space as a surrogate for
    substance 63
  universality of category of 63
  and Word become flesh 29
timelessness, and Barth's *theological
    circle* 26
totum simul, Boethian 28
transcendence 193
Trinity 6, 17, 19, 81ff, 87., 89–90
  and revelation 84
  in Hegel 66
  Hegelian doctrine of, and Barth
    89–90
truth, theological ix

values, Nietzsche's transvaluation of
    171
Virgin Birth 41

Wartburg Conference (1920) 128
Weimar culture 100, 169
Weimar Republic 102, 170
Word of God 5, 17, 129
Word, crisis of the 170

Zwischen den Zeiten (1922–1933) 13,
    102, 175, 184